OB in Action:
Cases and Exercises

Third Edition

Janet W. Wohlberg

Boston University

Scott Weighart

Boston University

HOUGHTON MIFFLIN COMPANY   BOSTON   TORONTO

Dallas   Geneva, Illinois   Palo Alto   Princeton, New Jersey

Senior Sponsoring Editor: Patrick F. Boles
Development Editor: Susan M. Kahn
Design Coordinator: Ellen Conant/Sandra Gonzalez
Ancillary Coordinator: Elena Di Cesare
Senior Manufacturing Coordinator: Marie Barnes
Marketing Manager: Mary Jo Conrad/Diane McOscar

Cover: Frantisek Kupka, *Disks of Newton (Study for Fugue in Two Colors)*, 1912. Oil on canvas. The Philadelphia Museum of Art. The Louise and Walter Arensberg Collection.

Printed in the U.S.A.

ISBN: 0-395-60610-1
Library of Congress number: 91-71971

ABCDEFGHIJ-PO-9987654321

To all our friends and colleagues who have taught OB221
at Boston University's School of Management
over the past several semesters:
Susan Bunker, Carol Carlson, Sandi Deacon, Gail Gilmore,
Ruth Kenworthy (alias The Steel Magnolia), Kathe Kirkman, Bruce Leblang,
Debbie Levine, Vicky Parker-Estey, Kent Seibert, Mary Young.
Thanks gang: We couldn't have done it without you!

Contents

Preface

Over the past several years, we have increasingly tried to practice in teaching about organizational behavior what we preach about managing organizations—that is, greater compliance and commitment to a concept come about when those who must act on the concept are involved in developing it. This is no less true for students taking a course in college than it is for employees working in organizational settings. *OB in Action* gives you, the student, a chance to have your say in how things should be done, to chart the depths of your existing knowledge, combine it with new knowledge, and put that synthesis into practice. This is a hands-on approach; it depends, for its success, on your being willing to get involved, to share your insights and experiences, and to take some risks.

OB in Action also introduces you to the vast possibilities and diversity of opinions that can be generated as valid responses to problems. Most of the cases and exercises in *OB in Action* have any number of possible solutions. This level of uncertainty, however, is often disconcerting to students whose lives have been driven by what's in and what's not.

Many of us reach late adolescence and early adulthood believing that our ways of doing things, or those of our family and friends, are the only "right" ways. There's a right way to talk, a right way to dress, and a right way to behave. Anything that departs from our concept of "right" is wrong, or possibly even "dumb."

I once tried to explain the problem in this kind of thinking to a medical missionary who had just returned from a remote village in an African country. "Those people are so ignorant," he told me, "that if they come to see me, and there's a perfectly good chair available in the room, they'll still sit on the floor." "Why," I asked him, "would someone want to sit on a hard object from which his or her legs dangle, which pushes the human back into an awkward position, and which feels unnatural and alien?" To the missionary's patients, the chair was an inappropriate solution to a problem they had long ago solved to their satisfaction by deciding to sit on the floor. They didn't have desks or coffee tables, cooking was done at floor level, sleeping was on mats, and therefore, chairs were irrelevant. In addition, there was a culturally imposed restriction on the patients to remain physically lower than the revered doctor. Without understanding his patient's interests and traditions, the doctor concluded that *they* were "stupid."

Many of the problems employees and employers often have with one another come from this kind of a "we-they" mentality and a lack of understanding of the motives, traditions, and ways of thinking each uses. The conclusion "that's dumb" is an offshoot of poor communication and an unwillingness to listen carefully to what others believe and say. In turn, this results in a vicious circle of employers trying to impose their will on their "ignorant" employees, employees failing to cooperate with their "idiot bosses," and employers taking even harder lines, having concluded that their employees are "too stupid" to follow a few simple orders. Sound familiar? This kind of thinking results in rigid hierarchies, low morale, the need to coerce workers in order to maintain productivity, high turnover, and other workplace problems.

In *OB in Action*, you will be exposed to real workplace problems and work in groups to find solutions that are acceptable to a wide range of employees. With the increasing diversity of the American work force and the increasing globalization of business, this is not only a desirable approach, but may be a matter of survival.

Before beginning with the cases and exercises, it is important that you be familiar with the methods for learning about behavior in organizations, such as case method and the various forms of experiential exercises. This information is presented in the Methodologies section. It also gives background on some frequently used techniques for problem solving. Following the methodologies are icebreakers—a number of short exercises to get you started in building the kinds of relationships that will be necessary for group problem solving.

The cases and exercises in *OB in Action* are grouped into eight sections. Part I, Individual Processes in Organizations, deals with our perceptions, where they come from, the impact that imposing our perceptions and stereotypes can have on others, and the issues of motivation—how we are motivated and how to motivate others.

The cases and exercises in Part II, Interpersonal Processes in Organizations, will involve you in exploring leadership styles and group dynamics. Part III, Enhancing Individual and Interpersonal Processes, deals with goals setting, performance appraisal and feedback, and group decision making. This part encourages the use of brainstorming as a problem-solving technique.

Part IV, Integrating Individuals, Groups, and Organizations, introduces the use of force field analysis for managing change. In this section, exercises that use concepts of organizational structure are also included.

Part V, written by Morris Raker, J.D., a practicing attorney who specializes in Litigation Cost Containment© through the use of negotiation and other forms of alternative dispute resolution, gives hands-on experience in both distributive and integrative bargaining.

Part VI, written by family business expert, Dr. Wendy Handler, deals with the kinds of business problems that specifically haunt family business situations—that is, succession, credibility of potential successors, planning, and family dynamics.

Part VII, International Aspects of Organizational Behavior, offers a case and three exercises for developing an understanding of the impact of cultural differences on conducting business across borders.

Part VIII, written by Bruce Leblang, a career counselor who also teaches career courses at Boston University, gives you the chance to evaluate interests and skills as an important first step in deciding on a career choice.

As in the "real" world, most of the cases and exercises in *OB in Action* have more than one theme. While a case or exercise may have learning about leadership, for example, as its central purpose, it will be important not to overlook secondary considerations that may be present, such as managing diversity, team work, ethics, sexual harassment, and so forth.

Even though each part of the book is introduced with a brief overview of the relevant topic areas and theories, we strongly recommend that this book be used in conjunction with a text and/or supportive readings that further develop the theories of the field of organizational behavior. These theories supply a framework within which you can begin to interpret and understand the world of organizational behavior.

Acknowledgments

Many people helped with this book, supplying ideas and useful critiques, as well as moral support. We want especially to thank the students who took OB221 at Boston University's School of Management for their candor in letting us know what worked and what didn't. Thanks to Lloyd Baird and George Labovitz for encouraging us to continually try new and different methods of getting our points across. Thanks also to Lani and Shira Wohlberg, who allowed themselves to be used as consultants on how college students think; to the folks in our undergraduate office who shared feedback; to Bernice Colt, Pat Boles, and Susan Kahn at Houghton Mifflin, who were patient and supportive; and most of all, to all the folks who have taught sections of OB221 over the past couple of years and to whom this book is dedicated.

JWW and SW

METHODOLOGIES

USING CASES IN THE STUDY OF ORGANIZATIONAL BEHAVIOR

Increasingly, managers are finding that their biggest problems are not balancing budgets or erecting buildings: the most complicated, the most difficult, the most time-consuming problems they face are people problems.

Every individual brings to the workplace far too many variables, many of which are never seen or only glimpsed, to allow managers to indulge in neat analyses and pat answers to these problems. Placing complex individuals in groups, setting them tasks and deadlines, and asking them to compromise much of their individuality for the sake of cooperative efforts multiplies infinitely the number of variables with which a manager must cope. The human urge to package vast numbers of variables into tidy bundles can be overwhelming. Unfortunately, doing so can also lead to answers that don't respond to the questions and problems raised.

Case studies offer you a realistic approach to the inexact science of understanding and dealing with people problems in organizational settings. Cases are microscopic cross sections of the real world in which the possibilities are seemingly endless. In analyzing cases, you will work with incomplete information from which you must extrapolate, generalize, and find meaningful answers. Because of the number of possibilities, missing information about people, and secret agendas, cases may often seem frustrating and irksome. However, in work as in life, we must make many decisions, some more critical than others, and probably never do we have *all* of the information needed with which to reach perfect conclusions. Instead, we make educated guesses, weigh the benefits and potential problems, and arrive, we hope, at those decisions that will bring the best possible outcomes. Cases give practice in doing just that.

What Is a Case?

A case is a story—usually a true story, but not always—that illustrates an idea, presents a problem, offers a dilemma, and leaves you hanging, wondering what to do next. Some cases give you all of the events that lead to a crossroad and then ask you to decide which path to take and to project what lies ahead on each road. Other cases tell you what was done and ask you to analyze what went wrong and what could have been done better.

Cases are tightly written. Virtually every word has a meaning, a point that should be considered by those seeking to analyze the facts and issues presented. Rarely may information presented in a case be disregarded.

Case Analysis

Case analysis requires reading a case several times—with an open mind to a virtually unlimited number of possible interpretations and outcomes—and leaving enough time in between readings to consider the issues and identify the problems. Often on first reading, you may identify as a problem an event or relationship that may be merely a symptom. Subsequent readings are generally helpful in sorting the symptoms from the problems, but you should not feel threatened by the possibility of confusion. The problems may be well camouflaged. For this reason, preparing a case with a case group of three to seven members may be helpful as a way to elicit the greatest number of ideas about what is really at issue.

There are many possible ways to approach case analysis, including the fairly straightforward method outlined below. Items one and two suggest ways to think about cases. They will help you put yourself into the role of a case character (or at least in the role of a fly on the wall), identify with the events taking place and in other ways involve yourself in the case. You will find them useful in oral case presentation, but in your ultimate write-up of the case, you should not try to describe the characters in the ways you have imagined them. This technique is meant only to give you a framework for thinking about the case.

1. *Do a stakeholder analysis.* A stakeholder is any individual or group that has an interest in your company or the ability to affect it. For example, if you work for a manufacturing company, your stakeholders include, but are not limited to, your CEO, your employees, your customers, your suppliers, your stockholders, your directors, the people who live in the area of your plant, and so forth. You may also count among your stakeholders such people as environmentalists, landlords, bankers, political groups, and a wide range of special interest groups.

   Begin by making a list of those stakeholders you believe are pertinent to the case. Be careful not to overlook the bit players, such as the secretary who is only referred to briefly and the people who are described in groups, such as the accounting team, the interdepartmental bowling league, or three friends who often get together next to the water cooler. List everything you know about each stakeholder, and then describe your mental image of each. Don't be afraid to generalize; sometimes putting faces and bodies on the case characters can help you analyze what is going on.

   Look for clues, and try to flesh out each stakeholder on the basis of those clues. Since it is likely that you will be making decisions that stem from assumptions about the characters involved, make a concerted effort to bring those assumptions into your conscious awareness. Don't just sketch the characters; draw them in full color and detail. Then, test out your perceptions of the characters against those of your study mates.

2. *Develop a chronology of events.* In this step, you can use a time line or other method to list the events in the chronological order in which they occurred. You will quickly note that cases often do not follow a chronological order, so it is up to you to tease out the events and order them. Some events may seem minor because of the way they are presented. Don't let this fool you; they can be significant and even critical turning points, and they should be listed in your chronology.

3. *Identify and list what you believe are the basic issues.* Note especially those problems, events, acts, values, and attitudes about which decisions need to be made, e.g., Do government restrictions preclude certain courses of action, and if so, what can you do? Is there a mismatch of leadership styles to employee needs? Does some group of workers have norms that differ from those of the prevailing organizational culture? Using your list, arrange the items in order of priority and strength and find the relationships among them.

   In addition, draw a diagram that depicts the flow of communication in the organization. Some cases include organizational charts, but communication doesn't necessarily follow the prescribed patterns. Finding out who talks to whom can be significant in identifying both problems and solutions.

4. *List as many positions as possible that a reasonable person might take in solving the case.* The mistake most case analyzers make is to assume that there is one, and only one, reasonable solution. In fact, part of the intrigue of case discussion is finding just how many possibilities there are for solving any single problem—many of them workable, usually more than one with excellent results.

5. *Play out some of the possibilities.* "If I do this, will someone else do that? And if so, what will happen next?" Again, write out your results, or depict them graphically.

6. *Make a recommendation.* What do you consider the best possible solution to be? Why? This step generally presents the biggest trap. When you make a recommendation, it is far too easy to begin to believe in the singularity of your approach. For case method to work, you must stay open to the possibilities; you must stay flexible and be willing to listen to what others have to say. Good case analysis often depends on synergy, that process in which a group of people working together can accomplish more than the same number of people working by themselves, so, unless instructed otherwise, go ahead and discuss the case with your friends, family, anyone who will listen, and get everyone's input.

You may find yourself feeling slightly inadequate after your first case discussion. "Why didn't I think of that?" is the usual question, as your peers seem to be making observations that never even occurred to you. Instead of dwelling on this question, learn to respect the power of the group, the importance of your role in the group in stimulating the ideas of others, and the role of the group in stimulating you.

Case Discussion

The presentation of a case in a classroom setting is an opportunity for peer discussion. To avoid having their opinions taken as fact, instructors act merely as facilitators, selecting the presenters and occasionally redirecting or refocusing the discussion.

Generally, the facilitator will begin the case presentation by asking one or more members of the class to state the problems and present the list of pertinent stakeholders. Sometimes writing the names of the stakeholders on a chalkboard, along with a brief description of each, can be enough to get the discussion going. Examining the differing interpretations of each stakeholder's persona most often leads into the necessary analysis of the case events. If not, move on to a presentation of the chronology, and so forth through the steps outlined above.

Case analysis can be a satisfying learning experience if you are well prepared and willing to participate. The field of organizational behavior, in which the variables seem infinite, lends itself particularly well to this method.

Writing the Case Analysis

In many courses you will be required to do a written case analysis. A thorough written analysis should include, but not necessarily be limited to, the following:

1. A clear statement of the problem(s)
2. A thorough analysis of the pertinent stakeholders and of the issues and the ways these combine to create the problem(s)
3. One or more suggested solutions, with clear explanations of the strengths and weaknesses of each solution and with each solution supported by one or more of the theories of the science of organizational behavior
4. An explanation of how the solution(s) can be implemented (by whom, etc.) and the problems that might be encountered in implementation

Occasionally, students allow themselves flights of fantasy into what "might be," adding events and other material to cases to somehow force-fit them into a selected theory. Unless such material can be solidly and logically derived from the existing case material, it has no place in a written case analysis. Even if such material is reasonably derived, it should be presented as tentative.

The quality of a written case analysis generally is judged far less on the solution(s) presented than on how well the case analyzer has supported his or her arguments with the use of case material, theory, and solid critical thinking. No statement should be included in a case analysis, whether written or oral, that is not thoroughly supportable and supported.

USING EXPERIENTIAL EXERCISES IN THE STUDY OF ORGANIZATIONAL BEHAVIOR

Experiential exercises offer ways to test out and get feedback on behavior—actions and reactions—in group situations. Management trainers have long used experiential methods for teaching personal skills, and these methods have become a standard teaching technique at many business schools. Because experiential exercises are simulations and not actual situations in which behaving in an unacceptable manner can negatively impact an individual's career path, they are reasonably safe. In fact, experiential exercises work best when participants use them to test behaviors that they might be too threatened to use in settings "where it counts."

More traditional teaching methods are what I call "filling station style." Used successfully in certain disciplines, these methods often start with the assumption that students arrive with empty tanks and that it is the instructor's role to open the cap and pour in the knowledge. According to the tenets of this methodology, students are passive recipients, and rarely do they need to interact with one another.

The responsibility for learning from experiential exercises, however, belongs to the students themselves. Exercise groups consist of two or more participants; the most common groups range in size from five to seven. The role of the instructor is to set a tone that encourages participation, interaction, and risk taking; to introduce the exercise and lead and focus the debriefing discussion; and otherwise to remain essentially neutral and on the periphery. With experiential methods, the assumption is that you, the student, have a wealth of material from which to draw, particularly when it comes to the study of human behavior. By probing this material, comparing it to the experiences and observations of others, and by being willing to accept feedback, you build on and enrich your existing base of knowledge and understanding.

Experiential exercises come in a number of forms. For the purposes of this book, we will look at six: role plays; decision-making and consensus-building activities; fish bowls; round robin interviews; identity group sorting; and self-assessment tools.

Role Plays

Role plays are among the most common of the experiential exercises. The exercises are structured for anywhere from two to seven participants, although occasionally they involve larger numbers. Each participant is given a description of the person he or she is to play. If role plays are to work, participants must take their roles seriously, thinking through just how, based on the description, the character to be played would behave. The purpose is to give you a chance to experience what it might be like to be in another person's situation. For example, you might be asked to take the role of a disgruntled employee who feels he or she is not being treated fairly, while one of your classmates might be asked to act the role of a manager who has to deal with you. Since good management skills often involve being able to assess how another person is feeling, role play will give you an opportunity to do so.

It is not unusual to feel awkward, or even a little silly, the first time you are asked to play a role. Having had some previous acting experience might help, but barring that, simply taking your role seriously should ensure that you play it convincingly. If you are willing to jump in, role plays can be fun as well as meaningful.

Decision-Making and Consensus-Building Activities

Many decisions, but by no means all, are best made to the mutual satisfaction of those who will need to implement the results. Decision making must be done through open discussion, since imposing a decision from the outside generally means less commitment and less compliance by those affected by the decision. Similarly, if a group resolves a problem by voting, the group members become either winners or losers; this can polarize the group and severely undermine future cooperation. Workers tend to be less motivated to carry out a decision in which they feel they had no say, and clearly this has negative implications for productivity.

Since the emphasis in business is increasingly on team approaches to problem solving, decision-making and consensus-building activities will give you a chance to refine the skills necessary for staying open to diverse viewpoints and reaching creative outcomes. These activities present a problem and require you to work with one or more of your classmates to reach a mutually acceptable resolution.

Initially you may find it difficult to let go of your own perception of just how a problem should be solved. It's not unusual to think that your answer is the best. Listening carefully to your group mates, however, will allow you to further understand the complex dimensions that a problem presents. Here the group serves to bring to light far more facets of a problem than most of us are able to recognize alone.

Fish Bowls

Fish bowls are highly structured exercises that are often used in the social sciences to explore feelings and reactions to situations. A small group of people, usually not more than five, is asked to sit in the middle of the room and discuss a topic, while everyone else sits around the outside. Those in the middle are the "fish." Fish bowls generally start with a statement such as, "Tell us about . . ."; the fish then describe the particular event, person, or thing being explored. In this book we ask students, "Tell us about a situation in which you think you had a bad leader." Other topics may include, but not be limited to, times you felt different, times you felt left out, times you think you were effective, and so forth.

It is the job of the rest of the participants, those on the outside of the fish bowl, to listen to the discussion of the fish and to try to isolate recurring and prevalent themes. Those outside of the fish bowl may not speak until the fish have completed their conversation. At that point, those outside of the fish bowl are asked to report on what stood out for them in the conversation. During the reports, fish are required to listen but may not speak.

Fish bowls tend to spark memories and reactions in those who listen carefully to the fish. They also afford opportunities to practice skills in giving and getting feedback.

Round Robin Interviews

Round Robin Interviews are data-gathering and consolidation experiences. A number of questions (about one per every seven to ten people participating) focusing on a particular topic area are prepared in advance and assigned to the participants. For example, if the topic is motivation, the questions might include "What role does your salary play in your life?" "How do you feel about working overtime?" "How would it impact the quality of your work to have an office in the basement?" and so forth.

Each question is identified by number, color, or some sort of visible code that participants display. Participants are then asked to conduct interviews with other participants who have a different question. In other words, if you have question one, you could interview someone with question two or three, but not someone with question one. The person you interview would, in turn, interview you with his or her assigned question. Interviews last about five to ten minutes each, with length and number of interviews depending upon available time.

At the end of the interviewing, all those with the same questions meet together to share their results and consolidate their findings into a report that is then made to the rest of the class.

These exercises help to bring out differences and similarities in responses to topical issues. They are also useful as ice breakers.

Identity Group Sorting

This exercise asks people to join others who identify themselves in similar ways. Categories of identification may be generated by the class or decided on in advance by the instructor. For example, if a topic is leadership, participants may be asked to sort themselves into democratic leaders, autocratic leaders, country club leaders, Theory X leaders, Theory Y leaders, and so forth. Each identity group then meets to explore such concerns as what it is like to belong to that group, how they perceive themselves and why, and how they believe others perceive them. Groups then report their findings to the rest of the class. Feedback from those outside of the group is especially important in this type of exercise, particularly since we know that the way we perceive ourselves is not necessarily the way others perceive us.

One interesting and frequently used technique with identity group sorting is to ask the group members to depict themselves graphically, using a large sheet of paper and marking pens. Each group then displays its drawing to the rest of the class, explaining the symbols used and the reasons for them.

Self-Assessment Tools

We are probably all pretty familiar with self-assessment tests: they're the ones that give us the correct answers and some feedback on why our answers are right, wrong, or have some particular meaning. We see them in magazines and newspapers fairly frequently, with the correct answers supplied by an expert. They're usually fun to do, but they should be seen only as giving limited insights and serving as jumping-off points for further self-exploration. Information from self-assessment tools is probably most useful when shared and explored with others.

TECHNIQUES FOR PROBLEM SOLVING AND HEIGHTENING CREATIVITY

Brainstorming

Brainstorming is perhaps the most common group problem-solving and decision-making technique used in business today; but if you ask ten different managers to describe the process, you will probably end up with ten different responses. *The American Heritage Dictionary* defines a brainstorm as "a sudden and violent disturbance in the brain" and "a sudden clever, whimsical, or foolish idea."[1]   The concept of brainstorming draws on these definitions and suggests that out of the violent disturbances and the whimsical ideas can come creative solutions to complex problems, especially when several brains storm together.

Most often, the word *brainstorming* conjures up an image of a casual process—people sitting around boxes of half-eaten pizzas and throwing out ideas as they come to mind. In fact, for brainstorming to be really effective, it should be highly structured and tightly controlled. Moreover, it should be made clear from the outset that every member of the group must participate and that, at least in the early stages, every idea generated will be deemed to have equal weight with every other idea generated.[2]

For every idea to be received and considered as being equal to all other ideas, strict rules must be followed. While an idea may seem absurd or amusing when given, laughing is generally taken personally by the idea giver and as an affirmation to all that the idea is nonsense. As a result, the idea giver feels diminished and is less likely to make additional suggestions. The idea becomes tainted and is not taken seriously. Laughing, or in any other way criticizing an idea, is sometimes called "discounting," since the value of the idea has been diminished.

The opposite is also a problem: Many of us automatically believe that complimenting someone on an idea is an act of encouragement. In brainstorming, however, compliments directed at an idea during the initial stages give that idea enhanced weight and credibility. This inhibits the generation of other ideas: participants consciously or unconsciously note that since an acceptable idea has already been generated, no new ideas are really necessary and that it is unlikely they will be able to think of anything as appropriate anyway.

Stopping idea generation either by discounting or complimenting often results in premature closure and can mean diminished creativity and mediocre decisions. When this happens, it is called "satisficing."

Brainstorming tends to be most successful when carried out in groups no larger than seven nor smaller than three, not including the facilitator.

The Facilitator

It is the facilitator's job to frame the problem, set out the limits and issues, see to it that everyone's ideas are accepted equally, control the schedule, and make sure that everyone participates. The facilitator should be equipped with an easel and pad, chalk board, overhead acetates, or other materials that will allow him or her to record, in a visible place, the suggestions generated. Ideas should be recorded, either by the facilitator or an

---

Definition of "brainstorm" is adapted and reprinted from *The American Heritage Dictionary, Second College Edition* (Boston: Houghton Mifflin Co., 1985) p. 203.

1. *The American Heritage Dictionary of the English Language*, 2nd coll. ed., s.v. "brainstorm."

2. See A. F. Osborne, *Applied Imagination: Principles and Procedures of Creative Thinking* (New York: Scribners, 1941), for additional information about brainstorming.

Facilitators should also learn a few simple techniques:

1. When a suggestion is made that seems unclear, the facilitator may request, "Please tell me more," or ask, "Could you tell me just a bit more about what you're suggesting?" The facilitator should avoid such phrases as, "I don't understand," since they can make a participant feel defensive or uneasy.
2. The facilitator also may give clarifying feedback to participants by rephrasing a suggestion, prefacing it with, "So you are suggesting that [. . . restatement of the suggestion in the facilitator's words . . .]?" This allows a participant to agree or further explain the suggestion as necessary.
3. The facilitator should also check frequently with participants for affirmation that what is being recorded accurately reflects the intention. This can be done by asking, "Is this fair?" or, "Is this an acceptable/accurate depiction?"

The Process

The following six-step technique is one of many possible variations of brainstorming:

1. *Defining the problem.* In this step, the facilitator describes the problem to be solved. He or she gives the background of the problem, explains why it needs to be solved, and describes who will be affected. The definition must also include an explanation of any limits that are inherent to the problem—for example, we must be able to complete the project within six months; the product must be fire resistant; or the product must be able to be operated by one person. At this time, participants may ask for any additional clarification.

    The definition should be kept brief: Too much information or too many restrictions can inhibit creativity. Step one is generally limited to about five minutes.
2. *Individual generation of ideas.* Each participant silently and independently generates three to four suggestions that he or she writes down without discussion with other group members.
3. *Round robin.* The facilitator begins by asking each member to give one of his or her ideas and continues to go around the room, in order, taking ideas from each of the members. After the initial round, participants continue to suggest ideas either inspired by those already raised or altogether new.

    Comments and criticisms of any kind are not allowed. Every idea is considered to have equal merit and potential. Step three should be time limited to twenty to thirty minutes so as to avoid boredom and frustration.
4. *Categorizing.* Sometimes called "idea structuring," this step involves examining the ideas that have been generated to find categories into which they can be sorted. Categorizing allows participants to begin to examine the distinct similarities and differences between the ideas. For example, if the problem has been to develop a vandal-proof public telephone,[3] solution categories might include limited-access telephones, telephones made of resistant materials, and telephones without moving parts. More than one set of categories may emerge; it is up to the group, with the leadership of the facilitator, to select the best ones, usually three to five.
5. *Discussing and synthesizing.* At this stage, ideas are looked at critically, and the process of eliminating the least ones acceptable is begun. In some situations, it will be possible to eliminate entire categories at once. For example, if one category of

---

3. New York employees of NYNEX actually used brainstorming to tackle this problem.

ideas is "things that require considerable research and development" and the project must be completed within a short time period, this category might be easily removed.

During this step, it is often useful to appoint a "devil's advocate." Historically, the devil's advocate was appointed in the Roman Catholic Church to find flaws and provoke controversy in discussions over whether certain individuals would be beatified as saints. The purpose of the devil's advocate was to ensure that saints would be selected on the basis of merit and not politics. This same function works well in brainstorming. As the field of suggestions is narrowed, it is the job of the devil's advocate to raise points about possible weaknesses.

6. *Closure.* The last step in brainstorming is to do one of the following:
    a. Select the single best idea by consensus or vote. It may also be desirable to select the top three to five ideas and rank them to create a back-up plan.
    b. Take the best elements of several ideas and develop a new, composite idea.
    c. Reject all of the ideas, redefine the problem based on new information gathered through the process, and start again.

Used correctly, brainstorming is a powerful tool. Remember that while it requires considerable time, brainstorming also encourages the generation of creative solutions to difficult problems.

Force Field Analysis

Force Field Analysis[4] is a kind of accounting system for breaking down problems to clarify which parts can be dealt with meaningfully and which cannot. The kind of breakdown required by a Force Field Analysis aids decision making as to the most cost-effective use of time and effort in effecting change. Force Field Analysis has an added benefit of being graphic; driving and restraining forces are laid out on a form, complete with arrows, that gives quick visual access to the problem and its component parts (Figure 1).

Driving forces are those factors that push toward making a change. Take, for example, the change that you made in your life when you graduated from high school and decided where to go to college.[5] Driving forces may have included your having gotten good grades in high school, a desire to meet new people, your parents' desires to see you receive a top-level education, your desire for further education, college parties and social life, getting a necessary credential for a good job, and so forth.

On the other side of the ledger, however, are restraining forces—those things that push away from making the decision to go away to college. These might have included the high cost of a college education, leaving friends behind, leaving family, having to have a roommate, fear of the unknown, fear of becoming "a small fish in a big pond," and so forth.

Imagine that these driving and restraining forces are pushing against one another and nothing is happening (Figure 2). The ideal situation may be to go to a college in another state, but there are many forces pushing away from that decision. Picture the driving and restraining forces as being at opposite ends of a big spring[6]: Pushing against the driving forces doesn't really do anything other than to increase the pressure from the restraining

---

4. K. Lewin and D. Cartwright, eds., *Field Theory in Social Science* (New York: Harper & Row, 1951).
5. Special thanks to Sandi Deacon for this suggestion.
6. Special thanks to Dr. Lloyd Baird, Department of Organizational Behavior, School of Management, Boston University, for this suggestion.

forces. You have to keep the pressure on at the driving end because, unless the pressure from the restraining forces is reduced, the spring will want to bounce back to its original shape.

How might you go about reducing that pressure? If money is an issue, you might apply for financial aid or a scholarship. If you're concerned about missing friends and family, you might call home a lot. If you're concerned about going to the unknown, you'll probably want to visit the school, talk to students, and attend classes. The point is, doing something about the restraining forces allows the driving forces to move ahead with less resistance.

Force Field Analysis

Goal

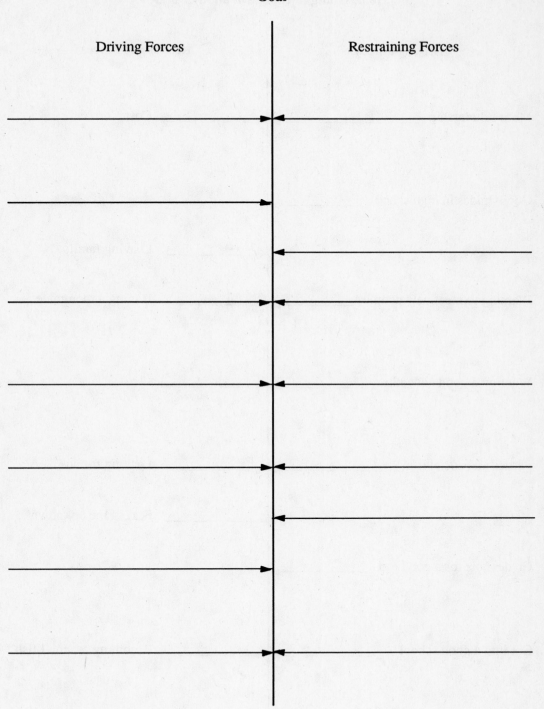

FIGURE 1

Force Field Analysis

Goal: Going to college in another state

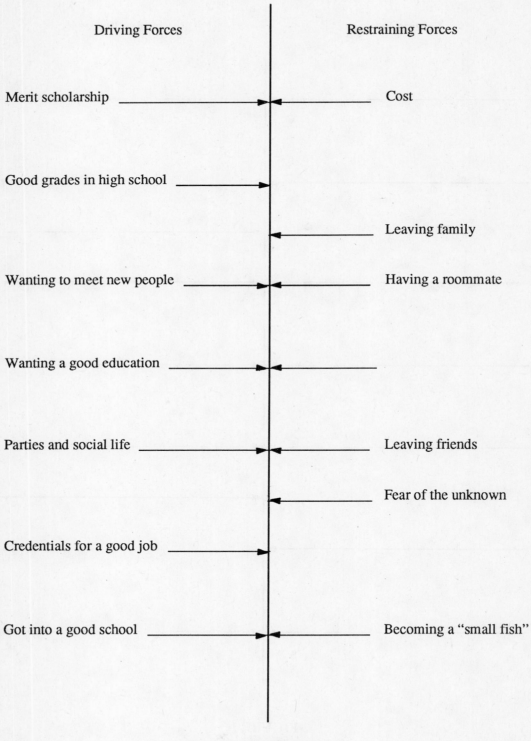

FIGURE 2

ICEBREAKERS

THE REALISTIC JOB PREVIEW

Most people have seen the old TV commercials that promoted the army, navy, air force, and marines. Ever wonder what those did for enlistment? Not surprisingly, those images of crashing waves on exquisite beaches, Tom Cruise look-alikes flying jets while enthusiastic admirers looked on, and other "see the world" scenarios increased enlistment. But the armed services also had the equivalent of an enormous turnover problem, and re-enlistments were fairly low.[1]

Step 1   Take a minute to note below why you believe the turnover problem existed:

_____

_____

_____

Chances are, you recognized that the actual experiences of recruits did not match their expectations and that therefore the recruits became disillusioned and angry. In an effort to turn this around, army recruiters started to give potential enlistees a realistic job preview. They showed them videos of what life would really be like in the service and in other ways tried to give them a balanced portrayal of military life.

Step 2   List below those positive and negative factors about military life that you think the army recruiters should have included in their realistic job preview:

Positive:

_____

_____

_____

Negative:

_____

_____

_____

Surprisingly, many of the enlistees found basic training to be nowhere near as bad as they had feared. However, the biggest and most unanticipated problem was homesickness. As a result of using the realistic job preview, enlistment did decrease to some extent. However, probably as a result of having given recruits an accurate picture of what to prepare themselves for, re-enlistment increased dramatically. The army gained considerable credibility and loyalty from the troops.

Realistic job previews were also used to try to decrease the turnover that airlines face with airport baggage checkers. Applicants were forewarned about the good and bad points of the job.

This exercise was written by Scott Weighart.

1. See B. Megliana, A. DeNisi, S. Youngblood, and K. Williams, "Effects of Realistic Job Previews: A Comparison Using an Enhancement and a Reduction Preview," *Journal of Applied Psychology* 73, no. 2 (May 1988):259–266.

Step 3   List below those positive and negative factors about the job of airport baggage checker that you think the airlines should have included in their realistic job previews:

Positive:

_____

_____

_____

Negative:

_____

_____

_____

What impact do you believe realistic job previews had on airport baggage checker turnover? _____Turnover increased _____Turnover decreased _____Turnover stayed the same

Unfortunately, realistic job previews don't always work, because a bad job is a bad job—previews can't change that. The job is boring and stressful; impatient passengers are rude and resentful. Thousands of bags must be examined, even though virtually none of them contain anything troublesome. Periodically, some handlers report, Federal Aviation Administration workers try to slip fake explosives past the checkers, and steep fines are assessed if they are caught napping. Realistic job previews can't help here.

Step 4   Try one more: If you were providing realistic job previews for applicants for the job of highway or bridge toll collector, what positives and negatives would you include?

Positive:

_____

_____

_____

Negative:

_____

_____

_____

Surprisingly, jobs as highway and bridge toll collectors are very popular, despite tedium and car exhaust. Why? Toll takers get a tremendous amount of feedback. Given the nature of the equipment with which they work, toll takers generally know precisely how accurate they have been in terms of giving out change. Some like being outdoors, enjoy the steady routine, and like the human interaction that comes with giving directions and otherwise helping travelers out.

If you went through steps 1–4 without peeking at the answers before supplying your own, chances are you got some of the important points but missed others. The moral is that while the fields of organizational behavior and management appear to be common sense, sometimes the things that drive human behavior are either outside of our immediate experience or are counterintuitive. For example, are satisfied workers more productive workers? Sometimes, but many researchers have found that there is no great statistical correlation between job satisfaction and productivity.

Step 5   (Optional) One of the things you might want to do is hold a realistic "job preview" for the course in which you are using this book. Consider what your expectations, hopes, and fears are, then take a minute to list what you believe the positives and negatives of being in this course are likely to be:

Positive:

_____

_____

_____

Negative:

_____

_____

_____

When you're done, share your list with others in the class and with the instructor. Use the course syllabus as a framework for developing a realistic assessment of what the course will be like and what the job of being a student in it will be.

NETWORKING

Since you'll most likely be working with one or more of your classmates over the course of the semester, it helps to learn a little about them from the outset. Following is an exercise to help you get to know some of the people with whom you will be working. This exercise will also give you an opportunity to practice your listening skills.

PROCEDURE

Step 1 (20 minutes)

Look around the room and find: someone who you do not now know but who you think would be interesting to know; or someone whose background or interests you think are the least like yours. In about twenty minutes, learn all you can about one another. Get general information about your partner's interests, background, hobbies, plans for the future, and so forth. Find out about three things that you and your partner have in common and three things that are different. Listen carefully to what your partner tells you about himself or herself but do not take notes or write anything down.

Step 2 (20–30 minutes)

When you and your partner have finished your mutual interviews, select another pair of students to join. This time, introduce your partner to the new pair, telling them everything you have learned about him or her. Continue to go around the group until all four members have had a chance to introduce their partners.

Step 3 (open-ended)

Option 1: When you have completed the introductions in your groups of four, join another group of four. This time, introduce a member of the new pair that you joined in step 2. Continue to join other groups until you run out of time.

or

Option 2: When you have completed step 2, introduce your original partner to the rest of the class.[2] This will give you an opportunity to practice oral presentation skills and give more people a chance to learn something about you and your partner.

---

2. Thanks to Gail Gilmore for this suggestion.

ROUND ROBIN INTERVIEW

Like the Networking exercise, this ice breaker will help you learn about your classmates. Knowing something about each other should help facilitate working together throughout the duration of this course.

PROCEDURE

Step 1 (30–40 minutes)

You will be assigned one of the following sets of topic areas (or others as may be selected by the instructor) about which to talk to other class members. In addition, you will be given a number, colored tag, or other item to wear that will identify you as having a specific topic area.

Possible topic areas

1. Describe a time when you felt uncomfortable or out of place, and explain why you felt that way and what you did about it.
2. Describe a time when you felt really proud of something you had done, and explain why and how you reacted.
3. Describe a time when you got very angry about something, and explain how you reacted and why.
4. Describe a time when you really disagreed with something but went along with it anyway, and explain how you felt and why.
5. Describe a time when someone important to you tried to get you to do something you really didn't want to do, and you said no. Explain how you felt and why.

Select a class member who has an identification other than yours and interview that person on the topic area you have been assigned. In turn, that person should interview you on his or her topic. You may take notes. Keep your interviews brief.

Repeat the interviewing with additional people, up to four, until time runs out.

Step 2 (20–30 minutes)

Working in a group with the others who were assigned your topic area, discuss your findings and consolidate the information to develop a summary of the topic. Consider what the responses had in common and how they differed.

Step 3 (open-ended)

Report your findings to the class. Discuss.

PART I

INDIVIDUAL PROCESSES IN ORGANIZATIONS

OVERVIEW

The two central areas of focus of the cases and exercises in this section are perception and motivation. As subsets of these themes, you'll be asked to consider the management of diverse work forces, sexual harassment, and cognitive dissonance. Most likely, you'll quickly note that the themes and their subsets are all closely intertwined. The way we perceive people, for example, is the way we treat them, and the way we treat people has a great deal to do with just how motivated they are to carry out the tasks we assign to them. But it isn't quite that easy: People are more likely to be motivated according to how they *perceive* they are being treated—which may be very different from the way we believe we are treating them—as well as according to what they perceive their needs to be.

Perception

Let's look into the crystal ball and consider what might be awaiting you in the business world after you graduate. You've been a reasonably successful student and are able to land a prestigious management job with a glamorous company. Three months after you've started your dream job, the national economy collapses. All of a sudden you're called into your boss's office. She concedes that you have been an excellent performer—one of the best she's got—but times are hard. She reminds you that you have the least seniority on the job. Then she says that you're laid off, shakes your hand, and shows you to the door.

Although you are upset, you are confident that you can get another desirable and professional job. No such luck: Nobody's hiring young business graduates. The only job offer you get is from a local grocery store called Shop Till You Drop. They want you to be a grocery bagger; you see no other choice, and you accept.

What would be going on in your head during this whole situation? Would you find it unfair? How motivated would you be about bagging groceries if this really happened to you? The answer to that is probably pretty obvious. What would someone else think about it? Answering that is not nearly as simple as you might think.

The fundamental rule of individual processes is that we are all different in how we perceive events and in what motivates us to work hard or hardly work. Our perceptions and motives are driven by what we have learned through our experiences.

Perception is the way we make sense of what we experience. Consider an American couple—Bruce and Sandi—who decide to see a bullfight at Plaza de Toros in Madrid. As they watch the matador stoop to one knee and twirl his cape, allowing the bull's horns to miss him by inches, Bruce feels anxious; Sandi is dazzled and awestruck. When the matador kills the bull by expertly thrusting the knife down through the bull's shoulder blades, Bruce can no longer look; he feels thoroughly nauseated. Meanwhile, Sandi stands up and cheers, not even flinching when someone cuts off the bull's ears and presents them to the matador in honor of his exemplary work.

In this example, Bruce and Sandi see the same reality: a bullfight on a hot day in Madrid. However, they perceive the bullfight very differently. Most likely, their previous experiences have caused them to react in contrasting ways. Perhaps Sandi loves Hemingway's novels and romanticizes the sport of bullfighting: Seeing an actual fight only reinforces how she already feels about the subject. Meanwhile, Bruce might have grown up on a farm where he was taught that needlessly killing animals is no sport at all. Regardless, past learning experiences have led them to develop different attitudes about their afternoon in Madrid.

Bring Bruce and Sandi back to the United States and put them in jobs in which they work for the same manager, a manager who sets high standards and is demanding. Bruce considers the manager to be inspirational, a great leader; Sandi, on the other hand, considers the manager to be overbearing and intimidating. The manager is the same: Sandi and Bruce simply perceive him differently.

Motivation

What drives us to do the things we choose to do each day? Lynn, a marketing manager for a shoe company, can't understand why her secretary, Miriam, doesn't go to graduate school and get a better job. After much arm twisting, she convinces Miriam to take the GRE test; Miriam gets scores of 790, 710, and 750. Lynn is thrilled for her, but Miriam asks her not to tell anyone else in the office about it, fearing that it might affect her friendships with other secretaries. Nothing Lynn says convinces Miriam to make the most of her intellectual ability. Lynn is completely puzzled.

Why are there such dramatic differences in what motivates people? Many social scientists have determined that we all have our own motivational needs: We try to act in ways that will fulfill our individual needs, but our needs may change frequently, depending on our life situations. If a professional couple decides to have a child, perhaps the husband will feel less inclined to strive for great achievements at work and want to stay at home to fulfill more basic affiliation needs. As a successful businessperson approaches retirement, he or she may stop devoting large amounts of energy to job achievements or personal friendships. Instead, the businessperson may concentrate on taking all the right steps to ensure that personal finances are invested properly, perhaps to make sure that there will be enough money available to survive retirement.

More personally, think about the bosses you've had on summer jobs or part-time jobs during high school. Did your bosses treat you as if you were a responsible adult, or did they watch your every move to make sure you weren't goofing off? Did they assume that you would want to do the best work possible, or did they act like you were a lazy kid who had to be forced to do anything and everything? Managers are no different from employees: They perceive things based on their experiences and may or may not have treated you in the way that you deserved.

A good manager recognizes that every human being is different and cannot be judged on the basis of age, gender, culture, race, and so forth. Only by recognizing and accepting people's differences can we treat them fairly. This is why it is so important to learn all you can about perception, motivation, and managing diversity.

Now reconsider our first example: How do you think a skilled and educated individual would respond to being laid off during a bad economy? How would he or she perceive it? How would this event affect this person's motivation?

This kind of layoff actually happened to a Scottish immigrant back in the 1930s. The man had an engineering degree and was earning a better-than-average salary after moving to the United States, getting married, and having two children. Suddenly he no longer had a job, and indeed, the only work he managed to get was as a grocery bagger at a local supermarket.

How did he respond to this disappointing blow? The night before he began work as a grocery bagger, he asked his wife and children to empty all of the groceries from the cabinets. He proceeded to practice bagging the groceries as fast as he could. Due to the discouraging economic environment and the responsibilities of providing for a family, he perceived the grocery store job to be a good one: It would help him fulfill what had become his most crucial motivational need—making enough money to survive and to have some sense of security.

When the Great Depression ended, he was again able to find work as an engineering draftsman and earned the respect of his colleagues for his professionalism and high level of motivation.

What You'll Need to Know Before Tackling the Cases and Exercises

Prior to reading the cases or exercises included in this section, you will need to have an understanding of perceptual processes and how they affect attitudes and motivation. You should also be familiar with projections for the American work force, which is becoming increasingly diverse as more women and minorities enter the job market. This development, generally referred to as Work Force 2000 (after a study undertaken by the United States government), will make an understanding of individual differences crucial to your future success as a manager.

Douglas McGregor's Theories X and Y are useful ways to describe the philosophies and preconceived notions of the managers illustrated in the cases and exercises. Remember that it is not worker behavior that McGregor describes, but rather managerial perceptions of workers—for example, workers are lazy and won't work unless pushed, or workers will work hard if given a chance.

You should be familiar with attitudes and the concept of cognitive dissonance. An individual experiences cognitive dissonance when he or she has contradicting thoughts, such as "I love smoking cigarettes" and "I don't want to have emphysema at the age of twenty-nine." The theory suggests that when people have these conflicting thoughts, they strive to *reduce* the conflict by changing their thoughts or behaviors: The person could quit smoking or could start thinking, "Well, the air is so polluted that I'm no better off if I give up the cigarettes."

It will be important, as well, to be fully acquainted with several theories of motivation. Specifically, you should understand Maslow's Hierarchy of Needs, Alderfer's ERG Theory, McClelland's Three Needs Theory, and perhaps Murray's Manifest Needs Theory. All of these theories suggest that human behavior is driven by various motivational needs. These needs can change rapidly, but often for an individual, one is dominant. Managers must be sensitive to these needs and address them directly when attempting to resolve any organizational problems, such as those illustrated by the cases and exercises.

Herzberg's Two-Factor Theory is also a valuable tool in understanding worker motivation. You should be able to identify the various hygiene factors and motivators, which basically illustrate that the factors that lead to job satisfaction are not the same as those that lead to dissatisfaction.

Equity and expectancy theories are two valuable diagnostic tools to consider. According to equity theory, workers will adjust their behavior to reduce any inequities (unfairness) that they perceive. The expectancy theory develops the link between performance in a motivational situation and expectations of whether that performance is likely to have a positive or negative outcome for the individual or organization.

Since individual processes are the most fundamental components of organizational behavior, be sure to devote ample time to mastering these theories. When we consider broader organizational issues and more complicated cases later in this book, a solid understanding of these concepts will greatly enrich your understanding and analytical base.

What You See Isn't Necessarily What You Get

PROCEDURE

Step 1 (5–10 minutes)

Read the situation to yourself, and decide who it is that is standing at your door and why you believe it to be that person. Make some notes as to your rationale for eliminating the other possibilities and selecting the one that you did.

Step 2 (10–20 minutes)

Working in small groups or with the class as a whole, discuss who might be standing at your door and why you believe it to be that person. In a place visible to all, reproduce the grid found with this exercise, and use it to record the responses of class members.

Step 3 (open-ended)

In class discussion, consider the stereotypes used to reach a decision, and consider the following:

1. How hard was it to let go of your original decision once you had made it?

2. What implications do first impressions of people have about how you treat them, the expectations you have of them, and whether the acquaintance is likely to go beyond the initial stage?

3. What implications do your responses to the above questions have to the way you, as a manager, might treat a new employee? What will the impact be on that employee?

4. What are the implications for yourself in terms of job hunting and so forth?

Situation

You have just checked into a hospital room for some minor surgery the next day. When you get to your room, you are told that the following people will be coming to speak with you within the next several hours:

1. The surgeon who will do the operation
2. A nurse
3. The secretary for the department of surgery
4. A representative of the company that supplies televisions to the hospital rooms
5. A technician who does laboratory tests
6. A hospital business manager
7. The dietician

You have never met any of these people before and don't know what to expect.

This exercise was written by Janet W. Wohlberg.

About half an hour after your arrival, a woman who seems to be of Asian ancestry appears at your door dressed in a straight red wool skirt, a pink-and-white-striped polyester blouse with a bow at the neck, and red medium–high heel shoes that match the skirt. She is wearing gold earrings, a gold chain necklace, a gold wedding band, and a white hospital laboratory coat. She is carrying a clipboard.

Questions for Discussion

1. Of the seven people listed, which of them is standing at your door? How did you reach this conclusion?
2. If the woman had not been wearing a white hospital laboratory coat, how might your perceptions of her have differed? Why?
3. If you find out that she is the surgeon who will be operating on you in the morning, and thought she was someone different initially, how confident do you now feel in her ability as a surgeon? Why?

What You See Isn't Necessarily What You Get

On the grid below, list the reasons that the woman standing before you is or is not each of the following individuals. Also, take a vote, and list the number of people in your class who select each possibility.

		Number who make this selection
Surgeon		
Nurse		
Secretary		
Television Representative		
Laboratory Technician		
Business Manager		
Dietician		

Waiting Tables for Godot

Instead of spending her summer vacation at her parents' house in King of Prussia, Pennsylvania, college student Diane Almeida decided to stay in Boston and take a job waiting on tables at La Maison d'Essence, a fancy French restaurant near the up-scale Faneuil Hall Market Place. Diane felt fortunate to get such a job: The pay was $2.35 per hour, plus tips. Considering that the average dinner for two, with wine, ran about $90, Diane thought that she could make big money if she worked hard enough to earn 15 to 20 percent tips.

When Jean-Pierre Godot, owner of La Maison d'Essence, hired Diane, he emphasized that he expected excellence from his staff. He spoke about his vision for his restaurant and the importance of working as a team. She decided right then that she would really give it her all to prove just how good she could be.

Godot seemed dedicated and industrious, but he was also prone to emotional outbursts. When the restaurant got crowded, and people got restless waiting for their dinners to be served, Godot would stomp into the kitchen and shout at the chef in French: "Dépêche-toi! Tu es un escargot paresseux; ma grand-mère peut faire la cuisine plus vite que toi!" (Hurry up! You are a lazy snail; my grandmother can cook faster than you!)

Godot essentially ignored Diane during her first several weeks on the job. Hearing how he spoke to the cook, she was actually a little relieved. Still, she was surprised that he hadn't said anything to her. As far as she could tell, she was doing a good job, and she was averaging close to 20 percent in tips. Customers complimented her on her efficient service—from previous experience, she had learned to balance several plates on her arms, so she didn't have to waste time making extra trips to the kitchen. She also knew that giving really good service meant doing a lot of little extras.

Diane was sure, as well, that she was helping La Maison d'Essence make more money from each customer. She had a knack for recommending the right wines to compliment meals, she frequently walked by to see if people needed to have drinks refreshed, and she tempted her customers into buying lavish desserts by describing them in sensuous detail.

Diane spoke French well enough to use it when the occasional French or French-Canadian diner ate at the restaurant. She displayed her excellent memory by always remembering who ordered what and handing out the entrees accordingly, and she remembered repeat customers and greeted them with "welcome back."

Despite all of this, Godot took little notice of her, merely grunting at her when she said hello or goodbye each day. Then, one night, he finally spoke to her. More precisely, he yelled at her when she dropped a bowl of bouillabaisse appetizer on the carpet. Diane was very apologetic and hurried to get a sponge, but Godot shouted at her in rapid-fire French and told her that he would be deducting $8.95 from her pay—the price of the bouillabaisse—plus $5 for the cost of cleaning the stain in the rug.

Walking home that night, Diane felt angry and confused. Sure, maybe she shouldn't have tried to carry out four appetizers at once, but it was just a small mistake. What about the things she did to give the customers great service? Godot never seemed to notice

---

This case was written by Scott Weighart.

those things. Waiting for Godot to give a compliment was like waiting for a million dollars to fall from the sky.

Diane decided to slow down a little on the next night, not wanting to inspire another outburst from her boss. It was a Friday night, and the place was packed. Diane brought out no more than two dishes at a time, and her tips went down to under 15 percent, much less than her one-night high of 23 percent.

Although she didn't break anything, Godot still got irritated with her and the rest of his staff. As the waitstaff almost ran in and out of the kitchen, Godot kept saying to them, "Vite! Vite! Avez-vous plomb dans vos souliers?!" (Quick! Quick! Do you have lead in your shoes?!)

By the end of the night, Diane was really sick of his griping, and she slowed down considerably. Unfortunately, this made her tips sag. Really needing to make money so she could afford to eat something other than rice or spaghetti during her next college semester, Diane forced herself to go back to her original fast pace, praying that she wouldn't drop anything. She could hardly wait for September. Waiting for Godot had turned out to be all work and no play.

Questions for Discussion

1. Consider this case in terms of operant conditioning: What positive and negative reinforcements are used by Godot, if any?
2. What impact does punishment have on behavior, and on Diane's behavior specifically?
3. Using the concept of cognitive dissonance, explain what you believe are Diane's perception of the events at La Maison d'Essence.

The Kidney Transplant

You are a member of the Ethics and Policy Committee of a medium-size urban hospital and teaching facility. Your committee is charged with making decisions about research proposals and innovative medical procedures. When resources are short, the committee must also decide which patients will receive special services. This last responsibility usually leaves you with the uncomfortable feeling that you are being asked to play God. You are painfully aware that many patients who are not selected for special services face almost certain death.

This is exactly the case before you now. Five patients in your hospital have been recommended by your hospital's kidney transplant team as having the physical and psychological stamina necessary for a transplant operation. Without transplants, *all* of them face about one hundred to one odds that they won't survive beyond another three months. In the five years that the transplant unit has been in place, kidneys have become available at an average of about four a year. At times, the unit has had to wait as long as four months for kidney availability. It is impossible to know just when a kidney will become available. When one does, it will be on such short notice that it is important to have decided in advance which patient will be the recipient. Because all of the patients are critically ill, it is conceivable that one or more may die before a kidney becomes available, or that one or more could develop complications from their disease that could render them unacceptable as transplant candidates. If either of these possibilities comes about for the individual who is number one on the priority list, your transplant team needs to know immediately which patient will be moved in to take his or her place. Because any number of the patients could become unacceptable, you need to establish the order in which you will consider the five patients for transplant.

The transplant team has given you histories on each of the patients, including their personal and family backgrounds. You must consider the information and make your decisions. Your committee should discuss each candidate and reach a consensus (based on discussion rather than voting) as to who will be first, second, third, fourth, and fifth in line for this life-saving operation.

Sandra M., Age 34, Black, Baptist

Sandra is a registered nurse with three children, all under nine. She had worked the 11 P.M. to 7 A.M. shift at your hospital for six years until four months ago when her illness became too severe. The money she had been earning, and her willingness to work the night-to-morning shift, allowed her husband, James, a full-time paralegal in a major law firm, to pursue a law degree at a local night law school. Over the past four months, James has had to stop his law school classes (in which he was consistently earning top grades) in order to care for Sandra and the children. During the day, home health aides come in to assist Sandra. James drops the youngest child off at day care and drives the two older children to school on his way to work. He leaves work at lunchtime to pick the older children up and take them to the day care provider, and in the evening he picks them up.

This exercise was written by Janet W. Wohlberg.

There are few community support services available to the couple. Sandra is an only child whose parents had her rather late in life: both have been dead for over ten years. James has one married brother, but he lives in another city seven hundred miles away, as do his parents, who themselves are not well.

When Sandra and James were married almost a dozen years ago, they were full of high hopes. James had just graduated from a major university with a degree in business and had taken a job with the law firm, initially in their bookkeeping department. Sandra had graduated from the nursing school of the same university. They have both sung in their church choir, and Sandra had organized a support group for young mothers in their community.

Now Sandra is scared and depressed. She is increasingly upset with the realization that her illness has drained their young family both financially and emotionally, and she worries about her children and the impact her illness is having on them. Sandra prays that she will be considered to be a viable candidate for a kidney transplant so that she and James can continue to raise their family and share the love they feel so deeply for one another.

Sara Y., Age 42, White, Jewish

Sara is an English professor at Boston University. She is popular with students, has won the Metcalfe Award for Excellence in Teaching, and consistently has received highest evaluations for her courses. In addition, she is a member of the Democratic Women's Caucus and The League of Women Voters and is active in the Planned Parenthood Association (an organization that supports a woman's right to make choices about pregnancy, abortion, and birth control).

Last April, Sara received both good news and bad news on the same day: her first book won a national writers' award, and her kidney disease was diagnosed. She is currently on a semester leave as her illness has left her physically exhausted and unable to concentrate.

Sara grew up in a middle-class family in the Midwest. She received her undergraduate degree from an eastern women's college, a master's degree in English from Stanford, and just after she turned twenty-four, she settled into the role of housewife, having married her high school sweetheart. At age 29, she became a widow when her husband died in a plane crash. She was left with three young children. A substantial settlement from the airline allowed her to live comfortably, care for her children, and return to school for a Ph.D. in English literature, which she completed in five years. During her Ph.D. program, Sara met and married a Boston University history professor fifteen years her senior. A widower, he had four children, two of whom are now students at the university, a sophomore and a senior respectively. The oldest child has completed college and works in Vermont on an experimental farm; the youngest is still in high school. Sara's children are also still in high school. The couple adopted one another's children, creating what Sara calls "sort of a Jewish Brady Bunch." Sara's second husband died suddenly two years ago when he had a heart attack during his tenure hearings.

"My work isn't over," says Sara. "I know I'm not the only one in the world who can teach English and write books. That's something I do for me, something I feel good about. But I am the only one left for seven terrific kids, and they just don't deserve this."

Peter V., Age 27, White, No Religion Stated

Peter is a college dropout who has never held a steady job. His father, a member of your hospital's board of directors, has been particularly useful in helping the hospital weave its way through local red tape and politics. Peter's father also has been a major donor and an invaluable fundraiser. His efforts have been critical to the continued operation of the kidney transplant unit, which year after year incurs an enormous operating deficit and even now operates under the constant threat of being closed for lack of funds.

Unlike his very generous father, Peter behaves in an arrogant, demanding, and entitled manner. Since his admission to the hospital four months ago, he has angered and frustrated much of your staff. His nurse call button always seems to be on, but the nursing staff complains that when they respond, his demands are for channel changes on his television, pillow adjustments, and other petty requests. In addition, many members of the staff say they're uncomfortable with the steady stream of questionable characters who visit Peter's room night and day.

You have known Peter since he was a small child. He was a sweet boy, bright, fair-haired, and lively. At age thirteen, Peter was sent to the finest private boys' school in your area. You have heard rumors that Peter was suspended several times for drinking on school grounds or coming to classes drunk and that each time his father pressured the school to take him back. Ultimately he graduated, although you suspect he was given "social passes" to get him through and out without alienating his parents. Peter went on to a local two-year college, and for a time it looked like he was really going to straighten out. His parents have continued to support him since he dropped out of college at age twenty. They tell you that they will never abandon their son and that they believe that their love and support will ultimately bring him around. Until his admission to the hospital, Peter had been living in his parents' home.

Peter's father appears despondent over Peter's medical condition. Peter's mother, however, is angry and seems to hold the hospital responsible for every ache and pain her son is suffering. She has stated openly to members of her various clubs that if Peter does not receive a kidney, she and her husband will "stop all financial support and see to it that the hospital is made to pay for its negligence."

Chris J., Age 37, White, Methodist

Chris holds a Ph.D. in biology and worked on a research team at a leading biotech firm until two months ago when health complications made further work impossible. Scientists at the biotech firm believe that, thanks in large part to a major breakthrough by Chris, they are close to developing a drug intervention for use when AIDS is diagnosed at an early stage. Largely on the strength of Chris's work, the firm has been able to raise considerable capital and two government grants to continue the investigation and drug development. You've had a recent visit from the CEO of the biotech firm, a personal friend and former member of your hospital's staff, who came to plead on Chris's behalf. "Without Chris," the CEO told you, "we would not be as close to a cure for AIDS as we are. We're on the edge here of being able to save thousands of lives, and Chris is important to us."

Chris has been in a stable, same-sex "marriage" for thirteen years with Lee, a social worker for a local "safe house" for battered women. Chris and Lee have established a home in the suburbs, and Chris's elderly mother lives with them. (Chris's father was an alcoholic who disappeared when Chris was nine.) They have been active in their community, where they are socially popular and accepted by most, although by no means all, of their neighbors. A year ago Chris and Lee cochaired their community's successful Red Feather charity drive.

As a scientist, Chris is philosophical about the likelihood of a kidney transplant. "Life is so fragile and uncertain," says Chris. "I see that every day in the laboratory. I desperately want to live because I think I have a lot to contribute, but I also know that I could walk across the street and get hit by a car. Who ever knows?"

Cuong Ti D., Age 34, Asian, Catholic

Cuong came to the United States from Vietnam, where his parents, brother, and one of his two sisters had been killed by Vietcong snipers during a raid on his village. Cuong and his younger sister, an infant at the time, had escaped and hidden in the jungle for over a month before American soldiers found them and helped them to safety. Though only a young boy, Cuong had become invaluable to the U.S. troops for his knowledge of the strategically critical area surrounding his native village. He served as a guide on reconnaissance missions and successfully guided the American soldiers on eight such missions before he was captured. His captors took him to a North Vietnamese prison camp, where he was beaten and tortured for more than five years before he was able to escape. With the help of therapy, he has been able to gain some control over the nightmares he has suffered from these experiences.

Members of the Lutheran Church who sponsored his immigration to the United States are proud of Cuong's accomplishments. He studied English and, within a year, was accepted at a top university. He completed his undergraduate degree in engineering in three years on an army ROTC scholarship, while also holding a part-time job and keeping house for himself and his sister, who is, as far as he knows, his only surviving relative. After graduation, he took a full-time job, pursued and completed a master's degree in metallurgy at night, and continued to serve in the army reserves.

In late January 1991, Cuong was called into active service in Operation Desert Storm in Saudi Arabia. The doctors in charge of Cuong's case believe that his kidney damage was probably caused by the beatings he suffered in Vietnam but lay dormant until dehydration, suffered while in the Saudi Desert, brought his condition to where it is now.

For Cuong, life has just begun. Despite all he has been through, Cuong is optimistic. Two years ago, he met a Vietnamese woman whose story paralleled his own in many ways, and they have just recently become engaged. "God didn't bring me through all of this to let me die now," he told your staff psychiatrist. "I've been to hell and back—and I'm just not ready for a return trip."

PROCEDURE

Step 1 (15–20 minutes)

Read the profiles on each of the transplant candidates and rank them from 1 to 5, with 1 being the patient you would give highest priority to for a transplant and 5 the lowest. Record the order on the grid below.

Step 2

Working in groups of five to seven students, discuss each of the patients and, as a group, rank the patients again from 1 to 5, again with 1 being the highest priority. Do this by reaching a consensus based on discussion, not by voting.

	Your Ranking	Group Ranking	Influence Score	Comments/ Reasons
Sandra M.				
Sara Y.				
Peter V.				
Chris J.				
Cuong Ti D.				

Linda Sifuentes

Chris Chuang continued to chew on an already well gnawed-on rollerball pen and to think back over the seven years since Linda Sifuentes had joined the accounting office of Maven Development. It was clear that Linda, who had just left Chris's office, was angry about her semiannual performance appraisal discussion and the news that her salary increase was to be just 4 percent. Attempts to assure Linda that she was being treated "just like everyone else," to encourage her, and to offer support for any problems she might be having at home had obviously not helped. Chris feared that Linda was going to continue in the less-than-optimal performance pattern she had begun just over five months ago and had tried to warn her that her work had to improve. Linda's reaction had been defensive and somewhat accusing.

Maven Development

Maven Development is one of New England's largest commercial real estate developers. The company had been started in 1968 by Dersh Maven. Originally from Brooklyn, Maven had stayed on in Boston after his graduation from Boston University's School of Management in 1964. His summer internship with Cabot, Cabot & Forbes had turned into a challenging and interesting full-time job and proved to be a good training ground for learning about the politics and finances of real estate development. But Maven had always wanted to be his own boss, so less than four years after graduation, he left CC&F and started Maven Development.

During the building boom of the late seventies and eighties, Dersh Maven had grown his company from what was, by that time, a mid-sized firm developing largely in the outlying suburbs, to a giant. From 1983 to 1988, Maven developed three of the new office buildings in Boston and had created similar projects in Providence, Hartford, and Nashua, New Hampshire. As with many of the developers doing business at this level, design and construction were done by hiring outside architects and general contractors. It was Maven's job to assess the financial feasibility of a project, assemble the parcel of land, get clearance to build from local authorities, get zoning and environmental clearances, arrange for construction financing with a major bank, arrange long-term financing, and then market and ultimately manage the new building.

With the onset of the current real estate downturn, Maven began to face financial setbacks for the first time. While the company stretched to complete ongoing projects, rental of the new space began to fall well behind projections. Dersh Maven was reasonably sure that if he could hold on, he would do well when the market again turned around, but, in the meantime, the drain on cash flow was significant. The falloff in the real estate market was severe in the Northeast, and in addition to problems with renting new space, leases on existing buildings were having to be renegotiated at substantially reduced prices to hold tenants. This further eroded the cash flow situation; without a doubt, Maven was being financially squeezed.

This case was written by Janet Wohlberg.

Dersh Maven was a real hands-on company president who was loyal to his employees and made a point of knowing them by their first names. When his company's profits began to sag, he imposed a wage freeze on upper management while trying to keep salary increases for lower-level employees at around 7.5 percent. Bonuses, tied to profitability, were eliminated. In addition, he had instituted a hiring freeze that was now in its second year. While most of his industry competitors had laid off up to 25 percent of their employees, Dersh Maven was determined not to follow suit. In order not to lay off, however, Maven realized that this year's salary increases for lower-level employees were going to have to be not much more than 4 percent for top performers and that mediocre performers would probably get a lot less. The *Wall Street Journal* had only recently reported that average salary increases nationwide had dropped to 5.6 percent, with increases in the Northeast averaging 4.4 percent.

Linda Sifuentes

Linda was one of those success stories about whom newspaper columnists love to write. She had grown up in Lynn, Massachusetts, a depressed manufacturing town just outside of Boston. She was the eldest of four children, three girls and a boy, whose parents seemed perpetually out of work.

In her sophomore year, Linda became pregnant and dropped out of high school, despite attempts by her guidance counselor to help her complete her education. Two years later, Linda had a second child. She lived in a subsidized housing unit in Boston with her children, not really making it on welfare.

At age twenty-two, Linda decided that she had to have a better life for herself and her children. With considerable effort, she finished high school, receiving top grades and a scholarship to study at Boston University. While it took her six years of attending night classes to complete her college program, working during the days to support her family and studying on weekends, Linda did well. She met Dersh Maven when he came as a guest speaker to one of her classes in her senior year, and he had been impressed enough to offer her a job after graduation.

In May of that year, Linda went to work in the accounting office of Maven Development at a starting salary of $19,785. From the beginning, Linda had loved working at Maven. She had quickly become friendly with the other nine people in her department with whom she often went out after work and on weekends. Several of the others had children around the same ages as Linda's, and family outings with them became the norm. For the first five years, Linda had enjoyed a close relationship with her supervisor, Pat James, who had been supportive and who Linda felt she could always count on to be fair in the treatment of workers in the accounting department. Linda believed that her hard work and diligence at Maven would allow her to be able to move ahead in the company, her next step being into a position like Pat's.

Linda's work record had been impeccable. Except for having taken two days off at the time of her mother's death, Linda showed up regularly, always on time, worked late, and would often come in on weekends to finish important projects. Her work was accurate and well above average. At the end of her seventh year with Maven, she was earning $32,225 and had moved from her dismal, subsidized apartment to a small but comfortable one in a pleasant section of Quincy. Her children were doing well. During the previous summer, she had begun to date a real estate broker with whom she was now making wedding plans.

The Accounting Department

Five years after Linda had begun her job, Pat James had left Maven for a middle management job with Beacon Construction. Around the same time, Lee Elsworth, who had joined the accounting team about a year after Linda, was promoted to a management position in another department. Two other employees, close friends of Linda's, left for jobs in other companies, one following a spouse to the West Coast.

Chris Chuang, Pat James's replacement as supervisor of the accounting department at Maven, was brought in just before the hiring freeze went into effect. Chris had an M.B.A. from Boston University's Graduate School of Management and three years of accounting experience. Single, and younger than most members of the accounting department, Chris liked to spend summer weekends sailing and winter weekends skiing. Notwithstanding some sense that commercial real estate development was a troubled industry, Chris had been satisfied that the supervisory job at Maven was, at least for the time, a satisfactory rung on the climb up the corporate ladder.

Other than Chris, no one else had come into the accounting department to replace those who had left. The department was unquestionably short-staffed, and work had begun to pile up. There was considerable pressure from upper management to produce the figures needed for reports to the banks, insurance companies, and other lenders, all of which were getting nervous over the downturn in the market. As each of the department's workers began to show strains from the increasing workload, the once-supportive environment became noticeably tense. Still, Dersh Maven was adamant about the hiring freeze. "Until we can return to profitability," he had written in a company memo, "no new workers will be hired. We must work together, support one another, and preserve Maven Development for the brighter future that lies ahead."

Chris's Problem

With added pressure from above, Chris thought this was no time for a reliable employee like Linda Sifuentes to become unreliable—but unreliable she was. Over the past five months, Linda had begun to come in late, take long lunch breaks, and call in sick, particularly on Mondays and Fridays. Chris had tried everything—threats, promises, you name it, but Linda's difficult behavior continued. "If I could only understand what's going on here," Chris thought, "maybe I could turn this around."

Questions for Discussion

1. Using at least two—but not more than three—theories of motivation, analyze and explain Chris's problem.
2. If you were Chris, given your analysis of the situation, what would you do?

Spanglemaker Publishing

For nearly twenty-five years, Marty Callahan had been the executive editor at Spanglemaker Publishing, a small company that specialized in children's books. Although Marty had had a long and happy career at Spanglemaker, he was headed for semiretirement.

The president of Spanglemaker, Lawrence Guthrie, had recently announced that the company planned a much more aggressive marketing strategy. Noting that a successful children's book—such as Chris Van Allsburgh's *The Polar Express*—could be on the best-seller lists for years, whereas adult literature had a much shorter life span for high-volume sales, Guthrie had decided to produce more innovative children's books in the hopes of discovering an occasional long-term "cash cow."[1]

While Marty understood Guthrie's rationale, he decided that the new goals and directions of the company were not consistent with his interests and that it was time to leave. Marty had always enjoyed the friendly atmosphere of Spanglemaker—how people would clip cartoons for him and how he and some of his colleagues would have long lunches in a nearby park, swapping book tips and jokes. As a sixty-two-year-old widower whose children had moved out of state, these get-togethers had become important to him.

Although Guthrie had said nothing directly, Marty realized that his boss's new expectations for the executive editor would mean a faster pace that would leave little time for friendly chats. Guthrie had hinted that Marty could step down and once again become a copy editor, a move that would allow him to continue his long lunches and coffee breaks. But, at his age, Marty decided to do freelance work at home for a variety of large and small publishing companies. It wouldn't be hard to get enough business; over the years, Marty had made many connections, and he was well liked and respected in the industry.

In a short meeting, Marty told Guthrie of his decision to take early retirement. Guthrie wished him luck and asked him if, before leaving, he would recommend someone to take his place. Three Spanglemaker copy editors had expressed an interest in the job. It would be a sensitive decision: Each candidate had a great deal of experience and was confident that he or she would be the best choice.

Initially, Marty eliminated Charles Langley from the list of candidates. Though they were good friends, Marty was sure that Charles would be obsessed with being in charge of his workers. Although he had more experience and seniority than the other two candidates, Charles would certainly be a big "rule maker" who might alienate the workers. He was bright and one of the better copy editors, and his people had the reputation of being highly productive. Charles was known to be hardworking and to expect nothing less from those who worked under him.

The maximum stay at Spanglemaker for most people who worked for Charles seemed to be about two years, considerably less than the company average. After getting some

---

This case was written by Scott Weighart.

1. A "cash cow" is a product that, after initial investment costs, continues to generate a high rate of income with only minimal additional expense.

really good training from him, the people who worked for Charles generally left to take higher-paying jobs with competitors. When Spanglemaker executives offered to match what competitors were offering, as an enticement to stay, few accepted. Having a fairly constant string of new employees meant a lot of fresh and new ideas, although Charles insisted that his people master the basics before getting involved in innovation.

Of the other two candidates, Marty decided first to interview Dominique Bernays, who had been with the company for more than ten years. In the past, Marty had been a reluctant admirer of Dominique's. She had shown a knack for discovering new authors and working with them. Many of her projects were unconventional but successful. For example, she had done well in helping an author develop a book for young children—a story about a little girl who had a single mother. Dominique believed that Spanglemaker should publish books geared toward the children of single parents, house-husbands, and even gay parents. Marty wasn't sure that the world was ready for such things.

Marty was also concerned that Dominique's personality would be problematic. He found her to be—well—"pushy." She was always deadly serious about her job and never seemed to have time for a friendly word. At work, she mostly stayed in her office, just chuckling and continuing to work even when someone told her she needed a breather.

"Tell me why you should get the job," Marty said during the interview.

"I think my record shows that I thrive on responsibility," Dominique replied, staring into Marty's eyes so hard that it made him uncomfortable. "As you know, most of the books that I've been involved with have been recognized by the critics as real breakthroughs in children's literature, such as the bilingual books for Hispanic families. Given my performance over the last several years at Spanglemaker, I feel I deserve an opportunity to grow while the company grows."

"Your individual performance has been outstanding," Marty admitted. "But how would you manage the copy editors?"

Dominique gave him a hard glance, and Marty wondered if he had sounded more skeptical than he had intended. But why not? He had legitimate doubts about her interpersonal skills.

"As executive editor, I would do several things differently," she began. "First, rather than just assigning people to an author, I would let them choose the projects that they would find most interesting. If a copy editor prefers to do primarily realistic fiction, or fantasy, or whatever, I'd let them do it whenever possible. At the same time, I would work closely with the copy editors so that I would always know what they are working on. If someone did a particularly good job, I would reward him or her—you know, a plaque for the office, his or her name displayed somewhere—or maybe just an occasional day off for anyone who doesn't seem comfortable about being publicly congratulated. Most importantly, though, I would emphasize that Spanglemaker should produce the best books possible—whatever it takes, I'll make sure that we publish the most dynamic books."

"As you know, sometimes the executive editor has to deal with support staff— temporary secretaries, receptionists, and various others—people who tend to be unmotivated. How would you deal with that?" Marty asked.

"It would really depend on the situation," she replied. "I think some people work fine without much input from a boss, while others are basically lazy and have to be ordered around if you want anything to get done."

Would Dominique be a tough, single-minded slave driver if she became boss? Marty couldn't be sure.

Next, Marty interviewed Lou Healy, another veteran employee of Spanglemaker. For twelve years, Lou had done more than work for Marty. He had frequently joined him for lunch, and they had even attended poetry readings and wine-and-cheese book signings together. Nonetheless, Marty was determined to be all business in this interview. He wanted to be fair and make the best possible decision for the company.

"Why should you become executive editor?" Marty asked.

Lou spoke in his usual relaxed and confident voice. "I believe that, above all, a manager of workers should be a "people person," much the way you, Marty, have been over the years. I get along with almost everyone here, as you know. I don't think I've had a single argument in all the years that I've been here."

Marty knew this was true, and this sentiment was even reflected in the kind of children's books with which Lou preferred to work. He liked books that were traditional, even nostalgic—warm stories about girls who owned horses, or realistic novels that supported the idea of family togetherness.

"What kind of manager would you be?" Marty asked.

"I would supervise everyone closely," Lou responded, "but in a friendly way. I believe that a close relationship between a boss and his workers is what motivates those workers to be the best that they can be. Under no circumstances would I yell at an employee or lower the boom on anyone. People basically want to do a good job. A manager should be a positive thinker and be supportive to help them do that kind of job."

Marty and Lou shook hands, and Lou left. Sitting alone amid the bookshelves in his office, Marty pondered the decision. He had to admit that Dominique had some interesting ideas that might prove to be effective—letting people choose their own book assignments, for example. But he still had serious concerns about her ability to get along with others. It seemed like work was the only thing that mattered to her: Wouldn't the other copy editors find her to be too "gung ho?" He knew that Lou wouldn't like her as a boss. And what would Charles Langley think about taking orders from a woman?

On the other hand, what would happen if he chose Lou? Would Dominique be able to accept that?

"Hell, I don't have a crystal ball," Marty said to himself at last. He didn't want to spend too much time making a decision. Already the pace had been picking up at Spanglemaker; the number of books in production had increased by 25 percent in the last two months. Soon the little publishing company he had loved would become a fast-paced marketing machine that would leave him in the dust.

The next morning, Marty called Dominique into his office. "I'm sorry," he said, "but I'm going to recommend Lou Healy for the job."

"It figures," she snapped.

Uncomfortable, Marty tried to explain the importance of having a people-person as a manager and how his decision in no way was meant to diminish the excellence of her performance. Her dark brown eyes stared at him in silent anger, making him stutter as he finished his explanation.

"Don't think that I believe any of that," she said. "We women have had to deal with this kind of treatment for centuries."

"That has nothing to do with it!" Marty insisted. "Charles has more experience and seniority than you do, and I still put you ahead of him in making my decision." With a sense of frustration, Marty realized that the last chapter of a successful career in publishing had revealed an unpleasant twist in the plot.

Questions for Discussion

1. Using the various theories of motivation, explain how the characters in the case differ both in they way they themselves are motivated and the methods they would use to motivate others.
2. Why do you believe Marty made the decision that he did?
3. Consider that you are Lawrence Guthrie. Would you accept Marty's recommendation? Why? If not, who would you select, and why?

Motivation at Bald Eagle Software

Martin Blanchard, vice-president for research and development at Bald Eagle Software, sat in his office staring at an urgent memo from his boss. Although the memo had been sent to all five of the company's vice-presidents, Blanchard assumed that there was something personal in it that had been directed to him.

The message was simple but intense: Orders were skyrocketing, but there was also a shortage of personnel to handle the demands of the high-tech company's rapid growth. "In short," the note said, "productivity has to improve."

For several minutes, Martin thought about his workers: Was there a bad apple who wasn't pulling his or her weight? Before long, he thought he knew who it was in his department who had inspired the memo.

Eager to take steps towards pleasing his boss, Martin buzzed his secretary. "Tell Hank Seaver I want to see him right away," he said. When Hank arrived, Martin told his secretary to hold all calls during their meeting.

"There are some important things we need to discuss," Martin began, drumming his fingers on his oak desk as Hank took a seat across from him. "First of all, I want to tell you that I'm giving the team leader position to Olga Richardson."

"Really?" Hank replied, smiling. "That's great! I'll be sure to congratulate her."

Martin raised his eyebrows.

"Do you understand what I'm saying, Hank?" he said. "Olga has only been working here for six months, and she's getting a raise and a promotion. You could have had that promotion if you had pushed yourself to earn it."

"Oh well," Hank replied, shrugging in his easy-going way. "I really wouldn't have wanted that job. If I got a promotion, I'd be stuck in an office with a pile of papers. I'd hate that. The best thing about my job is that I get to work with people. The guys in marketing . . . they're the best; they really make me happy to come in every morning."

Martin glared at Hank. "That's another thing I want to talk to you about, Hank," Martin continued. "It seems like you spend about an hour every morning chatting with the production workers, joking around with the marketing team. . . ."

Hank's smile faded, and he leaned forward in his chair.

"Well, sure . . ." Hank replied, "but I get the work done, don't I? Have I ever let you down by not getting something done?"

"No," Martin admitted. "In terms of output—both quality and quantity—you're one of the best in the department . . . but that's not the point."

"Then, what is the point?" Hank asked, looking confused.

Martin slammed his fists on the desk.

"You're undermining my authority—that's the point!" Martin blurted out. "I'm in charge of this department! How do you think it makes me look when the president of the company walks through the production line and sees you sitting around having coffee? I want him to respect the control I have over my department. I want to be recognized as one of the strongest managers here! It makes me look bad when one of my most

---

This case was written by Scott Weighart.

experienced software designers spends the whole morning making the rounds like a neighborhood gossip. You must become more productive."

"But, Martin," Hank objected, "I am productive—you said yourself that I'm one of the best in the department! Sure I like to chat with my buddies . . . but I also stay here past seven almost every night. I put in my hours just like everyone else."

"No, Hank," Martin replied, looking his subordinate straight in the eye. "From now on you'll put in your hours like everyone else. You're going to have to play the game by my rules."

Hank's face turned white. He loosened his tie before he spoke.

"What does that mean?" he stammered.

"First," Martin began, "it means you will work here from nine to five with a half hour break for lunch. That's it—no other breaks. Second, you can't go around visiting other departments unless you have my permission beforehand. I'll let you go—but only when a matter of company business is involved. Third, if you don't shape up, don't come crying to me next December when you don't get a bonus."

Hank was visibly shaken. "But, Martin," he pleaded, "you know I don't care about the money. . . . It's just. . . ." his voice trailed off, and he stared at the carpet.

"Look," Martin said stiffly, "I'm just trying to be fair to everyone who works here. I can't let personalities and relationships get in the way of these kinds of decisions. I'm even fair with Olga Richardson. Hey, I was skeptical when they hired a woman as a software designer, but she knows the boss is, and basically, she did what she had to to get ahead. She's growing with this company, Hank. You're at a standstill. I hope that what I've said today will help you turn yourself around. We need everyone here to be as productive as possible."

Again, Hank look confused. As he opened his mouth to reply, Martin stood up, clearly indicating that the meeting was over. Hank mumbled something about getting back to work and quickly left the room.

Alone, Martin strolled over to the bay window of his office. Clasping his hands together behind his back, he watched a group of Bald Eagle Software's second-shift production workers walk towards the building's entrance.

"Workers are like horses," he said to himself. "Leave them alone, and they'll wander aimlessly. You have to keep them on a tight rein," he thought, "if you expect to get any work out of them."

Questions for Discussion

1. On the basis of what you know about how people are motivated, what would you say motivates Hank? What about Martin?
2. Will Martin's efforts to make Hank more productive be successful? Why or why not? Explain what you believe will happen to Hank.
3. If you were Martin, what would you have done differently, if anything?

The Favorite Job

Background

Unlike many of your friends who have joined the ranks of the unemployed or who feel fortunate to have gotten a single job offer, you have recently had a number of really good job offers, all with real estate departments in banks. Now you must decide which one you will accept. Following is a brief synopsis of each of the jobs:

Job A is with a medium-size bank a short distance from where your family lives. The bank was recently taken over by a larger bank, and currently you understand there is some chaos and juggling of personnel. You have been told that your immediate job will be to help with the reorganization of records and to develop a foreclosure priority list. The job pays $26,500 per year.

Job B is with a large and quite stable bank in Detroit. The real estate department is located on three subterranean levels, and your office will be a large six- by eight-foot cubicle with five-foot-high frosted glass walls. Your immediate job will be to analyze data on a computer terminal. The job pays $37,000 per year.

Job C is with an international bank that builds, owns, and operates real estate all over the world. Your job will require you to travel about seven months of the year across the United States and to Europe and Southeast Asia, and it will bring you into constant contact with many different people. The job pays $18,000 per year plus travel expenses.

Job D is with a medium-size bank with eighteen offices throughout Utah. It has a reputation for being quite dynamic. While your entry level job will be fairly routine, the bank prides itself on its training programs and its policy of promoting from within. The job pays $26,500 per year.

Job E is with an inner-city, minority-owned bank that is socially active. You would be working with developers of subsidized housing units and running two programs for developing shelters for the homeless. Your bank has its own on-site day care center that takes children from the community as well as those of employees. The job pays $25,000 per year.

PROCEDURE

Step 1   (5–10 minutes)

Read the job descriptions and select the best job.

Step 2   (15–30 minutes)

In a group with those who selected the same job that you selected, discuss why you made the choice you did and why you would find the other jobs less preferable. Using any needs theory, analyze what personal needs you believe would be fulfilled by taking the job that you took.

This exercise was written by Janet W. Wohlberg.

Step 3 (open-ended)

Have a reporter from each group summarize your findings to the class. When every group has reported, discuss your findings.

The Maryland Institute for the Developmentally Disabled

Until recently, Candace Danielson's young career had been quite a success story. At the age of twenty-four, she had already completed her B.S. and M.S. degrees in rehabilitation counseling. Even more impressively, she had done all this while working at the Maryland Institute for the Developmentally Disabled in Silver Spring, Maryland, starting as an unpaid intern and working her way into a full-time position as a vocational counselor.

At first, Candace found this position extremely rewarding. Her main responsibility was finding appropriate jobs for individuals with special needs and limited abilities. Most of these people, her clients, had IQs of less than 70; some also had emotional difficulties. Candace would interview and work with her clients to learn about their capabilities; then she would try to find a good match for each one of them in the corporate world. After placing a client, she would help train him or her and find ways to ease the transition into the workplace.

"I guess you could call me a headhunter for the disabled," Candace said.

As a result of Candace's efforts, many people with developmental disabilities—who not long ago would have been institutionalized or idle at home—had found jobs that gave them a sense of purpose and belonging.

The Maryland Institute for the Developmentally Disabled was located inside the Lawrence Pediatric Hospital in Silver Spring; many of Candace's cases were referrals from members of the hospital's staff. Because special education programs are not provided for disabled people after the age of twenty-two, it was at this point that the institute would step in.

When she had first gotten her full-time position, Candace had been overjoyed. At that time, her greatest concern was that she would be expected to start paying back a mountain of student loans. Having chosen to work in the human services field, Candace had never expected to make a great deal of money. As long as she had enough for rent, food, loans, and a little extra, she would be content.

After a while, realizing that she was putting so much energy into doing her job that she wasn't getting to know her coworkers, Candace joined her department's softball team, where she quickly proved she could play a mean second base. Between that, and working closely with her disabled clients, she found that the job gave her plenty of people contact. Almost everyone was upbeat and friendly.

In fact, everything was fine until financial cutbacks started to affect her department: When one of her coworkers went on maternity leave, there wasn't enough money in the budget to hire a full-time replacement. And with the state economy doing poorly, it took longer to match clients to jobs. Working fifty hours a week and often coming in on Saturdays, Candace felt overwhelmed.

One year after becoming a full-time counselor, Candace found herself increasingly frustrated. She felt that much of her time was spent doing things that had nothing to do with the degrees she had received. Hours each day were devoted to completing tedious paperwork. Countless reports had to be filled out, and follow-up letters to companies had to be written. Each week, roughly fifteen data sheets would have to be completed in

This case was written by Scott Weighart.

which Candace was required to detail the number of daily hours she spent on her various cases. She was told that the data sheets were necessary because the institute always had to prove to the federal government that the operation was cost-effective and beneficial to taxpayers.

In spite of the fact that developmentally disabled individuals were now earning money and paying taxes instead of sitting at home collecting disability benefits, state officials had slashed the nstitute's budget by 10 percent, and more federal cuts were possible. As a result, the institute was understaffed. Candace felt overworked and underappreciated.

"I feel really committed to this field," she told one of her coworkers, "but these days it's getting to the point of sheer overload and complete exhaustion."

Worse, her supervisor almost never showed any sympathy for the counselors.

"A couple of years ago, around Thanksgiving, things were really crazy, so we each got a free mug. That's it, nothing since that. You don't expect bonuses or big raises— everybody knows that the money just isn't there for that—but it would be nice if they'd acknowledge what we've had to do. It could be anything: a pizza party, whatever. Just some small symbol of gratitude would be nice."

Candace went on to explain a typical dilemma: She'd often have to drive to various job sites in anywhere from Washington, D.C., to Baltimore. After a long day of fighting the traffic on I-95, she'd return to her office and the overflowing in-basket that threatened to turn her, literally, into a "basket case." Her superiors would complain that getting in touch with her always required a lengthy game of telephone tag.

Candace also felt that she had never been seriously considered for promotion when a more challenging position in an integration program had become available.

"I found out that I hadn't gotten the job through the grapevine," she said. "I think they didn't give me the job because I'm younger than a lot of my colleagues, but it could have been handled more professionally. Even if they won't promote me, I think I've at least earned the right to be treated with that much respect."

Another source of frustration for Candace was with benefits. Initially, she had been pleased to learn that she was eligible for six weeks of vacation each year—but it wasn't that simple. For the past year, Candace had only been able to take four days off: Given how overburdened the department was, finding someone to cover for her was almost impossible. The logistics of traveling around the state and the need for close rapport with each disabled person also made it tough to take time off. The thought of returning to an even deeper stack of paperwork and phone messages wasn't very appealing to Candace: It would keep her from doing the best job she possibly could, and that idea bothered her.

When Candace finally decided to take a week off, her supervisor discouraged it.

"I don't think this would be a good time" was the response, as usual. It would have been nice for her to at least hear that she deserved some time off, but nothing was mentioned about that. And what with cutbacks and the slow job market, it seemed like there would never be "a good time" in more ways than one, and the worst was yet to come.

In September, when raises were usually given, Candace was dismayed to hear that there was to be a wage freeze in her department. Her landlord had increased her rent by $50 a month, and she realized she would have to get a waitressing job on weekends. Although she'd always said money wasn't important to her, this was getting ridiculous. How could she possibly get by? While she drove around to check on her cases, she tried to think of other ways to make enough money to get by.

For Candace, it was tempting to think about leaving this job, but that would also mean leaving behind many of the colleagues and disabled people who had come to mean much to her. Charlie, her first client, had a long history of behavioral problems and a great deal of difficulty communicating because of Down's syndrome. At one time, he had worked in a sheltered workshop with other disabled people, but he had shown little progress. Candace was aware that people with developmental disabilities seldom improved or learned many new skills in sheltered workshops, settings in which they were surrounded by other disabled people. She had realized that Charlie would blossom only by joining the real working world. When interviewing him, she discovered that he had a great deal of determination; he badly wanted to earn a paycheck so he could be independent.

Although training Charlie took a long time, Candace helped him get a job mopping floors and keeping shelves neat at a local supermarket. He was a great success and, like many disabled people, had an outstanding attendance record. Once he mastered his job, he gradually became friendly with other employees, who appreciated his positive attitude. To the amazement of everyone involved, Charlie even improved his communication skills in this positive atmosphere. Working hard to earn the praise and recognition of his coworkers, Charlie could usually help customers find items like peanut butter or cake mix.

Although Candace no longer saw Charlie regularly, he called her frequently to tell her how happy he was and to thank her for her help.

"That's the kind of thing that really keeps me going," Candace said. Some of her other successful clients had taken her out to lunch to express their appreciation, a gesture she found touching and rewarding.

Of course, some of her cases were frustrating. One client's family wanted very much for their son, Henry, to get a job, but Henry knew that he had a large trust fund and would never have to worry about money or a place to live. Although Candace worked hard to push him toward getting a job, it became clear that Henry was really looking for a "day-hab" program where work would be secondary to socialization and where he would have the chance to meet people, play cards, and watch TV. There was nothing Candace could do about that.

Considering the pros and cons of her job, Candace was undecided about her future. Given the tough times in the job market, she didn't feel she could just quit. Making a change would be hard, especially given how much she liked the people with whom she worked. She also liked being part of a noble cause: She was helping people realize that there was a place for them in society, and she was helping organizations see that they could do something that was both humane and profitable. (In addition to being able to depend on developmentally disabled workers to be reliable, organizations are given substantial tax incentives for hiring them. In fact, recent legislation probably will require the hiring of specific quotas of the developmentally disabled by the year 2000.)

But Candace also recognized that there were large parts of her job that were neither satisfying nor rewarding and that she just didn't want to do. Just a few weeks earlier, in her performance review, Candace's supervisor had noted, "You need to become more organized and to schedule more time for phone calls and appointments. You have a tendency to let things slide rather than meeting them head on."

Candace had nodded. She knew that her supervisor's criticism had been warranted; she had let things slide because of her frustrations with the job.

Her supervisor had closed Candace's evaluation folder and added, "Perhaps you should consider whether this is a good job match for you."

Afterward, Candace had laughed at the irony: She had been so successful in helping clients find jobs that nicely matched their abilities and interests. And what had happened? Here she was: a vocational counselor who needed some vocational counseling.

Questions for Discussion

1. Using one or two theories of motivation, describe and compare the motivational needs of Candace, Charlie, and Henry. What are the interactions of Charlie's and Henry's needs to those of Candace?
2. Considering what you know about managing diversity, do you think that the developmentally disabled are being treated appropriately? Why?
3. If you were Candace's supervisor, how would you try to keep her motivated, given that both of you realize her performance could be better? Be specific and comprehensive in your recommendations, tying them back to the motivational theory or theories used in your analysis.

The Music Teacher from Hell

Joe Swanson, principal of the Cornelius Mercker Elementary School in Dacron, Ohio, was not a happy man on the first day of the school year. He had just learned that Martha Vandeberg had been assigned to the Mercker as a music teacher. Vandeberg was notorious throughout the school system; every principal who had supervised her told horror stories about faked illness and injuries, unexcused absences, and remarkably persistent attempts to do as little as possible without getting fired.

When she showed up for the first day at Mercker, Vandeberg told Swanson that she could not teach on the second floor due to a fractured toe. When he asked for a doctor's note, she became angry. "Fine then," she said, making a spectacle of hobbling up and down the stairs. On the third day of school, she called in sick due to a "bruised tooth root" resulting from excessive flossing.

When Vandeberg did work, she went from classroom to classroom, spraying Lysol on her hands and in the air before playing records at maximum volume. The children sang with their hands on their ears. She opened the windows as wide as possible—even in subfreezing temperatures, and the children either would have to put their coats on to avoid catching cold or sit shivering and with teeth chattering.

Unfortunately, the Dacron Teacher's Union was very powerful; Swanson did not have the authority to fire her. Even giving her an unsatisfactory rating would have no effect on her salary. He had no ability to influence her, and she treated him, as she treated all principals with whom she had come in contact, as the enemy from day one.

About all Swanson could do was to make life as miserable as possible for Vandeberg. If she had not signed in by 8:30, he wrote "LATE" where her signature would go. Instead of getting her own mailbox like most teachers, she had to share one with the custodian.

When it was time for the annual school Christmas concert, Swanson asked the school's substitute teacher to lead the chorus, while Vandeberg was given meaningless paperwork to fill out. She didn't dare defy him by refusing to comply. Although Swanson realized this was all very childish, twenty years as a school principal had taught him that this was the only way to get rid of someone who was incompetent. He had seen other principals try to be nice to her, and she had responded by getting away with as much as possible. He made sure to keep a file of every rule infraction that she made, in case she tried to sue him for any reason.

Vandeberg lasted the entire school year, taking every sick day available to her and basically giving the students the same records to listen to and sing along with week after week. Fortunately for Swanson, she didn't choose to return to Mercker the following year. Still, the year had been stressful and sickening. Due to the pay scale, based on seniority, the city of Dacron would be increasing her pay from $36,300 to $37,100 the following year. Many younger teachers—who earned just over half that amount—were angry to see that their hard work did nothing to narrow the vast difference between their salaries and those of the music teacher.

This case was written by Scott Weighart.

Questions for Discussion

1. What sources of power does Joe Swanson have in his dealings with Martha Vandeberg? Give examples of each. What sources does he lack? Why?
2. Consider what you know about motivation. What connections can you make between the sources of power and the impact they have on an individual's motivational profile?

PART II
INTERPERSONAL PROCESSES IN ORGANIZATIONS

OVERVIEW

In this section, we will look at what happens when individuals—each with their own perceptions and motivational profiles, as we saw in the previous section—are put into situations in which they must interact with managers and fellow workers. We will consider group dynamics, intergroup dynamics, power, political behavior, communication, and the match—or mismatch—between leadership styles and the needs of a work group.

Group Dynamics

Wouldn't it be common sense to say that a manager would always be fortunate to be in charge of cohesive groups, groups in which individuals have shared goals and work hard together to achieve them? Not necessarily? Some groups may have goals that have nothing to do with organizational success and everything to do with self-serving or undermining and destructive objectives.

For example, imagine a group of maintenance engineers working for a nuclear power plant. They are a great, fun-loving bunch. Instead of monitoring their computer screens to make sure the nuclear reactor is a glowing success, they take turns playing video games while one group member is assigned to watch out for the boss. When the boss approaches, the lookout person gives a quick whistle. The group has worked very hard in developing a system for not getting caught goofing off. They have designed a remarkable computer program that allows the user to simply touch a specific key to make the video game disappear and be replaced with a screen of nuclear facility data.

Of course, people who live near the nuclear plant may eventually wonder why they've started spotting rabbits as big as kangaroos, but no one can deny that the engineering group is very successful and productive in working toward its goals.

Organizations do have control over some group dynamics. Typically, managers create formal groups of people who must work together temporarily or permanently on some designated task. When management assigns people to these formal groups, they must make crucial decisions about size and composition.

However, informal groups still develop at organizations, and managers can't easily control their size, composition, or purpose for existence. Likewise, group norms, those mutually agreed upon and accepted ways of behaving, may fall outside of management's jurisdiction. Some group norms can be beneficial for the organization: For example, there are several religious cults in which members are expected to devote almost every waking hour to making money or recruiting new members.

Every time you walk into a classroom, sit down, listen, take notes, and ask questions, you are displaying several norms of student behavior. Likewise, the professor comes in and speaks, writes key points on the blackboard, and asks questions. All of these behaviors are norms: patterns of behavior that we have come to accept without question. If you fall asleep during a lecture on norms, the professor might single you out for violating the norms of the classroom. If a professor comes into class in the United States and speaks fluent Icelandic for ninety minutes, then the professor is violating a norm and may be fired and told to hop the next flight to Reykjavik.

Sometimes, students make the mistake of thinking that norms are nothing more than rules that the group chooses openly and consciously. For example, if an organizational behavior teacher creates groups and tells them they must create a firing policy before beginning a group project, the group will write a list of rules that could be considered norms. However, many norms represent unwritten and undiscussed rules for behavior: If an individual is late for a group meeting, the other members may joke about firing the person but quickly drop the issue. If the person continues having problems in meeting the expectations of the group, the joking may become bitter sarcasm. The other group members might retaliate for the breech of norms by assigning the most boring jobs to their problem member. Often there is no official decision to treat the person this way; this is a norm that has developed by itself.

Have you ever been assigned to a group project? If you have, you might have noticed that group development goes through several stages—sometimes referred to as forming, storming, norming, and performing.[1] In the first stage, people try to find out facts about each other and form tentative alliances. Secondly, some issues must be resolved: personality clashes must be dealt with; the authority hierarchy must be established; and the roles of each of the group members must be determined. In the third stage, norming, groups are consciously or unconsciously developing ways of getting things done, and they create their unwritten rules of conduct. An unsuccessful group may fail to get through a stage and never reach the point where everything is in place and the group is performing adequately.

Intergroup Dynamics

In terms of intergroup dynamics, groups from different divisions or functions may recognize their interdependence and collaborate to accommodate the best interests of their company. Sometimes, however, they may see other groups as their enemies or competitors, perhaps vying for limited funds or supplies, and avoid contact whenever possible.

In 1987, a plant manager at a large company spent a great deal of time studying a revolutionary "Just-in-Time" manufacturing system. Because the manager appreciated the role of another functional group—the finance department—he liked the idea that the "Just-in-Time" system would save his company millions of dollars in inventory costs while freeing valuable warehouse space. This made the company's product much more accessible for the trucks of the distribution department. Collaborating with other functional groups, the plant manager made the best of intergroup dynamics.

However, some of his superiors in production were unhappy. His innovative process made production's efficiency numbers worse in the short run. The superiors put pressure on the manager to abandon his plan, fearing that the efficiency figures would upset the company's executives: They didn't want production to look worse than the other divisions, and they didn't care that the system would greatly benefit the company's overall functioning.

Situational Leadership

Clearly, the plant manager was disappointed in the behavior of his bosses. As a college student, the odds are good that you've also seen bad leadership in action. If your manager at your summer job treated you like you were no more intelligent than a household appliance, you're not alone.

---

1. B. W. Turkman, "Development Sequence in Small Groups," *Psychological Bulletin* 63 (1965): 384–399.

One problem is that some managers are not given their jobs because they have the charisma of Mother Teresa, the inspirational power of Martin Luther King, Jr. or even the questionable counseling knowledge of a newspaper advice columnist. How do individual workers become managers? Sometimes people with good technical skills get promotions, regardless of their interpersonal skills.

Several leadership theories can be used to help explain mismatches between workers and managers, and why a leadership style can be effective or ineffective in any given situation. Inexperienced workers may require a more directive, hands-on style, while more confident or competent employees may resent such hand holding.

Hersey and Blanchard's Life Cycle Theory helps us to understand how and why managers need to use different styles with different employees, depending on their job maturity. Likewise, the Path-Goal Theory suggests that leaders may need to use different styles to help different individuals achieve their goals. Failing to use appropriate leadership styles can lead to problems.

Fiedler's Contingency Theory may also prove valuable to you as you work through the cases and exercises. This theory suggests that there is a direct link between a leader/situation match or mismatch and the performance of the affected workers. The Vertical Dyad Linkage Model suggests that there are "in-groups" and "out-groups" in leader-member relationships. Some employees are more likely to have close contact with their managers; some have little interaction, a factor that can have considerable impact on worker perceptions and performance.

Power, Politics, and Conflict

Power sources and political behavior also come up frequently in the cases and exercises that follow. John R. P. French, Jr., and Bertram Raven describe five distinct types of power that individuals derive from different sources.[2] All bosses have legitimate power, which comes simply from holding a position of authority. Managers also have coercive power. This means that they are able to force employees to do things by using threats, warnings, and punishments. While workers may accept such treatment, this clearly is not a tool that builds employee commitment.

A boss may or may not have referent and expert powers. It might be useful to think of referent power as "rock star" power: People want to follow you because you have a charismatic personality or characteristics that others admire and may wish to imitate. As for expert power, many managers do get promoted because of their expertise; however, it is not unusual for a leader to manage people who know considerably more about the details of the work than the leader does. The last power tactic is reward power, which most managers have. This refers to the ability to give promotions, raises, bonuses, praise and recognition, and special benefits.

Managers are not the only ones who have power in organizations. Workers, while not necessarily having the legitimate powers of managers, can definitely have expert or referent powers that can turn them into informal leaders. This can cause friction if they are behaving in ways that aren't consistent with organizational goals. Informal leaders can also use reward power by giving their peers praise and attention.

Political behavior and conflict are usually thought of as negative forces, but this need not be the case. NASA's space shuttle *Challenger* tragedy is a sad example of an organization failing to have *enough* conflict. Despite warning signs that should have been

---

2. J. R. P. French, Jr., & B. Raven, "The Bases of Social Power," in D. Cartwright, ed., *Studies in Social Power* (Ann Arbor: University of Michigan Press, 1959), 150–167.

taken more seriously, NASA authorities—fearing the political ramifications of another flight delay—failed to stop the fateful event. In short, conflict can be functional or dysfunctional, and having too much or too little can be hazardous.

Communication

How has the communication process functioned in organizations in which you have been employed? Did the boss have countless meetings with an inner circle of employees while ignoring all others? Did the boss bark out orders and instructions, or did he or she ask you for feedback or input? Did the boss stay closed up in an office and dictate enough memos to wipe out a small rain forest?

In some organizations, communication can be strictly a one-way process: Some managers are order givers who tell people what to do. They are not particularly interested in whether the employee thinks the manager's approach is the best one. We already know, from studying motivation, that workers are more willing to commit to their tasks if they have had a say in decisions that have to do with their work.

Does this mean that managers should never use one-way communication? Imagine this: You're a driving school instructor. Preparing for sixteen-year-old Rodney Maxwell's first driving lesson, you strap yourself into the passenger seat, put on your crash helmet, and gulp down a handful of antacid tablets.

The first ten minutes go better than you expect: There have been no fatalities, mainly due to the surprising agility of the local pedestrians. You have been successfully using two-way communication with Rodney, encouraging him to ask questions, such as "What are you supposed to do about all these red lights, anyway?"

Then you face a major crisis: Rodney seems to think that the ringing bells at a railroad crossing mean that he should speed up so he won't have to wait ten minutes for the train to go by.

At this point, you *could* decide to use two-way communication. As Rodney speeds toward the crossing, you could say: "Now Rodney, what are the various alternatives you have as a driver right now? I value your input, and I'd like to hear your rationale for risking our necks at this particular juncture."

Alternatively, you could use one-way communication and scream, "Hit the brakes!!!" Of course, you will run the risk of hurting Rodney's feelings by not engaging him in the decision-making process, but this may be preferable to turning the railroad tracks into a demolition derby. In short, one-way communication does have one big advantage: It's fast.

Karen Carlin

Karen Carlin graduated from Plympton University's School of Management in 1985. Though she was a top student and planned someday to get an M.B.A., she wanted for the moment to work in Manhattan. Karen grew up in the small town of Mechanicsburg, Pennsylvania, and she was excited at the idea of living in the big city. She figured New York was the next logical step after going to school in Pittsburgh.

Having heard many horror stories about the cost of living in Manhattan, Karen wasted no time trying to find a job. While working at the *Daily Free Press,* Plympton's student newspaper, Karen had learned a great deal about word processing. Accordingly, she went to Temployee Specialists and applied for a job.

The interview was high pressured. The woman in charge of Temployee Specialists, Jane Thorley, gave her four consecutive timed typing tests, followed by a Dictaphone test. She asked Karen unusually specific questions about her education and her work background. Finally, Thorley brought her to a Wang computer.

"Have you ever used one of these?" she asked. Karen reluctantly admitted that she hadn't.

"Well, you seem bright enough," Thorley told her. "Sit down, and give it a try."

Although Karen felt a little intimidated, she tried calling up files and doing simple commands. It was different from the Free Press's Varityper system, but she managed to figure out the basics.

Fifteen minutes later, Jane Thorley came in and watched over her shoulder. Although it was hard to tell from her all-business expression, Thorley was apparently pleased. She told Karen that she had a long-term assignment for her at Hepplewhite & Boyce, a large accounting firm in a huge office building near Canal Street. Karen was shocked and thrilled to have gotten a job so easily. However, there was a catch.

"If they ask you if you've used the DataLogic computer, just tell them that you have," Thorley said. "You're a quick study; you'll pick it up right away. If you get stuck, just ask if you can take a look at the manual. Tell them you need to refresh your memory. If you could photocopy the manual for us, that would be even better."

Karen felt uneasy about deceiving her first client, but she also felt she couldn't afford to pass up a job offer. In Manhattan, who could tell how long she might have to wait for another one. She had found a great apartment in the West Village through a Matching Roommates agency. Her room was claustrophobically small, and her rent was $575 a month, but she wanted to be in the heart of the city. She decided she couldn't afford to pass up this opportunity.

By the time she was sitting behind her computer at Hepplewhite & Boyce, Karen was a nervous wreck. She typed frantically, certain that someone would find her out. She had been assigned to the schedule typists' office, where there were three other women, all sitting at desks with computers and all studying her out of the corner of their eyes. Their job was to update lengthy tax schedules for the fifteen accountants who worked in their department.

This case was written by Scott Weighart.

After half an hour of typing as fast as possible, Karen was interrupted by Pauline, a thirtyish woman sitting across from her, who walked over to her with an annoyed expression on her face. For ten long seconds she stood and watched Karen work. Finally, she spoke: "What in the world do you think you're doing?"

Karen turned bright red. She was sure her charade had been discovered. Instead, she was amazed as Pauline scolded her for working too hard. "Would you please slow down?" she said. Then she shook her head, and as she walked back to her desk, Karen could hear Pauline mutter, "Can you believe these eager beaver temps?"

Before long, Karen was almost fascinated by how little work was done in the office. The system was almost ingenious. When the accountants needed work to be done, they sent it to the schedule typists through the internal mail system or dropped it by personally. Either way, the work piled up in the office in-basket. The office supervisor, Keith Frazier, would stop by every day or two. If there was only a small pile of work in the in-basket, Frazier would get extra work from another floor to keep them busy. If there was a large pile of work in the in-basket, he would take some of it to another floor to be done. Sometimes, instead of taking the extra work elsewhere, he would hire an additional temporary employee to deal with it.

Karen realized that this was why she had been hired. Two of the women in the office, Pauline and Pat, had purposely been doing the bare minimum of work for the last few weeks. They had correctly realized that the more of the tedious work they did, the more they would have to do. On the other hand, if they spent all morning getting coffee, chatting about their weekends, and so on, Frazier would take the work elsewhere. It was unbelievable.

The third woman in the office, Myra, was different. While Pauline and Pat were white and from England, Myra was an Indian immigrant who commuted from the Stuyvesant area of the Bronx. Although she laughed at Pat's off-color jokes, Myra kept working away while the others dawdled. She never criticized them for fooling around even though their lack of effort generally meant that she was the one who did most of the schedule preparation.

When Karen started working in their office, the others were polite to her but not very friendly. Slowly, Pauline began asking her questions. What did she think about Manhattan? Where was she living? and so on. The others eventually joined in.

After a while, Karen started to enjoy working in this group. Pauline and Pat, who lived in Brooklyn, were very quick witted and entertaining. In particular, things seemed to revolve around Pauline, who was the ringleader behind most of the mischief making. When Pauline started coming to work at 10 A.M., Pat did the same. After a week, even Myra and Karen were coming in late, around 9:15. Myra was shy and quiet, but sometimes Karen had good conversations with her when the others took one of their ninety-minute to two-hour lunches at a nearby café.

Even though the four of them were very different in terms of race, nationality, and background, Karen was intrigued to find that they each stuck up for one another. If Frazier stopped by while Pauline and Pat were taking an extra long lunch, Myra would tell him that they were checking on work with an accountant on another floor or that they were getting supplies from the stationery center. Karen learned that Pat had occasionally taken a whole day off to go shopping uptown—and been paid for it—while Frazier thought she was up in the schedule typists' office, working away.

Karen believed that the Hepplewhite & Boyce employees in other departments didn't like her or anyone else in the office. If she sat down in the cafeteria at lunch and told someone where she worked, she felt she was treated like a nobody. When she asked

Pauline about it, Pauline just chuckled. "We're what you might call the Black Sheep Office. No one wants to have anything to do with us because they know what we do is just busywork, something that any moron can do."

As Karen listened, she glanced out the window of the office, which overlooked an ugly jumble of back alleys and construction projects. Pauline went on to explain that they had initially pushed Frazier to give them a little more free rein in how they did their work.

Karen was confused. "Don't you have free rein already?" she asked. "Frazier only comes to check up on us about twice a week."

"Yeah, right," Pauline said. "But he still tells us we have to do things his way." The current procedures were rigid and monotonous. Pat had suggested that the schedule typists should be able to fix obvious mathematical errors without sending them back to an accountant, and Pauline herself had asked if they could each be responsible for working with three or four specific accountants so that the schedule typists could get used to the style and handwriting of each one. Doing that, Pauline had told Karen, might save time.

Pauline was certain that they could have come up with many more ideas, but Frazier had assured them that his way of getting the work done was the most efficient. Using his system, for example, it wouldn't matter if one person was absent, because someone else would just do her work. Since absenteeism was high, he felt this was an important consideration.

"After a while, we stopped complaining," Pat said, "because, number one, he wouldn't listen, and, number two, it's easier to do less work his way."

Pauline nodded. "Why should we knock ourselves out? This way we have a lot more time to chat and have long lunches. The day goes by just as fast either way."

Within a few weeks, the typists began having more and more serious conflicts with Frazier. He had started to receive some complaints from the accountants about the delays in getting tax schedules updated. Then he succeeded in tracking down a bunch of international phone calls that were being made from the schedule typists' office. Pat had a sister who was married to an air force colonel in Keflavic, Iceland, and she had been calling her regularly. Frazier's solution was to change the phone system so that it was impossible to make anything but an internal phone call from the schedule typists' office.

Pauline, angered about this development, took it as a personal challenge to beat the system. Within twenty-four hours, she discovered that it was possible to make international calls from the emergency telephone in the office elevator. She and Pat commandeered the elevator for a half hour, while Pat called her sister. By now, Karen, also annoyed because she couldn't even call her temp agency without using a pay phone on another floor, was fully willing to cover for her new friends.

One Monday morning, Frazier called Karen to his office, a spacious corner room with a beautiful view of the southern tip of Manhattan and the Hudson River. When Frazier asked about whether everyone was pulling their weight in schedule typing, Karen said they were.

During the course of the conversation, it became clear to Karen that Frazier had found out about the elevator episode and that he intended to take action. Still, Karen was astonished by his plan.

"Some people around here need to learn a few lessons," he said. "Since you've been here, Karen, you've worked hard, and you're certainly qualified." Karen blushed, knowing how untrue that was.

"Frankly, Karen, I don't have time to babysit certain individuals in certain departments. So, I'm putting you in charge of the schedule typists. You can do whatever you want, be as tough as you like. Just don't fire anyone. As you probably know from your management background, that's an expensive alternative, a last resort."

Frazier went on to add that he was responsible for over thirty workers so he hadn't been able to give the schedule typists the iron hand of discipline he felt they needed. "Still, I've always spelled out for them everything they had to do. They just don't want to listen. They need someone like you to slap their hands as soon as they get out of line."

Karen accepted the position, figuring it would be a good opportunity to find out if she could apply what she'd learned in her management courses at Plympton. Nonetheless, she had many doubts and anxieties. Regardless of what Frazier had said, she knew that he wasn't making her leader because of her ability. He was probably more interested in embarrassing Pat and Pauline by appointing someone who was much younger and much less experienced than they, and someone who came in from a temp agency to boot. If Karen made their lives miserable, it was clear that that would surely be fine with Frazier.

What could she do to make the group productive? Frazier would probably laugh in her face if she suggested raises and bonuses for the "black sheep" group. Besides, the salaries were already more than reasonable, given the nature of the work. After all, the women would have probably quit long ago if money were the issue.

Another worry was that Pauline was unquestionably the informal leader of the group. She had been there the longest and knew the most about the computer system, and she was well liked. Karen liked Pauline and couldn't really blame her for most of what she had done. Still, how could she keep Pauline from being a problem?

There was another dilemma. After work, Karen took the subway to the midtown office of Temployee Specialists so she could tell Jane Thorley about her promotion. Thorley thought it was a wonderful thing. "Now we can deal with you directly when Hepplewhite & Boyce needs another temp!" she said.

Karen smiled weakly, knowing that Temployee Specialists would probably continue to send inexperienced but eager college graduates who would cheerfully lie about their computer ability to make it past the personnel department. When tax season arrived, Karen knew she would probably need to hire one or two temporaries, regardless of how successful she was in managing Pauline, Pat, and Myra. If she did use Temployee Specialists, she would be encouraging more lying, which didn't seem right.

Karen had made a regrettable decision at a time when she felt desperate for money. Now that she was a manager in a position of responsibility, she felt she should be a good role model and earn the respect of her business associates. At the same time, she would feel like a hypocrite if she told Jane Thorley that she wouldn't go along with the scheme. It would mean that she had been willing to lie when her own selfish interests were at stake, but not when someone else was involved. Admittedly, Thorley had put her through a tough selection procedure, Karen thought. Maybe Thorley was actually able to identify workers who could do good work, even if they weren't technically qualified. Still, did the end justify the means?

Karen now believed that she shouldn't have jumped at her first job offer, but at the same time there was no way to make that decision over again. She realized that she had been naive. Now, in many ways, she had to grow up in a hurry.

Questions for Discussion

1. Using what you have learned from your readings about organizational behavior theories and principles, analyze and explain the situation in the schedule typists' office of Hepplewhite & Boyce.

2. What is the central problem here?
3. Pretend that you are Karen Carlin, and write a specific and comprehensive action plan that you would use to correct the problem.
4. Regarding Karen's ethical dilemma with Jane Thorley and Temployee Specialists, what should she do?

Picking the Project Team at the Ozark River Bank

BACKGROUND

Two years ago, the Ozark River Bank, the largest commercial bank in a six-state area, became a major lender in a worker-led leveraged buyout. To finance the buyout, the workers pledged the assets of the company as collateral for their loans. Now it has become clear that the business plan on which the buyout was based is not meeting projections. Although the new owners have been able to turn the company around from a losing situation to one that is marginally profitable, it is unlikely that cash flow will be sufficient to meet debt-service requirements when a large issue of zero-coupon bonds matures in about eighteen months.

The original worker buyout was a highly publicized event in which more than a thousand jobs were saved, financial disaster for a community was averted, and the bank was hailed for its assistance and support. To let the company go under because it is unable to meet its financial obligations on the loans would throw the community into a severe recession, increase joblessness, and put the bank in a bad light. Therefore, the bank needs to explore a creative plan for the workout in which the various lenders, including a group of other financial institutions that hold unsecured debt (debentures), and the stockholders (both management and the workers) arrange a restructuring that would reduce debt-service requirements consistent with current cash-flow projections. This could involve a variety of techniques, including the conversion of some debt into equity, salary reductions for management, and efficiency cuts in the work force.

Dealing with this kind of situation is sensitive, high in stress, and severely time constrained. You have found that the most successful approach to doing this kind of work is to assign it to a project team. The job of the team will be to put together a restructuring plan that meets the needs of the bank and the other lenders and that can be put into place quickly at the time of default.

Five people in your department have the knowledge and ability to do the kind of work necessary. Your job is to decide which three will work best together to accomplish the stated objectives. The success of this team will be important to its members' career paths and to yours. The following people in your department are available:

HAROLD, AGE 52

Harold has been a loyal employee of the bank for twenty-six years. He is respected by his peers and his superiors, and he has a solid understanding of the industry involved. In addition, he has worked successfully on smaller but similar projects. Harold sets careful time lines for work in projects and pushes the members of his teams to be fastidious about meeting deadlines. Over the years, he has proven himself to be both a leader and a team player. Recently, Harold returned to the bank after a six-month medical leave of absence

This exercise was written by Janet W. Wohlberg.

because of a heart attack. He is anxious to get back into work and is actively looking for something to do.

JOAN, AGE 41

Joan is a detail person. She understands the fine points of leveraged buyouts and reorganizations better than anyone in your department, and when she is on a team, it is rare for there to be any loopholes or glitches in the final results. Through hard work and determination, Joan has risen in the company fairly quickly. She is an outspoken feminist whose sexual harassment case against the bank, brought seven months ago as a reaction to a situation with a prior project team, has still not been resolved. Apparently, the two men with whom she had been working used a great deal of locker-room language, persisting in this practice despite her objections. The previous manager of your department, your immediate predecessor, failed to take her complaints to him seriously.

CYNTHIA, AGE 31

Cynthia is married and has two young children. She came to work in your department five and a half months ago, just after receiving her M.B.A., and is still learning the ropes. Her job prior to and during her M.B.A. program was as a project manager with the company that is now the object of the workout. She was there throughout the leveraged buyout proceedings and had been part of the group that developed the original business plan. You had hired Cynthia to replace Harold, who you hadn't expected to return; however, some people also believe that she was hired specifically to undercut the credibility of Joan's case. For the last three months, Cynthia and Joan have been working together on a plan for an on-site day care program at the bank.

JACK, AGE 35

Jack is a bachelor who likes to spend his free time at sporting events or at a local bar with his friends. Of all of the people in your department, Jack is probably the most knowledgeable about workouts on complex loan defaults. He has an excellent reputation for being innovative, but he is also known to be a procrastinator—one of those people who likes to push deadlines, waiting until the last minute before he really gets going. Then, Jack works virtually round the clock, pushing his coworkers to do the same. In the end, he always seems to come through.

JOSHUA, AGE 62

Joshua has an air of Old World chivalry and is very conservative about women. He has been outspoken in his belief that women belong at home taking care of their husbands and children, but he makes his comments with such charm that most people don't take offense. Having been at the bank for more than thirty years, and being an active member in the local community, Joshua knows just about everyone and has ready access to a wide range of resources. He knows how to work the system to get what he needs when he needs it. This kind of networking ability could prove to be an important factor in the ultimate success of this project.

THE PROBLEM

It's important that the three people you select for this team be high functioning and successful. They must be able to work well together to accomplish the task accurately, quickly, and without delay.

Questions for Discussion

1. In what ways would the various people described work well together? In what ways might they have problems?
2. Given the answers to question 1, which three people described above will you select, and why?

Picking the Project Team at Ozark River Bank

	Reasons to include in project team	Reasons not to include in project team
Harold		
Joan		
Cynthia		
Jack		
Joshua		

Leadership Fishbowl

PROCEDURE

Step 1

Option 1: Think about people for or with whom you have worked and who you felt were good leaders.

Option 2: Think about people for or with whom you have worked and who you felt were poor leaders.

Step 2   (20 minutes)

Five students will be selected randomly or by volunteering to be the "fish." Sitting together in the middle of the class (or in a central place where they can be seen and heard by the other members of the class), the fish should tell the stories of their experiences with bad or good leaders and then discuss them with the other members of the fish group only.

Students on the outside of the fishbowl are *not* to speak while the fish are speaking. Their job is to observe, listening for common threads as well as differences in what they are hearing. Those outside of the fishbowl should listen carefully but not take notes.

If there is a lag in conversation, it is important for everyone, including the facilitator, to resist the temptation to jump in and help. It is not unusual for such a lag to occur at the very beginning of the exercise and again after each individual fish has told his or her story and prior to the onset of their general discussion.

Step 3   (15–20 minutes, depending on size of group)

Going around the class, every student on the outside of the fishbowl should report on one thing that he or she has heard about the elements of leadership discussed by the fish. During this phase, the fish are not allowed to talk. These common elements should be listed in a visible place.

Step 4   (10–15 minutes)

When the observation list has been completed, exchange and general discussion between the fish and the observers may take place.

Step 5   (10–15 minutes)

When the first four steps have been completed, the class should be divided into groups of five or six. If possible, there should be at least one fish in each group.

Working in these small groups, do one of the following:

This exercise was written by Janet W. Wohlberg.

Option 1: Develop a twenty-five- to fifty-word definition of leadership that begins with the phrase "A good leader is . . ." and incorporates at least three to five elements of good leadership.

Option 2: Develop a list of the personal and interpersonal traits, skills, and abilities you would like to see in a leader.

Step 6 (open-ended)

Report your results to the class. Discussion should follow.

Leadership Fishbowl
Step 5, Option 1

Drawing on what you have learned about leadership from personal experiences, readings, lectures, and the fishbowl exercise, discuss your ideas with the other members of your group, and together develop a definition of leadership in twenty-five to fifty words.

Step 1   List the elements of good leadership that you believe should be included in your definition.

_____

_____

_____

_____

_____

_____

_____

_____

_____

_____

_____

_____

_____

_____

Step 2   Write a definition of leadership beginning with the words "A good leader is . . ."

_____

_____

_____

_____

_____

_____

_____

_____

_____

_____

_____

_____

_____

_____

Leadership Fishbowl
Step 5, Option 2

Drawing on what you have learned about leadership from personal experiences, readings, lectures, and the fishbowl exercise, discuss your ideas with the other members of your group, and together develop a list of the personal and interpersonal traits, skills, and abilities that you and your fellow group members would like to see in a leader.

Briefly describe each item on your list and explain why it is important.

Personal:

_____
_____
_____
_____
_____
_____
_____
_____
_____
_____
_____
_____
_____
_____
_____
_____

Interpersonal:

_____
_____
_____
_____
_____
_____
_____
_____
_____
_____
_____
_____
_____
_____
_____
_____

Gadgets USA Goes International

BACKGROUND

Gadgets USA, makers of high-quality kitchen and home shop implements (paring knives, chisels, etc.) has decided to market its products abroad. The initial organizing and planning team for the new division to be created, Gadgets International, will be composed of four high-level marketing executives from Gadgets USA, whose experience is limited to the American market, and three new people hired from the outside: (1) a recent M.B.A. with a degree in international marketing; (2) a former top-level finance manager from Eurokitsch of Switzerland, manufacturers of major kitchen appliances; and (3) a distant relative of the Kuwaiti royal family who most recently served as vice-president of marketing for a now-defunct Kuwaiti farm implement manufacturer. Some of the issues still to be determined for this project are what the target markets are to be; how the organization will be structured; what additional people will need to be hired; which of the company's products will be marketed; what the time frame ought to be for introducing the products, and so forth.

An as yet unnamed individual will serve as the president of Gadgets International. Your job is to develop a profile of the kind of person who should be hired for this position.

PROCEDURE

Step 1   Work with three to four of your classmates. Based on the background given and what you know about leadership theory, develop a list of five to ten leadership characteristics that you believe the president of Gadgets International should have. Explain why you believe these are necessary and how they will be used. Be specific.

Step 2   Select a reporter from your group to report your list to the class. The list should be recorded in a place that can be seen by all.

Step 3   Since it is unlikely that you will be able to find someone who has everything on the composite list, in class discussion determine which of the characteristics you consider to be primary and which you consider to be secondary.

This exercise was written by Janet W. Wohlberg.

Who Works Saturday Night?

The purpose of this role play is to give you an opportunity to explore the effectiveness of different leadership styles—in this case, autocratic, democratic, and laissez faire—in decision-making situations. Autocratic leaders generally impose their decisions without considering the interests of their subordinates. Laissez-faire leaders, on the other hand, relinquish their decision-making powers to the group and its members. Democratic leaders clarify the goals to be met by the decision and work with subordinates to find a decision that best meets those goals.

As you do this exercise, consider the leadership style being used by your group's manager and the ways in which you believe that style to be appropriate or not.

BACKGROUND

Your small company, Turnem, Inc., a manufacturer of valves that have a wide variety of uses, including use in several aspects of the aerospace industry, is on a tight deadline to complete a project. The prototype product is due to be demonstrated to the leaders of your aerospace industry the following Monday.

To finish on schedule, it will be necessary for *one* member of your team to work this Saturday evening from about 5 P.M. to midnight and for the entire team to work at its most productive and cooperative level for the full day on Sunday. The budget allows for *only one* member of the team to be paid to work on Saturday night.

The contract for this project, although not your company's only source of revenue, is important.

Review and plan out your role thoroughly. *Do not discuss your role* with any of your classmates until you have been told to do so.

This exercise was written by Janet W. Wohlberg.

Who Works Saturday Night?
Observer Sheet

1. Briefly describe the manager's dilemma.

2. Were the employees given a fair chance to explain their concerns?

3. How would you rate the manager's overall listening skills and why?

4. What factors do you think the manager failed to consider in making a decision?

5. What factors did the manager appear to use in reaching a decision?

6. How did the employees react to the manager's leadership style, and why?

Questions for Discussion

1. Given the problem presented, did the manager of your group use an appropriate leadership style? Why or why not? (If you were the manager in your group, how did you feel about the effectiveness of the leadership style you used?)
2. What do you think the manager should have done differently?
3. Did the manager listen to and consider each employee's arguments?
4. How was the decision made? Did the manager elicit input from the employees?
5. What are the implications of the decision for each member? For the effectiveness of the team on Sunday? For the ultimate success and quality of the project?

Who Works Saturday Night?
Score Sheet

Rate your group manager on the following scale:

Autocratic	10	Laissez faire	5
	9		4
	8		3
	7		2
	6	Democratic	1

Calculate the average rating in your group (not counting the manager's opinion!) by adding all ratings and dividing by the number of workers in the group.

Rate your satisfaction with the decision on the following scale:

Very dissatisfied	10	Indifferent	5
	9		4
	8		3
	7		2
	6	Very satisfied	1

Calculate the average rating of satisfaction in your group by adding all of the ratings and dividing by the number of workers.

Generally, groups that perceive their leaders to be autocratic will be more dissatisfied with decisions made about who works Saturday night. Laissez-faire managers can also be frustrating to groups. Keep in mind that this may vary depending on the composition of the group: Some people actually like to be told what to do. In some cultures, managers who involve workers in decision-making processes, such as those represented by this exercise, are considered to be ineffective; in other cultures, managers are expected to seek input from subordinates regularly. The occurrence of and acceptance of laissez-faire styles of management, however, tend to be rare compared to that of more autocratic styles.

How did your group feel about the style of your manager, and why?

In what situations would you consider autocratic leadership to be both appropriate and acceptable, and why?

In what situations would you consider laissez-faire leadership to be both appropriate and acceptable, and why?

Who Types the Group Project Paper Thursday Night?

BACKGROUND

Your group project paper for your management class is due early tomorrow morning. You and the other members of your group have all worked on it for the past month and have spent many hours together over the past several days trying to agree on the content. Now it is Thursday afternoon, and you are trying to decide who will type, edit, and proofread the final copy tonight.

To start, read your part and explain to your group who you are and what you think your role should be in getting this paper typed.

This exercise was written by Sandra L. Deacon. Used by permission.

About the author: Sandi Deacon has taught organizational behavior at Boston University's School of Management and Northeastern University. She is a doctoral student in counseling psychology.

United Dynamics
Downsizing—Firing by Any Other Name

Within an hour of the announcement, the news had spread throughout the work force at United Dynamics (UD)—the government had selected a competitor to develop a new generation of jet engines for the military. It was no secret that UD had been counting on this contract, and that without it massive cutbacks would have to be made throughout the organization. This would, by necessity, include laying off not only many of the people who had been brought in to work on the development of the engine prototype, but cutting many who had been with the company for longer periods and in different capacities as well.

Your unit is composed of ten engineers specializing in cooling and heating systems: you have been instructed to lay off three of them immediately. You have also been told that further layoffs are likely should other contracts not come through.

Over the past several years, you have been able to build an almost perfectly functioning team. Your unit is highly cohesive. The engineers cooperate with one another's efforts and act as sparks for one another's creativity. In addition, their friendly and supportive relationships go beyond the limits of the workplace.

You have heard from other managers about just how difficult it is to lay off employees, especially when they are as good as those in your unit, but you never really believed you would have to wield the axe. You know that the negative effects on morale will be devastating, and you realize that the layoffs are also going to cause work overloads for those who remain.

On the following pages are the names of the engineers in your unit and the things that come to mind about each of them as you contemplate your task. Who will you lay off, and why?

In making your decision, consider the following:

1. How your choices of lay-offs will impact the group's ability to function effectively both in the near and long terms
2. What the impact will be on diversity, creativity, and socialization
3. What the effects will be on the group's cohesion

Other issues to consider are short- and long-term costs, ethics, politics, seniority, corporate image, social responsibility, legal issues, and ability to meet organizational goals.

This exercise was written by Janet W. Wohlberg.

PROCEDURE

Step 1 (30 minutes)

Read the background information and the profiles on each of the engineers. List the reasons for retaining and for laying off each of the engineers.

Step 2 (5 minutes)

On the main score sheet, note who you will lay off and who you will retain.

Step 3 (40 minutes)

Divide your class into groups of five to seven students. Discuss the characters and come to a group consensus as to who you will retain and who you will lay off.

Step 4 (15–30 minutes, depending on the number of groups)

Report to the class who your group agreed to lay off and why. The instructor should record each group's responses in a visible place.

Step 5 (open-ended)

Class discussion.

United Dynamics
Main Score Sheet

Engineer	Lay Off	Keep
Harold Aldrich		
Jane Calloway		
Lloyd Hunt		
Zelda Karas		
Murray Mangino		
Matt Peebles		
Robert A. Selkirk		
Eugene Stapleton		
Wei Tan		
Adam Twersky		

United Dynamics

Wei Tan

Tan has been at UD and with your unit just over two years. He came to the United States as a political refugee from China, not having been able to readjust to China's social system when he went home after receiving his engineering degree from an American university. Tan left China with his wife, who speaks no English, and two young children, with three suitcases of clothing and little else. It took him nearly a year, while living at virtually poverty level, to find the job with UD after arriving here. Tan and his family just recently moved out of the tiny apartment they had been sharing with another family.

Tan is an excellent engineer, and he has always been willing to work nights and weekends as project deadlines approached. Occasionally, Tan's English has led to some communication problems within the department; once the wrong equipment was ordered because someone misunderstood what he was saying. However, the other engineers like Tan, and feel protective toward him. Several have made concerted efforts to help him and his family. Eugene, particularly, passes his own children's outgrown clothing on to Tan's children.

Reasons for Retaining	Reasons for Laying Off

United Dynamics

Eugene Stapleton

Eugene is a single father whose wife died of lupus seven years ago and left him with three children, then ages two, three, and six. At that time, Eugene took four months of leave from UD, some of it in accumulated vacation days, to get himself and his young family settled into their new way of life. You know that child care costs still take a large part of Eugene's salary and that he has put a fair percentage of his flexible benefits package into the company's voucher system for helping to cover those costs.

Eugene is another genuinely good engineer and your only real expert in the design of cooling systems for boats, a steady 20 percent of your business. His efforts have been major factors in winning several large-sized contracts.

Because of his child care responsibilities, Eugene is rarely able to stay at work after five or to come in on weekends. However, he does have a computer at home on which he often works nights and weekends.

Reasons for Retaining	Reasons for Laying Off

United Dynamics

Zelda Karas

Zelda is a star performer and one of only two women in your department. When she first came to UD, almost fifteen years ago, she was actually the first woman employee in the company above the clerical level. She has consistently turned down managerial level jobs, preferring hands-on engineering instead. She has been the leader on a number of successful projects and is seen by the younger engineers as a mentor; when they have a problem, they generally turn to Zelda for help. She is also frequently consulted by engineers from other units.

Zelda is married to a successful ophthalmologist, her children are grown and off on their own, and she and her husband travel frequently. About every three or four years, Zelda takes an extra month of vacation—without pay—to go to Europe or Southeast Asia with her husband. She has always been careful to delay this until after the completion of whatever project she has been working on.

Reasons for Retaining	Reasons for Laying Off

United Dynamics

Murray Mangino

Murray has solid engineering skills. Over the past twenty-two years, he has been in a number of departments throughout UD, having originally started as a draftsman with an associate's degree from a nearby community college. Murray was the first one in his family to go to college. In his early years at UD, he continued with his education by going nights and weekends, ultimately getting both undergraduate and graduate degrees in engineering.

Because of his career path at UD, he knows the company well and can sometimes perform what no one else can for your unit. When your unit has needed special items or people, it is Murray who gets them even when you have been told that it is impossible. It never ceases to amaze you just how many people Murray knows who are willing to do favors for him.

While Murray is generally well liked by the others in the unit, he often gets tense and edgy when time is short and deadlines are tight.

Murray and his wife have two children in college and one about to graduate from high school. Murray's wife, Cynthia, has a full-time job as the manager of a small dental office, and her income helps to pay the bills. Not long ago, Murray confided to you that he also took out a second mortgage on his house to help pay his children's tuition.

Reasons for Retaining	Reasons for Laying Off

United Dynamics

Matt Peebles

Matt is one of the UD engineers who has been closely mentored by Zelda. Under her tutelage, he has become a first-rate engineer with an eye for detail. On a number of occasions, Matt has picked up design problems that the others in the unit have overlooked, and when problems arise, he is a valuable and reliable troubleshooter. He is also the best on-site person in the unit, overseeing the installation and start-up of systems. In this area, Matt has been able to develop good working relationships with a number of major clients.

Matt recently tested HIV-positive—something you think the others in the unit probably don't yet know. Being laid off will mean that he will lose his health benefits and will not get the support he is probably going to need during the critical stages of the AIDS disease.

Matt lives with his mother and is her sole source of support.

Reasons for Retaining	Reasons for Laying Off

United Dynamics

Jane Calloway

Jane is the sister-in-law of the UD vice-president, within whose span of control your unit falls. She is an average engineer and is well liked by the others in the unit. In many ways, Jane sets the mood tone for the group. She is virtually always upbeat and always ready with a joke or a story. When something goes wrong or the stress of deadlines starts to get to people, it is Jane who helps the others find the humor in the situation and who helps the group get back on track.

Jane and Matt are good friends and often go out socially. She has also been very helpful to Eugene and has volunteered from time to time to take care of his kids to give him some time off. Just recently, Jane spent her long holiday weekend with Eugene's kids while he went fishing with a friend.

Jane is the one in the unit who volunteers to chair the annual Red Feather and other charity drives, and she also organized the unit's recycling program.

Reasons for Retaining	Reasons for Laying Off

United Dynamics

Harold Aldrich

Harold has the most seniority at UD, having been with the company for over thirty years. He joined the company right out of the armed services, where he had received his education and had been a member of the Army Corps of Engineers. Harold still maintains contact with some of his old buddies from the military, most of whom are now retired from the service and working in private industry. One of his army friends is now a congressman and another is on the staff of a cabinet secretary in the present administration.

Harold's history of employment at UD has been solid. While never a star like Zelda or some of the others, he has been reliable and loyal. On any number of occasions, he has taken voluntary pay cuts and worked extra hours, always expressing concern for the "good of the company." Harold is a real team player.

The social activities in the office revolve around Harold. He and his wife always hold the annual unit outings at their house as well as numerous barbecues, birthday celebrations, and special events.

Harold is scheduled to retire in four years. Being laid off now will result in a significant loss of retirement benefits.

Reasons for Retaining	Reasons for Laying Off

United Dynamics

Robert Anderson Selkirk

Robert is the newest member of your engineering team and the only black. He is an excellent engineer —a member of the "star" category—and he has fit right into the group. Robert was specifically recruited in order to fill the government mandate for racial diversity in companies that receive government contracts. You are aware that this is closely monitored.

At present, Robert, Harold, and Zelda are in the middle of an important project for the air force. Zelda keeps telling you how impressed she is with Robert's skills and that the success of the project is largely going to be the result of his efforts.

Robert's wife is a lawyer; she is pregnant with their first child.

Reasons for Retaining	Reasons for Laying Off

United Dynamics

Adam Twersky

Adam was hired away from a competing company with promises of more money and a brighter future with UD. He came in just a few months before Robert and at a higher salary. At the time he was brought in, a note from the executive vice-president of UD made clear that Adam was being groomed for a higher position. You have no idea of just what that position is to be.

Adam is far from your most talented performer. As an engineer, he is little better than adequate. He does seem to be hard working, however, and the others in the unit often request him for their project teams because of his strengths during planning stages.

Adam is unmarried. Last Friday, he let you borrow his new sports car so that you could take a friend for a ride.

Reasons for Retaining	Reasons for Laying Off

United Dynamics

Lloyd Hunt

Lloyd is an average engineer who is somewhat on the fringes of the group. He has the second most years in service of anyone in the unit.

Lloyd is litigious. It seems that every time you turn around, Lloyd is suing someone for something. The amazing thing is that he very often ends up settling his cases for substantial amounts.

In the early 1980s, while working as an engineer in another unit at UD, Lloyd found a defect in a product that was being built for the U.S. Navy. His supervisor, who no longer works for UD, told Lloyd that the product was fine and that Lloyd should mind his own business. Lloyd's response was to write a letter to his congressman detailing the problem and expressing his opinion that the defect could put the lives of navy personnel in danger. During the investigation of UD that followed, Lloyd's supervisor fired him, ostensibly for chronic lateness and absenteeism from work.

Lloyd successfully sued UD for wrongful dismissal; he was awarded punitive damages, his lost wages, and the court ordered that he be reinstated. Since assuming your position as manager of the heating and cooling engineering unit, Lloyd has regularly reminded you of his triumph.

Reasons for Retaining	Reasons for Laying Off

Frederick Engineering

In 1971, Gordon Frederick founded Frederick Engineering in Brookfield, Connecticut. For the first three years, the company designed, produced, and sold only one item, a safety product called a Proxagard, which was used to protect people's hands around dangerous machines such as punch presses. Even as late as 1980, the company had only nine employees. Management was straightforward: Most personnel decisions were made by Frederick himself, or by his vice-president, Lewis Naehring.

By 1989, the situation had changed dramatically. In the mid-1980s, the company's sales had skyrocketed, largely due to landing an enormous contract with the Crown Company, the world's largest maker of ice cream and frozen yogurt machines. Frederick designed a soft-touch electronic master control for the machines that made many sophisticated operations simple.

However, life at Frederick Engineering was now far from simple. The company had moved to a new building and almost immediately had found it necessary to build an addition that tripled the size. By 1989, there were roughly eighty employees. The company had to hire an unusual number of young or inexperienced workers to meet the demands of building thousands of master controls. Despite the addition of fourteen assembly workers, the company was still not keeping up with orders, and more workers soon would have to be hired.

In production alone, there was a safety products group, a master control division, a proximity switch group, and a special orders group. Most of the experienced workers belonged to the safety products group or the special orders group. The latter did highly customized work for companies like Maine Potato and Star Oil.

All of the groups were responsible for product assembly. This involved following the guidelines of a schematic blueprint that specified the exact type and placement of electronic components into printed circuit boards.

Each group had a leader who regularly met with Larry Browning, a middle manager with more than twenty years of experience in operations. He was a positive thinker with an especially good knack for developing innovative production solutions. The previous year, for example, he had purchased a wave-soldering machine that had dramatically cut labor hours.

Browning would get sales orders from Lewis Naehring and help the group leaders with planning production, troubleshooting, and process improvement. In addition to meeting with Browning and managing a group of seven or eight people, each group leader was also expected to do assembly work—no leader was simply a supervisor. The company focused its efforts heavily on meeting the demands of the Crown Company.

In August 1989, Gordon Frederick walked past the benches of the safety products group and was surprised to see how disorganized things seemed to be. Tools were on the floor; microchips had been misplaced, a problem that could lead to defects that would waste the time and money of the repair department.

Frederick spoke to Browning about the problems, and he learned that Ellen Grassley, the group leader, had been wrestling with many personal problems. In fact, she had given

This case was written by Scott Weighart.

Browning her two-week notice just that morning. Frederick reminded the middle manager that he preferred to promote from within, if possible. Browning agreed.

"I think that there are two women in safety products who would make excellent leaders," he told Frederick.

Unfortunately, neither of the women—Laura Nishigaya nor Juana DeJesus—had any interest in becoming group leaders. Browning was disappointed. Both had been at Frederick for over four years, and they could build a Proxagard without looking at the blueprint or skipping a beat in their friendly conversation. The whole group seemed very close; Browning and Frederick wondered if this was why they didn't want the position of boss over the others.

As a result, Browning placed an ad in the *News-Times*. After several interviews, he hired Patrizia Rossini, an Italian-born woman with a fair amount of supervisory experience. For the previous six years, Rossini had managed a group of assembly workers at QDC, a company of similar size in nearby New Milford. QDC was a one-product company that had built quality stereo cartridges for turntables. With the compact disc boom, QDC had gone out of business.

In her interview, Rossini was very impressive. Apparently upper management at QDC had been unusually cheap when it came to paying assembly workers—Rossini had not had control over that. As a result of the low pay, Rossini had had to contend with extremely high turnover as well as a constant stream of thoroughly inexperienced men and women who were barely out of high school. Nonetheless, she had managed to take these raw recruits and make them into productive workers. She worked closely with them; she had mastered the process and had made sure to tell each worker the specifics of her approach. The QDC workers apparently respected her a great deal; Rossini showed Browning an engraved bracelet they had given her when the plant had closed.

Above all, Browning was impressed by Rossini's conscientiousness. "If the boss says to do something, I do it," Rossini told him. She explained that she had been brought up in a strict Italian family where respect for one's elders or superiors was considered extremely important. She assured Browning that the interests of Frederick Engineering would come first, saying, "I'm not the kind of supervisor who pals around with her workers and lets them do whatever they want."

Browning hired Rossini, thinking that she would be a dynamic group leader. He also decided that she would keep the workers from being slipshod, something Frederick had complained about. Giving the workers a new boss would be a good opportunity to change some of the lingering problems of the past few months. Therefore, he told Rossini that her first task would be to make sure that all tools were stored properly and that components, such as transistors and resistors, shouldn't be mixed haphazardly. Also, he had thought up a number of new assembly procedures he believed would increase efficiency and he wanted her to implement them.

In little more than a week, all kinds of problems had erupted in the safety products group. Rossini's requests had resulted in bitter arguments, and that was the least of it: Her workers questioned everything she did.

Apparently Nishigaya and DeJesus were the most vocal critics of Rossini. Browning asked the three of them into his office, hoping for a civil discussion. Before long, he was shaking his head, disgusted at the pettiness of the workers.

"She yelled at me!" Nishigaya said, "and she acts like I don't know how to do anything. 'Do it this way, do it that way,' she says. Plus, she never says anything nice when I do a good job."

Rossini didn't look at Nishigaya. Turning to Browning, she explained, "My experience has been that Asians don't like to be publicly recognized for doing good work—it makes them uncomfortable."

Nishigaya rolled her eyes and let out an exasperated sigh.

Then DeJesus chimed in. "Then she tries to tell us to build the motion detectors some new way, as if she knew anything about that. I've built them for over three years, and I can make one twice as fast as she can."

"We can probably make them three times faster," Nishigaya said.

Browning was dismayed. He told them that the new methods were his ideas. This quieted them down. Then he encouraged them to try to get along with each other as best they could.

When Browning told Naehring what had happened, Naehring was angry. He couldn't believe that the two workers were being so petty. Just two months earlier, Frederick had singled them out at the monthly meeting for being top producers. He thought they were being immature. Naehring told Browning to give Rossini all the support she needed through these difficult days.

"They didn't want the job," Naehring reminded Browning, "so they'd better learn to accept having someone else as their boss."

Every day seemed to bring a new problem. A major uproar occurred when the workers found out that Rossini couldn't read the color code, an extremely basic aspect of assembling electronic components. For example, Rossini didn't know that if a resistor had a brown, black, or yellow stripe, it was a 100K resistor. Through the grapevine, Browning heard that the workers were really irked by this. Of course, he had known that Rossini lacked this knowledge, but he was sure it was unimportant and that, like the others, she would pick it up within a few weeks. What was the big deal? All it seemed to be was more pettiness.

Already, Rossini had learned a lot. Several times each day, she knocked on Browning's door to ask him questions about Proxagard assembly. She apparently felt too uncomfortable to ask her subordinates for assistance when she got stuck. Given the resentment her arrival had caused, Browning thought this was understandable.

Then there was a major conflict. Rossini and Nishigaya got into a squabble because Rossini felt that the women's frequent conversations were causing mix-ups with tools and components. She warned that this could lead to no pay raise at their next review—Browning had given her full authority over pay and bonuses. Nishigaya told Browning that Rossini was like Mussolini and called her "an Italian dictator who likes to hear her own voice." Dramatically throwing back her hair, Nishigaya announced that she quit. DeJesus quit as well.

Browning felt badly about losing two productive and experienced workers. He briefly wondered whether he had made the best choice when he had hired Rossini. He decided to call Oanh Ng into his office. Ng was now the most experienced worker left in the group.

"As you know, Laura and Juana quit," he said. "Are you happy with your job?"

"Yes, Mr. Browning, I like my job very much. Mrs. Rossini is a very good boss, a very nice lady."

Browning's worries about performance vanished. He and Rossini interviewed and hired two new workers—one Hispanic and one Cambodian—and they learned their jobs with unusual speed. It was obvious that they respected Rossini and had learned a great deal from her. Pleased and proud, Browning went to Naehring. "I guess we had a few troublemakers, a few rotten apples ruining the bunch," he said.

But the peace didn't last long. The performance of the six veteran workers—even Oanh Ng—seemed to be suffering. Although there weren't many arguments after the departure of the two "troublemakers," there was still tension in the group. Gradually, Browning heard bits and pieces of the veteran workers' complaints:

"Even if I find a better way of making something, she doesn't want to hear about it. It's always 'follow company procedure.' "

"At this point, I just wish she'd leave me alone to do the work. I don't need a babysitter."

"Even though Ellen Grassley was doing practically nothing by the time she left, I felt like we were better off."

This attitude was reflected when Rossini was out of the office for three days for her father-in-law's funeral. During this time, the performance of the group as a whole was better than it had been since she had arrived.

Browning and Naehring resented having to deal with such petty problems while they were struggling to keep up with the huge demands of the rapidly growing master control group. They felt they had been sympathetic to Rossini, and they had told her that she had their support every step of the way. Now the "troublemakers" were gone, but only the two new workers were doing well.

When Frederick learned about this, he was concerned. "Of course the new workers are doing well—everyone's on their best behavior when they start a new job. I tell you, I'm getting impatient with this whole situation," he said to Naehring and Browning. Browning knew that Frederick would not suggest firing Rossini—his boss considered that to be a desperate measure, a last resort. Still, Browning wondered what could be done. Deep down, he believed she had what it takes to be a good manager. What could have gone wrong?

Questions for Discussion

1. Knowing what you do about leadership theories, what do you believe is wrong in the safety products division at Frederick Engineering? Why? In answering this question, consider not only Rossini's role, but those of her superiors as well.

2. Keeping in mind that Frederick considers firing an employee to be a last resort, if you were Naehring, what would you do?

Frederick Engineering

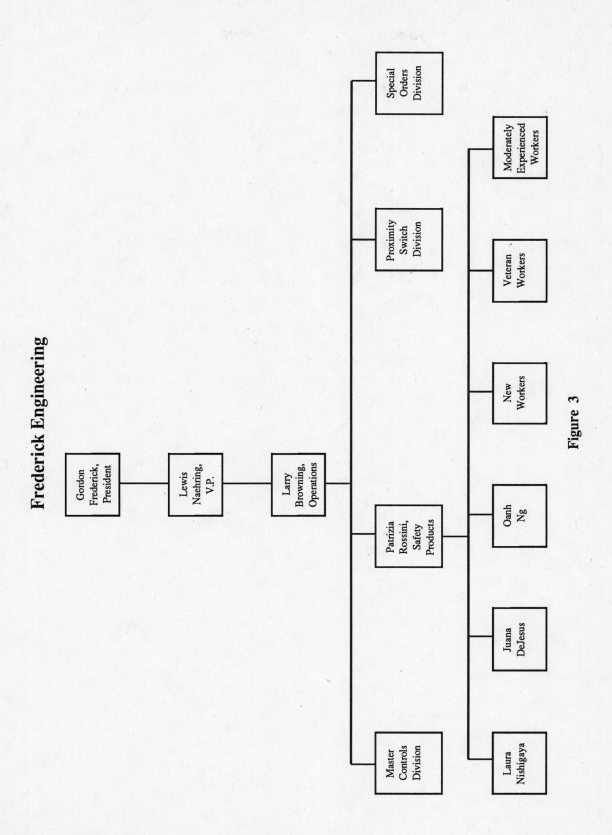

Figure 3

Leadership at Prodigy Electronics

Dennis Jackson couldn't understand what had gone wrong. Jackson, vice-president of marketing for Prodigy Electronics, had recently hired Tony Cafasso as marketing manager for the Robotic Controls Division. This division was responsible for developing road show presentations and marketing plans tailored to a great variety of world markets. The marketing team members needed to have considerable creativity, as well as sensitivity and awareness of cultural differences and global issues, to do their jobs well. Accordingly, there was substantial ethnic diversity in the department: Seven of the marketing representatives were white, five were Asian, three were black, and two were Hispanic. In addition to being specialists regarding the cultural differences of specific markets, most of the marketing representatives were fluent in at least two languages.

Jackson had hired Cafasso because of his impressive track record as a manager. Jackson often played tennis with Cafasso's former boss, who described Cafasso with glowing praise and as a nice guy who got results.

At his former job, Cafasso had managed an assembly line at a watch factory and had been charged with carrying out regular performance appraisals and making salary and promotion decisions. Faced with a team of veteran employees who had apparently lost the desire to work, Cafasso had turned them around by letting them make changes to the assembly line and giving them a say in how things were done. He also joined the group's softball team and was often invited to their regular parties after work and on weekends. Under Cafasso's management, productivity on Cafasso's line at the watch factory had increased dramatically.

Jackson was sure he had hired a great leader. But, he couldn't understand why the performance of Tony Cafasso's marketing team wasn't better. The team members were working, but their ideas lacked the kind of creative spark that Jackson had sought. He decided to speak with some of Cafasso's subordinates individually to get their perspective on Cafasso's management style.

Jackson decided that he should speak to the more experienced employees first. He called Chuck Pritchard, a white, forty-nine-year-old man who had worked for Prodigy for seventeen years.

"Tony is a great guy and a super manager," Pritchard assured Jackson. "Whenever I go to him for advice, he always turns my questions around and asks me what I would do. When something major is happening in my area, we work as a team to figure out what we should do. And you can't argue with the results. Sales in my area have gone up 20 percent since Tony joined the team."

When Jackson spoke to Nancy Bartels, another white employee who had been with Prodigy for thirteen years, she was equally as enthusiastic.

"Last month my region had the highest sales in the office, and Tony made a point of singling me out in our monthly strategy session. He told me he wished he had the authority to give me a raise or promotion. It made me feel really proud. I have more enthusiasm for my job than I've had in quite a while."

This case was written by Scott Weighart.

Next, Jackson decided to speak to Amanda Chan, a thirty-five-year-old Chinese-American woman who had been with Prodigy for just over seven years.

"I think Tony's very nice and everything, and I really don't have any problems with him, personally. I like the fact that I have a say in how things are done. But, sometimes Tony doesn't think. Last month he praised SooAe at the strategy meeting. She was so embarrassed that she didn't come to work for over a week, and I got stuck covering both of our territories. Plus, he keeps telling her that he wants her to make important decisions. She lacks the experience needed to make the best decisions, and she's terrified of making a mistake. I try to help, but I can't afford to let my area slip, too."

Jackson called SooAe Kim into his office. A twenty-six-year-old Korean woman, SooAe had joined Prodigy less than a year earlier. Jackson found himself more confused than ever as SooAe told him that she thought Mr. Cafasso was a very good manager. Jackson pressed her with questions, but she had absolutely nothing negative to say about her boss. When asked about her absence earlier in the month, Ms. Kim lowered her head, apologized, and said it wouldn't happen again. Finally, Jackson shrugged his shoulders and said she could leave.

Alone in his office, Jackson tried to make sense of what he had heard. He was sure Cafasso wasn't a racist. After all, he had praised SooAe, given her encouragement in a time when she was struggling, and was even giving her a chance to control her own destiny. He decided he had better speak with some of the other employees.

"Do you think Tony is fair to everyone, regardless of race?" Jackson asked Lou Andrews, a thirty-eight-year-old black man who had been at Prodigy as long as he could remember.

"Of course he is!" Andrews replied. "Tony treats everybody the same. Race doesn't make any difference to him. The guy goes out of his way to make sure that everyone makes decisions. And if something does go wrong, he never gives anyone a hard time about it. He usually doesn't even mention it. Tony's a positive thinker. The best thing this company could do would be to give Tony a raise, or at least give him the authority to hire and fire people. Otherwise, things are great."

Jackson was starting to think that there wasn't a problem. He wondered if it was just a slowdown in the marketplace. However, he knew that other divisions were soaring along. It didn't add up. He decided to speak to some of the younger workers, starting with Katie Langston, a twenty-seven-year-old black woman who had joined the company after getting her B.S./B.A. six months earlier

"I think Tony means well," she said. "But I hope he knows what he's doing. I'm still learning the ropes around here. It's exciting to be given so much responsibility so early in my career, but I'm really not sure if I'm doing a good job. With this kind of work, rules and methods seem kind of vague. It's an art, trying to match robotic controls with the needs of customers in some specific part of the world. I like the work, but I'm always worried that I might be making some kind of huge mistake."

Juan Delgado, a recent M.B.A. who had just joined the company as the coordinator for the South American marketing strategy, had somewhat similar concerns.

"Sometimes I just wish somebody would tell me what to do," he said. "In business school, we learned how great it can be to let workers make decisions for themselves. Now that I'm in the real world, I don't think it's so great! Tony is always pushing me to make my own decisions. Maybe if I had more experience, I would like it, but right now, it's driving me crazy. Sometimes I think I'd be better off making my strategy decisions by throwing darts at a dart board. I just hope I'm doing a good job. I'll never find out from Tony. He's always chatting with the guys who have been around here for a while—

brainstorming, he calls it. Anyway, I never get invited to join in. He must have something against me."

Again, Jackson was confused. Perhaps Cafasso had trouble dealing with Hispanics? Next, he invited Pedro Mantilla, a Mexican-American, into his office.

"I've been with this company for sixteen years," Mantilla began, looking Jackson straight in the eyes. "And I tell you, Tony Cafasso is the best manager I've ever had."

"Now what?" Jackson thought to himself after Mantilla left his office. He decided he had better interview the new marketing representatives, almost all of whom had been hired within the previous six months. Jackson was dumbfounded as one after the other the employees stated that they found Tony Cafasso to be a poor manager. They all mentioned that he pushed them to make their own decisions in spite of their inexperience, and most said they felt unsure about the level of their own performance.

"Tony likes to pretend that mistakes don't exist," one worker said. "He seems to think that if you don't talk about them, mistakes will just go away."

Most of the other recently hired employees seemed to share this view as well.

Dennis Jackson thanked the last worker for coming to his office, closed the door, and tried to make sense out of everything he had heard.

"It seems like the older workers—the few that we have—think that Tony is great," Jackson said to himself. "Meanwhile, the young people think he's terrible. I wonder why that's the case?"

"And what about the question of racial and ethnic differences?" Jackson thought. "What's going on here?"

Questions for Discussion

1. Are there problems with the kinds of leadership being displayed in this case? What? Why?
2. Compare what appears to have been Tony's success in his previous job with what you believe his level of success is at Prodigy. If you see a difference, what do you believe the basis of that difference to be?
3. If you were Jackson, what would you do?

Getting Ahead

PROCEDURE

Step 1 (10 minutes)

The facilitator will distribute role 1 to half of the class and role 2 to the other half of the class. Read the role you have been given and the observer sheet.

Step 2 (20–30 minutes)

Perform the role play. While doing so, stick to the facts that have been given in the role, and attempt to make the experience as realistic as possible. Try to reach a point at which you understand one another's positions and can reach a mutually agreed-upon resolution. If you are an observer, pay close attention to how each of the players seems to feel about the responses of the other role player and whether ach of the players has been effective.

Step 3 (45 minutes)

Class discussion.

Questions for Discussion

1. What outcome to this problem would best serve the purposes of the organization?
2. If the manager fails to give support to the worker's request, what are the outcomes likely to be:
   a. for the subordinate?
   b. for the manager?
   c. for the organization?
3. If the manager is supportive, what are the likely outcomes:
   a. for the subordinate?
   b. for the manager?
   c. for the organization?
4. Can you suggest any ways that this problem might have been handled differently or avoided altogether?

This exercise was written by Janet W. Wohlberg.

Getting Ahead
Observer Sheet

What you are witnessing happens more often than you would guess. As the discussion progresses, consider the following issues to report to the rest of the participants:

1. What are the personal interests of each of the parties?
    a. Manager

    _____

    _____

    _____

    _____

    b. Subordinate

    _____

    _____

    _____

    _____

    _____

2. Are both players stating their interests clearly and honestly? Why or why not?

    _____

    _____

    _____

    _____

3. Are the players listening to and hearing one another? Are the messages being sent also the messages being received? Why?

    _____

    _____

    _____

    _____

    _____

4. Were the players able to arrive at a solution? Why? Why not?

    _____

    _____

    _____

    _____

Danger: Radio Activity Hits Country in Long Island

Barbara Lankford and Max Vaughn looked at each other uneasily as they walked through the hallways of the radio station where they worked. They were about to meet Rex Honeycutt, the new owner of WPOP Radio, 98.6 FM on your dial, in Smithtown, Long Island. Although she didn't look forward to it, Barbara figured she'd find a way to handle the new boss; Max was more apprehensive, wondering what his fate would be.

Many rumors had been going around the office: Some said that Honeycutt planned radical changes for the station. When they sat down in Honeycutt's office, Barbara and Max's worst fears were confirmed. Honeycutt greeted them, giving Max a handshake and a hard slap on the back. Barbara noticed a brass spittoon on the floor alongside Honeycutt's desk. As he laid out his plans for the future of the radio station, he paused occasionally to spit out a mouthful of juice from the wad of tobacco he had stored in his cheek.

"Well, boys and girls," Honeycutt said. "I reckon you're mighty curious about how things are gonna be with a new cowboy leading the herd down here in Smithtown. So here's the big news: This here station is about to be turned upside down. I got an idea that's hotter than Alabama asphalt."

Barbara and Max glanced at each other in despair.

"First off, as of next week," Honeycutt said, "we are gonna have the first all-country music station in all of Long Island! From now on our official call letters are gonna be WAOK. Has a nice ring, don't you think?"

Honeycutt explained that he had done a great deal of industry and demographic research about making such a move. WPOP's ratings—and advertising revenue—had reached an all-time low. Up until just over a year ago, WPOP-FM had been a big hit. More recently, ratings had sagged as listeners began to tune into a more powerful, all-mix station from New York City.

DJ "Mad Max" Vaughn had been an extremely popular local celebrity for quite a number of years. Lately, though, fewer fans had been asking for his autograph when he walked through the Smithtown Mall. Hospitalized teenagers no longer requested his autographs, and one sponsor had recently cancelled Max's on-air endorsements of their products. Still, Vaughn liked to think that there was a "silent majority" of Long Islanders who loved him.

As for Barbara Lankford, advertising sales manager, she was horrified to think about what the change would mean for her. She had built up great relationships with the advertising executives of local companies; now it seemed as if all her hard work would be wasted.

After meeting with Rex Honeycutt, first together and then separately, Max and Barbara went out for a long lunch to discuss the situation.

"This guy's going to make me pull all my hair out within two weeks. I can't believe I'm saying this, but already I miss Craig," Barbara said, referring to the station's previous owner.

This case was written by Scott Weighart.

Max nodded. "Yeah, I know," he said sadly. "Craig didn't treat us like we were in some kind of radio kindergarten."

Max and Barbara had both been offended by Honeycutt's order-giving style during their first meeting. Handing a pen and a pad to Barbara—which made her feel like a secretary—Honeycutt had named a long list of companies and had told her to call their advertising managers immediately.

"I used to work at a country station in Virginia," she said. "You wouldn't believe the kind of 'folksy-folks' you have to deal with."

Barbara pulled a paper out of her purse and read Honeycutt's list of potential advertisers: Red Snake Chewing Tobacco, Real-Valu Hardware, QTP and Puritan Motor Oil, the Crawfish County Tourist Bureau, and John Foxe Tractors.

"I'm surprised he didn't name any chain saw companies," she said.

"You're still better off than I am," Max responded. "He told me he was changing the name of my show. Instead of hosting 'The Mad Max Hit Parade,' I now get to be DJ for 'The MAXimum Country Hour.' He also said that I had to start my next show with that song 'I Don't Care if It Rains or Freezes, as Long as I Got My . . . .' well, you know. Plus he's going to decide on my whole play list—every song—every day—for our first week of playing country."

"Ridiculous," Barbara said. "The guy's been in Long Island for two weeks, and he acts like we're the ones who are clueless about local radio."

Craig Sugerman had taken a very different approach to running the business. At first, Barbara had found him to be frustrating. He had constantly given them extremely vague memos. "Sell a few ads this morning" was the memo he sent to Barb on her first morning at the job. She walked to his office, hoping he would give her some idea of exactly how she was supposed to go about doing this, but his secretary had told her that he was meditating and couldn't be disturbed. When Barbara tried again in the early afternoon, she was told that Craig had invited some electronic engineers over for a "power lunch."

This lack of interaction was especially frustrating, since Craig's memos generally ended on some inspirational note: "I expect you to do everything possible to make us the best radio station west of Syosset."

Eventually, Barb realized she would have to do as well as she could by learning from her mistakes. She stopped seeking advice or attempting to confront her boss with complaints. After six months on the job, she was no longer bothered by his lack of specific instructions, and until just about a year ago, she had been the top-grossing radio time salesperson on Long Island. Several competing stations had tried to woo her away, but she realized that she appreciated the autonomy of her job at WPOP, and she knew she could handle it.

Still, Barb often had wished that Craig would meet with her once in a while, give her some feedback, or work together with her to brainstorm about new ad possibilities. She felt somewhat unappreciated, and sometimes she had trouble getting out of bed to go to work.

As for Max, he thought Craig had been the perfect boss: As long as you didn't interrupt him or waste his time with idle chitchat, he had no problem with you. Max had devoted his life to radio. In seventh grade he had built a small radio for a science fair. Max had been a DJ for almost twenty years and took great pride in his ability to predict the songs that would top the pop charts. He was rarely wrong and loved to introduce a song by reminding the listeners about his predictions: "This is Mad Max, the Radio Warrior, playing this week's number one song. Remember, you heard it here first!"

The thing Max liked most about being a DJ was that his days were pleasantly predictable. He had regular hours, and his play list was largely structured by the songs he liked that were popular at the time.

As for country music, Max didn't mind listening to it while sitting alone in a bar, drinking martinis and brooding about his three failed marriages; but, he didn't follow the Nashville scene and couldn't tell if he was listening to the Judds, Dolly Parton, or Tammy Faye Bakker. Being a country music DJ would be like starting a whole new job.

On the other hand, Barbara had worked for three different radio stations and sold ads for five different formats: all-news, Top 40, classic rock, classical music, and country. Her days were unpredictable. She would make numerous phone calls to advertisers, visit local businesses, and try to come up with new ideas for attracting clients, sometimes taking them out to dinner and then taking time off the following morning. She felt humiliated by the way Honeycutt had ignored her considerable experience. He acted as if she were a college intern with no mind of her own.

Despite her strong negative feelings, Barb was afraid to openly complain about the way he treated her. After all, Honeycutt was now responsible for any raises she might or might not receive in the future, and in fact, he controlled her job. If she complained about the new format and the amount of work needed to reestablish contacts with the appropriate advertisers, he could certainly just fire her.

Honeycutt had told Max and Barbara that he had an "open barn door" policy as a manager.

"If any of you farmhands find yourselves gettin' in deep manure on the job, you just make sure to stop by for a good heart-to-heart so we can pull out the weeds before they start smothering the vegetables. And if you've got some fine ideas, well, we can just put 'em out on the porch and see if the cat licks 'em up."

From Honeycutt's point of view, the first few weeks of the job had gone quite well. He had enjoyed meeting Barbara and Max, and he was glad when they told him they thought a country format would be just fine. Now, however, he felt that there were some problems with the pair of veteran employees.

During the first week of the job, Barbara barely talked to him and seemed moody. He asked her if anything was wrong, and she hesitated before saying no. What was eating her?

Max was even more of a mystery. During the first week, he had done a terrific job. He had followed Honeycutt's play list and had acted like a real professional all week. Rex figured that Max was a pretty sharp DJ and told him he could make up his own play list for the second week. On that Monday, Max had seemed tense on the air and had fumbled lines repeatedly. His choices of music were sometimes good, sometimes strange.

While driving his 4WD to work one morning that week, Rex had turned on the radio and had been surprised to hear an obscure country song called "Pa's Got Cancer, Ma's Got the Flu, and Me I'm Just Plain Missin' You." It turned out that Max had accidently cued up the flip side of a new 45. How could such an experienced guy make such a bonehead mistake? Rex had crunched the numbers and knew that switching to the country format was a good idea. Still, he noticed that Barbara was not working as well as she had under the previous owner, and her sales attempts were yielding only mediocre results.

Rex had offered both workers many chances to talk, but they never took advantage of the opportunity. Still, he could spot a problem that stuck out like a ten-gallon hat. Things could be better between himself and his employees, but how could he go about turning around a situation that appeared to be headed for disaster?

Questions for Discussion

1. Using one or two situational leadership theories, analyze the main characters of the case and explain, in theoretical terms, just what has happened to them since WPOP became WAOK.
2. Using the same theory or theories, compare the present situation with the situation that appeared to have existed when Craig Sugerman was the boss.
3. What sources of power have an impact on the present situation, and how are they being used?
4. Develop a comprehensive and specific set of recommendations for what you believe Rex should do as the new leader of WAOK based on the theories of leadership and power that apply.

Trouble with an Old Friend

It was a Friday afternoon when Dana Newell and Chris Decker came to see Ginny Fentross in her office.

"Pat Skinner is alienating everyone from design to purchasing to sales," Newell, vice-president for marketing at Ely Industries, told Fentross.

"It isn't that we don't like Pat as a person," added Decker quickly, "but we can't stand having such a troublemaker nosing into our business all the time and telling us what to do and when. It started virtually from the time Pat came here, and it hasn't gotten any better. If anything, things have probably gotten worse."

"Pat is your friend," Newell continued. "You did the hiring, and this problem is yours. If you don't do something pretty soon, there's going to be a revolution around here, and I'm not sure I want to be here to witness it. This whole thing is not my responsibility."

Fentross had been aware of the problem, the gathering storm surrounding Pat Skinner, but she was unsure of just what to do. In six months, since coming to work for Ely Industries, aggressive, intelligent, and hard-driving Skinner had achieved an outstanding record. There was no doubt in Fentross's mind that Skinner's unit, which produced excellent reproductions of antique toys, would soon be the top grossing unit at Ely—but she wondered if it was worth the headache and what increasingly felt like holding the proverbial tiger by the tail.

Fentross had tried talking to Skinner about the problems over a drink after hours. Skinner reacted with surprise, mildly suggested that the others weren't very efficient or were jealous, and made half-hearted promises to try not to step on people's toes. For about a week, things seemed a bit better, but then the undercurrent of resentment toward Skinner started to be felt by Fentross again.

BACKGROUND

Ginny Fentross had been out of her M.B.A. program eleven years when, with the help of some bank loans and a substantial inheritance from her grandfather, Clayton Harrison Ely, she formed Ely Industries. Ely, manufacturers of rustic crafts, was the result of Fentross's having purchased six growing cottage industries in Southern Vermont, to which she had added her own, a company that she had begun and had run out of her garage until it became too big. She then had purchased an abandoned sawmill near her home, had begun renovations, and had moved her original company to this site. It was shortly afterward that Fentross had purchased controling interest in the other companies, moving them to the sawmill as areas of the building were completed.

Within five years of consolidation, Ely had close to $12 million in sales. Along with the moves, Fentross had automated many of the crafts' manufacturing operations and centralized many of the business functions, most particularly purchasing, sales, and

This case was written by Janet W. Wohlberg.

research and development. Inventory and supplies were also centralized. However, each of the companies had its own space and worked as an independent production unit.

Fentross has retained most of the employees of the original companies, including several at the upper management levels, many of whom had been with their companies ten years or more.

Newell had been the marketing manager with Fentross's original company, and the two knew each other well. They had a comfortable working relationship, and Fentross found Newell, while not particularly aggressive or creative, to be loyal, steady, and reliable.

Decker, now manager of the purchasing department at Ely, had been treasurer and a kind of "chief cook and bottlewasher" in one of the other original companies. Decker was known for efficiency, accuracy, and an ability to work well with suppliers.

Ginny Fentross, forty-two years old, was dynamic, enterprising, and driven in comparison with most of Ely's former cottage industry employees, who appear somewhat laid back. With a reasonably sophisticated understanding of manufacturing and marketing, Fentross had consistently increased the company's efficiency and earnings and had still managed to keep most of the workers happy. Recognizing that most worked to fulfill their social needs, Fentross had instituted regular parties, had encouraged participation in local charity drives, and had set up the shops in such a way as to enable the workers to chat while they worked.

Only the antique toy division had continued to be a management headache. Now, it appeared that Pat Skinner was making the problem even more complex.

At the time of the buyout, the workers in the antique toy division had made it clear that they were unhappy with the changes being made in their lives, including the move to the sawmill. Many of them ignored the new company structure and were resistant to taking orders from new managers. Among the problems was that they often helped themselves to materials that were earmarked for other divisions, seemingly oblivious to the issues of supply inventory control. Fentross thought that as the older workers began to retire and new workers who identified more with Ely Industries were brought in, these problems would be worked out. In the meantime, the antique toy division was nearly impossible to control.

Pat Skinner

Fentross had hired Pat Skinner, an old college classmate, to head up the toy division, where production had often lagged behind schedule and anarchy was the rule. Skinner was just the kind of person she had thought she wanted at Ely.

While in college, Fentross and Skinner had been close and had worked together on various class projects and school activities. Fentross had found Pat to be reliable and ambitious, a self-starter with a great deal of follow-through. In addition, Pat Skinner had a lot of natural charm and seemed the perfect person to work with the old-timers. Indeed, Fentross had been right about that: production was up, and most of the workers even had agreed at least to try the new automated systems.

"Sure," Chris Decker admitted, "the toy division is more productive than it has ever been. But people around here are fed up, and we're getting a lot of complaints."

"Pat seems to think that the rest of us are either invisible or are just here to serve the interests of one Pat Skinner. When Pat gets a big order, process gets by-passed. Instead of filling out the necessary forms and passing them through the system, Pat goes straight to purchasing and starts making demands. Our purchasing and inventory systems get totally thrown off, and orders from other divisions get put aside."

"The salespeople are complaining, too," Decker continued. "They say that Pat is pushing them to give priority to toy sales. In addition, Pat is constantly haranguing R&D to push toy designs ahead of everything else."

"You know," Newell said. "If this was anyone else, most people would ignore the demands or fight back. But everyone knows that Pat is your friend, so they feel like they can't do that."

"I guess the other thing is," Decker piped in, "that we know that Pat has been good for business, and nobody wants to do anything that's going to hurt that. But if this keeps up, there might be more harm done than good."

"Right," said Newell. "Pat sure is a dynamo when it comes to motivating people in the toy division. I guess if you force a change, it might really ruin Pat's enthusiasm and undercut the support of the toy makers. But you're letting Pat run roughshod over a whole lot of people around here, and you have to do something before you have an all-out mutiny on your hands."

Questions for Discussion

1. In what ways are the various group dynamics at Ely Industries contributing to the problem faced by Ginny Fentross? Consider the stages of group development as well as the varying group cultures.
2. If you were Ginny Fentross, what would you do?

The Hands-on Manager

Leland Mansfield felt he was unusually well prepared for his new job as corporate communications manager at Excelsior Investment Services (EIS). In addition to an undergraduate degree in American literature from Colby College in Maine, he had recently received a master's degree in communication from the prestigious Reilly Institute in Wisconsin. The master's program had been extremely rigorous; it had begun with what Leland describes as a "boot camp" for writers. All new students had been taken off to a cabin in the Wisconsin woods, sent off into the wilderness with notebooks and pens, and told not to come back until they had written something good. Should they write about the omnipresent birch trees? The solitude of the writer? Smokey the Bear? No one seemed to know.

When the writing students trudged back to the cabins, they gathered together and proceeded to have almost everything they had written severely criticized by their instructors. It was an experience Leland would never forget. Over the next two years, he devoted himself to meeting the high expectations of the Reilly Institute. When he graduated magna cum laude, he considered it one of the best achievements of his life.

After working for three years at a variety of "stepping stone" jobs, Leland was hired in November of 1990 by EIS, a small organization with thirty full-time employees and about eighty part-time instructors. The mission of EIS was to train and inform people in the real estate industry and the investment community. EIS closely monitored the constantly changing world economy and ran frequent seminars to keep its clients informed and advised about what to do with their investment portfolios.

When Leland was initially interviewed by Teri Magnusson, the president of EIS, he was extremely impressed. Teri was clearly bright and educated; she had both an M.B.A. from Northwestern and a Ph.D. from Cornell in English literature, which Leland thought was a remarkable combination. Teri was dynamic, quick-witted, personable, and eternally optimistic. Leland was amused to notice that she nonetheless was a "touchy-feely" type: She was always patting employees on the back when they did a good job, and sometimes it seemed as if she were trying to set a record for the world's longest handshake.

Leland couldn't believe his good fortune: He had found a high-paying job that would also be challenging and fun. As corporate communications manager, Leland would have a great variety of duties. He would write the biweekly newsletter, which would inform clients about upcoming seminars and provide articulate tidbits of information to deepen their commitment to EIS. He would also be the official company representative when dealing with the press. More importantly, Leland was responsible for handling internal publicity—doing everything he could to keep clients coming back for seminars, the big moneymakers for the company. His job would require spending much of each day preparing mailings for customers and talking with them on the phone to answer questions and solve problems. Leland was placed in charge of a secretary—who had recently announced she planned to move to Pocatello, Idaho, and had given her two-week notice—and three employees who worked with desktop publishing programs to produce the newsletters and mailings.

This case was written by Scott Weighart.

At first, the job went well. Teri worked closely with Leland during his first two weeks; knowing how busy she was, Leland was surprised but appreciative. She practically did his first newsletter for him, going over exactly what should be included in each article.

With her positive attitude and energetic presence, Teri clearly had a vision for EIS. She made people—from the EIS employees to the CEOs of some of Boston's largest insurance companies and venture capital firms—believe in her and her company.

"You didn't feel like you were just part of some insignificant little company," Leland recalls. "She made you feel that you were in a cutting-edge organization, a dynamic and growing company."

After three or four weeks, however, Leland had begun to feel somewhat confused about what was expected of him.

"In many ways, things really hadn't changed from the first day I was hired," he says of his relationship with Teri. "I still felt like I was spending a lot of time listening to her 'advice' on how to do things. She'd take me out to lunch to talk about the clients or the newsletters, always emphasizing what my next move should be. I was flattered to get so much attention, but I sometimes felt she was treating me like an airhead."

By now, Leland felt he was capable of handling the job without much assistance. When he told Teri this, her usual smile turned into a sulk.

"Well, it's just that we both have writing backgrounds, and we approach things the same way," she said. "So why not work together, as a team?"

Leland felt frustrated and confused. True, Teri always seemed willing to listen to his ideas, but she rarely used them. Although the newsletter he was hired to write and edit was a new publication, Teri had already decided on the newsletter's name, typeface, style, and, now was dictating its content.

Worse, Leland felt that she was not always making the best decisions, perhaps because she had more important matters on her mind. Teri devoted most of her time to trying to please the CEOs and CFOs of many prestigious Boston companies. Leland had mixed feelings about her relationship with these powerful individuals. He admired how she could "spellbind them like a snake charmer," but he also felt she pandered to them shamelessly while treating smaller clients with impatience.

Teri would stop at nothing to fit into this precious circle of important men. In early 1991, the economic picture of Massachusetts had become cloudier; as a result, many Excelsior clients were adopting a wait-and-see attitude toward the future. Excelsior's seminar business dropped 40 percent in one month. Teri announced that there would be a salary freeze for the foreseeable future and that the company would be drastically cutting costs, eliminating such things as free coffee and tea as well as subsidized parking and subway passes.

Although Leland and his colleagues were disappointed, they realized that times were bad; sacrifices would have to be made. Then, a few days later, they were astonished when two burly deliverymen arrived with a new dishwasher for the private kitchen of the executive boardroom. Clients were entertained in this boardroom, and Teri had clearly bought the dishwasher so they would be impressed with Excelsior's facilities. However, clients only used the boardroom a few times a year. Leland began to have the feeling that while Teri could sweet-talk the CEOs and corporate moguls, she was somehow insecure and perhaps felt deep down that she could not match their prestige or knowledge of the field.

"It was as if she felt she had to compensate for that by kissing their feet with VIP treatment to a ridiculous extent," Leland says.

The mood in the office was bitter that day; everyone was complaining about their salaries and the dishwasher. Stacey, the marketing manager, said, "Teri is treating us like doormats: We're all supposed to cheerfully greet her and the clients while they wipe their feet all over us."

Not two minutes later, Teri walked in, pumped up and excited.

"I just set up a golf trip with the three biggest names in Boston real estate," she said. As usual, she was overflowing with optimism.

"Isn't it great?" she asked. "Isn't everything great?"

Leland couldn't stand to see her put her foot in her mouth. Remembering that she had once put her arm around his shoulder and told him that she wanted him to "open up with her," Leland pulled her aside.

"Actually, Teri," he said, "things really aren't that great. Everybody's pretty discouraged about the cutbacks, the dishwasher. The golf trip is not what people want to hear about right now."

Teri was furious. She proceeded to pull all of the personnel into the office one by one, demanding to know if they were unhappy. Under the circumstances, they all kept their mouths shut, saying that everything was just fine. Teri then brought Leland into her office and accused him of lying, badgering him about it until he began to cry.

Eventually that incident died down and was seemingly forgotten. A week later, Teri and Leland were joking with each other as they once had. Teri asked Leland to go out to lunch at a sushi restaurant.

"It was odd," Leland says. "It felt like a date. At one point, she told me I was wearing a really sexy tie; it was a silk one with swirling shades of purple. She said it reminded her of van Gogh."

Leland was unsettled. On the one hand, he felt that going to lunch with the boss was potentially a smart idea: "Maybe I was naive. I thought maybe this was just 'networking' and just a part of the corporate game, the way things were at a small professional company." Yet he also thought that something was very inappropriate about it.

Walking back to the office, Teri pointed out a large hotel by the Boston Common. "Gee, it's too bad we don't have a corporate suite, isn't it?" she asked, squeezing Leland's forearm. Leland was startled and didn't know what to say. He didn't want to believe that she was making advances. Was it only his imagination?

Leland's performance began to decline. He was sure he was spending too much time worrying about Teri and wondering about the motives that lay behind her "intimate lunches," but that was not the only problem. He felt he had all the credentials and training necessary to do a good job. Since Teri had a sharp mind and a knack for evocative language, he would have liked the chance to bounce ideas off of her when he wanted a fresh perspective, but he never really felt she allowed him any input into how he did his job. When it came to work, Teri made it clear he was not to veer far from how she wanted things done, even down to petty details such as the color of envelopes used for mailings. With no opportunity to use the skills he had worked so hard to acquire at the Reilly Institute, Leland had now lost much of the energy that he had had upon starting with Excelsior. Initially, he thought Teri was a great manager; now things had changed.

Perhaps sensing something was wrong, Teri called him into her office.

"Leland, I've noticed that you're ditzing out; you're not doing the kind of work that I expect of you."

She leaned over and ran her fingers through his hair. "Let's go out and have a quiet lunch so we can talk about what's bothering you."

Leland declined, and tears welled in his eyes. Seeing this, Teri seemed to grow impatient with him.

"Well, this is another problem you've been having, Leland: You're too emotional, too sensitive. You take everything too personally, and this is costing the company, I'll have you know. You've let yourself become distracted for some reason, and now you don't even know what your subordinates are doing. You've totally ignored the mailing list producers, and you've spent all kinds of time with that secretary, Linda. Don't you have better things to do than showing her how the fax machine works?"

Leland was astonished and hurt; his employees were hard workers and very loyal to him. For Christmas, they had chipped in to buy him a gift certificate at a local men's shop.

"Linda's only been working here for two days; somebody has to show her the ropes," he said. "I have no intention of doing this for weeks on end."

For the next ten minutes, Leland went on to defend himself. He told her that the mailing list workers were extremely experienced and didn't need him looking over their shoulders at all times.

"If they weren't doing a good job, I wouldn't hesitate to fire them or eliminate the possibility of salary increases at their next reviews. But they don't need much input, just somebody to occasionally ask them if they need any help or if they have any problems. Otherwise, they can just be given a general list of what needs to be done, then basically be left alone."

Teri shook her head and sighed, clearly annoyed. "That's hardly what I would call leadership," she told him. "A good leader has to have a hands-on approach."

Leland stood up, enraged, and kissed his job goodbye.

"I wouldn't say you're a good leader, Teri," he said. "But I must admit that—in more ways than one—you certainly do have a hands-on approach."

Questions for Discussion

1. Using one or two leadership theories, what leadership styles are used by the main characters in this case?
2. How are French and Raven's sources of social power used and/or abused by the main characters?
3. Has anything unethical happened? Why? Why not? If so, who is to blame?
4. In terms of power and leadership, what should Teri have done differently in this case? Be specific and comprehensive in your recommendations.

Isolating Team Task Elements

This exercise provides a format for identifying the positive and negative elements of group or team experiences and for setting priorities for their management. Nearly everyone has had some sort of group experience—playing on a sports team, trimming a Christmas tree with family members, doing a school project, and so forth—some of which were fun and successful, but many of which resulted in stress, broken friendships, and anger. We know that "something went wrong," but pinpointing the problems—that is, poor goal definition, poor job definition, unclear communication flow, group composition, and so forth—is a good first step for knowing how to plan and manage group tasks in the future.

PROCEDURE

Step 1 (10 minutes)

Briefly describe a successful group project in which you have been involved. Include when and under what circumstances you were working—that is, in school, at a job; with whom you were working; what your job was in the group; and what the overall goal was.

_____
_____
_____
_____

List six elements you consider the most important in making that project work. Then, number them in order of importance, with one being the most important, six the least.

_____
_____
_____
_____
_____
_____

Step 2 (10 minutes)

Briefly describe the least successful group project in which you have been involved.

_____
_____
_____
_____

_____

This exercise was written by Janet W. Wohlberg.

List six elements that you believe contributed the most to the failure of the project. Then, number them in order of significance with one being the most significant cause of failure, six being the least.

_____
_____
_____
_____
_____
_____

Step 3 (30 minutes)

Working with three or four of your classmates, discuss the positive and negative experiences of each participant. Select the top six positive and top six negative elements, number them in order of importance, and list them below

Positive   Negative

_____   _____
_____   _____
_____   _____
_____   _____
_____   _____
_____   _____

Step 4 (open-ended)

Present your findings to the class. In class discussion, examine which elements are common to both experiences and which are dissimilar. For example, was clear communication one of the elements on your positive list and unclear communication one of the elements on your negative list?

Questions for Discussion

1. Which of the negative elements appear the most frequently? Why do you think this is the case? Using your experience as an example, how do you think things could have been done differently to have avoided this problem?
2. What role did having a tangible goal—such as the gain or loss of money, a good or bad grade, a gift or no gift—have in the successful situation? the negative situation?
3. What elements showed up in your individual lists that seemed of little or no concern to others? Why?
4. What was your behavior in the two situations? How did your behavior in the positive situation differ from that in the negative one? What could you have done differently that might have changed the course of the negative situation?
5. If you were to manage a group/team project, what do you believe the key elements of your job would be?

PART III

ENHANCING INDIVIDUAL AND INTERPERSONAL PROCESSES

OVERVIEW

This section demonstrates ways in which managers can use their human resources to make both dollars and sense. We will examine how managers go about using their financial resources to reward their human resources and the rationale for goal-setting and managing by objectives (MBO).[1] Additionally, the section deals with group decision making and how it affects the speed and quality of decisions; and brainstorming and its relationship to creative problem solving. We hope this section will also help you learn about performance appraisal as a motivational tool and as an equity issue, and about stress as something that can inhibit managers as they try to get the most out of their human resources.

Goal Setting and Reward Systems

How should companies go about setting goals? In your experience, have your employers effectively communicated the company's objectives to you? Or have they told you what to do without specifically saying what you should strive to achieve?

Research done by Edwin Locke in the 1960s led to his development of the Goal-Setting Theory. Locke believed that establishing specific, difficult goals—but ones that are achievable—would lead to performance. In other words, a manager would be smarter to tell assembly workers to try to have fewer than 1 percent defects instead of just telling them to give it a good try. All the evidence indicates that this is true, but only, Locke concludes, when employees have accepted the goals because they have been involved in helping to set them or have some other good reasons for goal acceptance.[2]

Imagine that you have a job working at a Detroit automobile factory and that your job is not particularly complicated. Each time a car comes down the assembly line and stops at your station, you screw four bolts into each of the two axles on the passenger side of the car. Then the next car comes along, and you screw four more bolts into each axle. This is all that you do—eight hours a day, forty hours a week, fifty weeks per year.

Let's say you've had this job for twelve years. You just might have mastered the fine art of screwing bolts into axles.

Then your hot-shot M.B.A. manager comes along and tells you that he or she has a new and challenging goal for you: He or she wants to speed up the assembly line. Now, you have to screw in 20 percent more bolts each day—at your present salary, of course. You probably begin to wonder just how long it would take to screw eight bolts into your manager's mouth.

Obviously, there has to be an incentive to make you want to reach goals and objectives. This is why many American companies have begun to use goal-setting methods such as participative management and MBO. Surprisingly, even though these concepts originated in this country, they have been more widely used in Japan.

---

1. For additional information on MBO, see P. F. Drucker, *The Practice of Management* (New York: Harper & Row, 1954) and P. F. Drucker, *The New Realities* (New York: Harper & Row, 1989). Mr. Drucker is generally credited with having developed the concept of MBO.
2. E. Locke, K. N. Shaw, L. Saari, and G. Latham, "Goal Setting and Task Performance, 1969–1980," *Psychological Bulletin* 90(1): 125–152.

Participative Management and MBO

The key component of participative management is that workers are much more likely to reach a goal—even a difficult one—if they have a say in what kind of goal should be set. MBO, the mutual setting of goals by employees and their supervisors, is a specific kind of participative management that takes place at both the macro and micro levels of the organization. At the macro level, managers, working with one another, attempt to set organizational goals. If a company is suffering from excessive turnover, for example, the management team might set a new quantifiable, specific, and time-bounded goal (e.g., "let's reduce turnover by 9 percent within the next six months"). Ongoing feedback will be sought from all involved in implementing the goal, so that adjustments can be made along the way. This ensures that there will be no unpleasant surprises at the end of the target period.

When MBO is used to help an individual focus on achieving specific and quantifiable goals, this is referred to as the micro level of MBO. How is this implemented? A manager meets with his or her employees individually, and the manager and employee set goals together. First, they define the employee's job. Second, they set priorities and determine new performance expectations. Then they compare current performance with expected performance. If there is a large gap between these two performance levels, they discuss performance obstacles and what can be done about them. Then, over time, continuous feedback is given so that the individual knows if he or she is making appropriate progress toward the desired objectives.

Job Design

Let's, for a moment, reconsider life on the automobile assembly line. Frederick Taylor, the father of scientific management in the early 1900s, devoted himself to the notion that there are specific and scientific ways to maximize performance.[3] His approach was to break down complicated tasks into a series of small, simple ones. He found that such specialization could dramatically increase productivity. As a result, many organizations adopted assembly line tactics in manufacturing.

Regrettably, the principles of scientific management have also resulted in jobs such as "Axle Bolt Installation Specialist." As you might expect, many workers find such jobs about as interesting as watching grass grow. Accordingly, researchers have sought alternatives to job simplification or specialization.

In the 1950s, job enlargement was a new approach toward delegating work.[4] This widened the range of tasks for which employees were responsible. While increasing task variety can be helpful, there are limitations to such an approach. If you're a custodian whose job has been to mop floors, it is unlikely that you will enjoy your job more if your duties are expanded to clean the company's restrooms. Most likely, you would start thinking that there is something to be said for monotony.

Job enrichment has proven to be a more effective solution to the problems created by job specialization.[5] In contrast to job enlargement, job enrichment gives an employee significantly more control over how his or her work is to be done. Some large manufacturers have used this concept to radically alter job design. Let's say that a novelty

---

3. F. Taylor, *Principles of Scientific Management* (New York: Harper and Row, 1911).

4. See also J. Carlzon, *Moments of Truth* (Cambridge, Mass.: Ballinger, 1987), 60.

5. See F. Herzberg, "One More Time: How Do You Motivate Employees?" *Harvard Business Review* (January–February 1968): 59.

products factory has an enormous problem; production workers consistently make too many defective rubber Halloween masks. Under the old system, the defective likenesses of politicians and other monsters were carted over to the repair department, where three repairpeople worked full-time correcting the masks.

To the astonishment of the workers, management decided to completely eliminate the repair department. Instead, the three repairpeople become production workers. If they and the other workers make defective products—if the gash on Frankenstein's forehead isn't quite gory enough—they have to correct their own errors. Additionally, their pay and bonuses are closely linked to the quantity and quality of their output. As a result, the workers have a greater sense of ownership and responsibility; this makes them better at their jobs.

Hackman and Oldham's Job Characteristics Model (JCM) suggests that any job can be described in terms of five basic job dimensions: skill variety, task identity, task significance, autonomy, and feedback.[6]

Let's reconsider our Halloween mask example in terms of the JCM: Under the new system, the workers have much higher *skill variety* since they both produce and repair the masks. *Task identity* has also been improved considerably. Since workers now own the responsibility of the whole process and are held accountable for their performance, making the best rubber masks is more important to them.

Since making goofy-looking masks may not seem quite as purposeful as seeking a cure for cancer, flying a jet, or teaching sign language, the *task significance* of this job may be relatively low regardless of management's changes. Nonetheless, *autonomy* has been improved by the changes, since workers now have more control over how work is done. However, since rubber masks are produced by following a highly standardized series of steps, autonomy is still not incredibly high. Since workers are now being judged on the basis of the quality and quantity of Halloween masks produced, *feedback* increases significantly.

Performance Appraisal

We live in an era in which employees are increasingly likely to sue employers because of unfair pay. Many organizations are recognizing that to protect themselves and to be sure that employees are being treated fairly, they must have structured performance appraisal systems.

Performance appraisals can have dramatic impact on employee productivity and job satisfaction. Some interesting examples are evident in the sports world. When baseball players negotiate contracts with the general managers of their teams, they frequently disagree about how to determine a fair salary. Let's say the general manager only gives a minimal raise to a player because his home run and stolen base totals are low.

During the following season, the player's teammates and manager complain that the player is striking out too often because he "swings for the fences"[7] every time, and he tries to steal bases even when he has a pulled hamstring. The team is behind 11-0, and he should be running the bases conservatively. Can we really blame the player for trying to do what will be rewarded by the performance appraisal system?

A major performance appraisal issue is equity, which we have already discussed as a motivation issue. When a fairly average free-agent pitcher signed a $3 million per year

6. J. R. Hackman and G. R. Oldham, "Development of the Job Diagnostic Survey," *Journal of Applied Psychology* 60 (1975): 159–170.
7. Tries to hit home runs.

contract before the 1991 season, better pitchers started demanding that they receive similar or better contracts. Some claimed that they were "insulted" by being offered a mere $2 million per year, and sports fans across America began wishing that their bosses would offer them a similar insult.

Organizations have to carefully consider many questions when it comes to performance appraisal systems: who should perform them? Should there be more than one evaluator? Can the appraisers be objective and fair? How often should the evaluations take place? How much input should employees have in determining performance appraisal measures? There is no simple "right" answer to these questions; the "best" performance appraisal system appears to be one that is customized to the company's objectives and human resources.

Stress

Stress occurs when we are unable to adequately confront demands due to various limitations. It would be extremely difficult to put a precise dollar figure on how much stress costs companies today. Stress can be reflected by low productivity, high absenteeism, low quality of work, and high turnover. For the employee, stress on the job has been found to be directly related to high blood pressure. Researchers have found that the amount of stress experienced by employees can be controlled or reduced by giving workers greater control over their jobs.[8]

There are two primary types of stressors: organizational stressors and life stressors. How would you like to be an air traffic controller at a busy metropolitan airport? You have dozens of planes flying in various directions at various speeds and altitudes. You know that their fate depends on your skill and alertness. But you never have contact with the people in the planes; all you see are blips on a screen. It's like a video game, except for the fact that you have thousands of lives at stake instead of 25 cents. As you might imagine, air traffic controller turnover is quite high; people get burned out quickly. This is an example of an organizational stressor.

Although life stressors happen outside of the work place, their presence can strongly affect employee performance. Divorce, the death of a loved one, marriage, injury or illness, problems with children, and many other personal factors can have a strong impact on a worker. Life stressors are also trickier problems for supervisors who may want to be supportive and understanding but must also respect the individual's privacy and not try to be the employee's psychotherapist.

In order to prevent the problem of managers inappropriately crossing boundaries to address their workers' personal problems, many companies now rely on Employee Assistance Programs (EAPs). EAPs are outside agencies that provide confidential counseling for employees with problems; employers pay for these treatment services.

Decision Making and Creativity

Although group decisions are usually better than individual ones, managers should hesitate before involving a group in the decision-making process. According to Frohman and Frohman, managers should consider the importance of decision quality and employee

---

8. R. Winslow, "Study Uncovers New Evidence Linking Strain on Job and High Blood Pressure," *Wall Street Journal*, 11 April 1990, B8.

acceptance before using the group process: If both of these are of low concern, a manager might as well flip a coin instead of wasting company time on small matters.[9]

When a manager is looking for a creative solution, a heterogeneous group can be an excellent resource. Brainstorming is one decision-making technique that creates synergy. A leader throws out a problem, and individuals throw back ideas that are recorded without being praised or criticized. Eventually, individuals begin to build on each other's ideas, and the power of putting so many heads together is reflected in an imaginative solution.

Group decision making can have drawbacks in addition to being time consuming. A phenomenon called groupthink can occur if no individuals in the group are willing to criticize a group decision.[10] This may happen for a number of reasons—for example, too much emphasis is placed on group harmony; the group allows itself to become insulated from outside opinions; or individuals fear that their status in the group will be diminished if they are the lone voice of disapproval.

9. M. A. Frohman and S. W. Frohman, "When Are More Heads Really Better than One?" *Training* (September 1988): 65–68.

10. I. L. Janis, "Group Think," *Psychology Today* (November 1971): 43–46, and I. L. Janis, *Victims of Groupthink* (Boston: Houghton Mifflin, 1972).

The Work Station Bonus

PROCEDURE

Step 1 (20–30 minutes)

Read the background information and the profiles of each of the team members. Using the individual decision worksheet, list the amount of the bonus you would give to each and the reasons for your decision.

Step 2 (40–60 minutes)

Working in groups of five to seven students, discuss the problem and come to a group consensus on how the bonus money should be divided and why. Generally it is useful to discuss the philosophy on which you will base your decision prior to making it.

Step 3 (15–30 minutes)

Report to the class how your group divided the bonus money and why. The instructor should record each group's response in a visible place.

Step 4 (open-ended)

Class discussion.

BACKGROUND

You are the manager of the high-technology department in an industrial design firm. Several months ago, your company decided to bid on a project to design the housing for a new generation of computer work stations to be based on the latest RISC technology. Realizing that this could ultimately turn into a million-dollar contract, you carefully selected two three-member teams and set them to work to design the prototype, giving each team the customer's specifications and the following clear instructions: the housing had to be designed quickly; it had to be high in quality and durability; it had to be aesthetically distinctive; and it had to be modular, cost-effective, easy to assemble and service, and easy to ship.

Yesterday, you were excited to learn that your company got the job. Your very happy CEO has authorized $35,000 in bonus money for you to divide among your employees in any way you deem to be fair. You know that the way you give out the bonuses can have a serious impact on the morale and motivation of your employees and can impact their participation on future projects. Knowing something about equity, expectancy, and other theories of motivation, and understanding the basic tenets of performance appraisal and feedback, you know that you have to have a clear basis for apportioning the bonuses. In addition, you know that this project would never have gotten done well and on time

---

This exercise was written by Janet W. Wohlberg.

without a team approach. The way you give out the bonuses may impact how well your employees work together in the future.

TEAM A

You had assigned the following people to Team A:

Jennifer

Jennifer had worked off and on for you on a part-time basis for five years. A divorced mother with two young children, it had been impossible for her to come on full-time until both of her children were in school. Jennifer began full-time this past September. You were pleased to hire her, because she is an unparalleled designer with a sense of the practical. Indeed, you weren't let down by her abilities on this project. Her initial sketches served as an excellent starting point and also as the basis upon which the housing was ultimately designed. What did cause some problems, however, was that her children both came down with the chicken pox in the middle of the project, causing her to miss almost a full week at work. During that time, she came in nights, weekends, and whenever else she could find child care.

Abdul

Abdul is a true workaholic. Whenever you have assigned him to a project, he has worked virtually seven days a week, twenty-four hours a day, until completion. This project was no different. Abdul is pretty much of a loner, and you're aware that he frequently made his teammates angry when he made changes to their design plans without consulting them. When confronted, Abdul always acted disgusted as he pointed out just why the changes were necessary; more often than not, his teammates grudgingly went along with him. Unfortunately, you ended up spending a lot of time putting out the emotional fires that Abdul regularly seemed to start. Abdul is a job hopper; he has been looking for another job since he started with your company just eight months ago.

Hank

Quiet, competent, and self-assured, Hank goes about his business as business. You wanted Hank on this team because he is stable and reliable. He isn't, however, particularly creative and innovative. What he does best is to take other people's ideas, refine them, and execute them. He is also an excellent model builder, and the models he produced for this project are meticulous. Hank rarely stays late or works overtime, unless absolutely pushed. Instead, he prefers to spend nights and weekends with his family and in community activities. He is very active in his church and occasionally gets calls during working hours from church members who have pressing questions. In the past, you have asked Hank to limit his nonbusiness telephone time. Over the course of this project, you have noticed that he has had few calls, and those he has had have been brief. Hank has been very understanding about Jennifer's problems and has done everything he can to help her out and cover for her.

TEAM B

You had assigned the following people to Team B:

David

When David first came to the company, you were concerned that he wouldn't work out. He had been fired from his previous job. You were told by a friend that it was for frequent absences; however, David tells you it was because his boss didn't like him. While he hasn't been absent very often since joining your department, he has come to work late on a regular basis. David never did very much actual work on this project, and he couldn't be counted on to meet deadlines; but he is the only person other than Jennifer who has the design expertise and an understanding of aesthetics necessary to do this job. He is a brilliant innovator, and he came up with some terrific ideas, a couple of which were incorporated into the final design. They may have been the reason that your company got the contract.

Mei-Ling

Mei-Ling is your most reliable materials expert, but she knows little about design. She selected the materials for the project's prototype, and Hank tells you that her ideas were brilliant. Thanks to Mei-Ling, the work station is durable, lightweight, and can be broken down into modules for easy assembling, servicing, and shipping. You're not sure whether it is out of modesty or loyalty to her team that she tells you that she selected the materials based on David's suggestions and that she couldn't have chosen the correct materials without him. Mei-Ling has been excited about her project and about her team. She has asked that the three members be allowed to work together again on any upcoming projects.

Maida

Maida is one of those people who organizes things, gets after people to do their jobs, and picks up the pieces for others when they don't follow through. She generally does this without complaining, and she constantly praises those around her as knowing more and being more able than she is. On this latter point, she may be right—she isn't particularly brilliant or creative, but she is a plodder. So long as Maida is around, things get done and generally on time. When projects bog down or team members become upset with one another, Maida is there with support, homemade brownies, and occasionally a joke— she's a real team player. You put Maida on this team because you thought she would be able to offset some of David's irregularities, and that is exactly what she did. Maida, Mei-Ling, and David generally eat lunch together, and you have overheard them making weekend plans with one another on a number of occasions.

THE RESULTS

Team A finished their project in seven weeks, and it was largely their design, combined with a few of Team B's innovations, that resulted in the company's winning bid. Team B had actually finished ten days earlier than Team A, but there were a number of small flaws in their design that resulted in its being rejected. The $35,000 in bonus money is ready to be distributed. You suspect that giving everyone who worked on the project the same amount might be perceived as rewarding some questionable behaviors and failing to reward adequately some other positive behaviors.

Questions for Discussion

1. How much, if any, of the $35,000 will you award to Team A? How will you divide the amount among Team A's members? Why?
2. How much, if any, of the $35,000 will you award to Team B? How will you divide the amount among Team B's members? Why?
3. What do you believe the positive and negative effects on employee behavior and productivity, as individuals and as team members, will be as a result of the way you have allocated the bonus money?
4. Would it be possible and advisable to bring the team members into the decision-making process? How?

The Work Station Bonus

Worksheet
for Use in Individual Decisions

1. List the general criteria on which you will base the bonus awards.

   _____
   _____
   _____
   _____
   _____
   _____
   _____

2. How much will you give to each employee?

Abdul	$_____ or ____ % of $35,000	_____
David	$_____ or ____ % of $35,000	_____
Hank	$_____ or ____ % of $35,000	_____
Jennifer	$_____ or ____ % of $35,000	_____
Maida	$_____ or ____ % of $35,000	_____
Mei-Ling	$_____ or ____ % of $35,000	_____

3. Why?

   _____
   _____
   _____
   _____
   _____
   _____
   _____

The Work Station Bonus

Worksheet
for Use in Group Decisions

1. List the general criteria on which you will base the bonus awards.

    _____

    _____

    _____

    _____

    _____

    _____

    _____

2. How much will you give to each employee?

Abdul	$_____	or _____ % of $35,000_____
David	$_____	or _____ % of $35,000_____
Hank	$_____	or _____ % of $35,000_____
Jennifer	$_____	or _____ % of $35,000_____
Maida	$_____	or _____ % of $35,000_____
Mei-Ling	$_____	or _____ % of $35,000_____

3. Why?

    _____

    _____

    _____

    _____

    _____

    _____

    _____

Flying Down to Rio

Today is Thursday, and you have just learned that there is a school trip leaving first thing Monday morning for Rio de Janeiro, Brazil's famous coastal city, where the beaches are white, the sea is clear blue, and the night spots are jumping. The trip is being sponsored as a field trip by your school's sociology department. Over the ten days in Rio, you will have to attend a couple of lectures—although you've heard from friends who have been on this trip before that no one really pays much attention to whether you're at the lectures or not. Best of all, the trip is subsidized by a grant, so that for a mere $400, you'll get everything—transportation, meals, and deluxe hotel accommodations (four to a room) at a hotel on the beach.

The problem is that you don't have $400. You have already spent your entire year's allowance, and your parents say "not one penny more." Your grandparents are living on their social security, and while they really love you, there isn't much they can do. You really want to go on that trip!

PROCEDURE

Step 1 (5 minutes)

Read the problem to be sure that you understand the issues and limitations of the possibilities.

Step 2 (40 minutes)

Using the six steps in brainstorming, find a way to raise the money. Either the instructor or a class member should serve as facilitator. Be sure that the ideas are recorded in a visible place.

Questions for Discussion

1. Was the process successful? By what means did you measure its success?
2. Did ideas emerge that you hadn't considered? Were you able to keep an open mind to the ideas of others?
3. To what degree did you use the ideas of others as sparks to your own creativity?
4. In what ways do you think use of brainstorming helped with problem solving?

This exercise was written by Janet W. Wohlberg. Special thanks to Kent Seibert for this idea.

What Do You Make Out of This Junk?

You are an executive management team of Old News, Inc. Until recently, your company has been able to generate a substantial profit by producing and selling cellulose insulation for buildings. Your primary production materials have been old newspapers, purchased at low rates from recycling programs, and lock-top-style plastic bags. Recently, however, a new form of insulation has been sweeping the market, and you see your market share steadily decreasing.

You have several warehouses full of your basic materials and an ample and inexpensive supply of more of the same readily available. Your job is to come up with (1) a new product for your company to produce that uses both of these available materials, and (2) a name for your product.

Several management teams from Old News, Inc., have been assigned to brainstorm and come up with suggestions for the most marketable and most profitable product. There will be a large financial bonus for the group that comes up with the idea that is ultimately adopted.

PROCEDURE

Step 1   (40–60 minutes)

Working with three to five of your classmates, assign a facilitator, and go through the six steps of the brainstorming process (see Methodologies) to find a product and then to decide on a name.

If you finish early, use the time to generate a backup concept in case your primary product proves to be impractical.

Step 2   (10–15 minutes)

Report your decision to the class, and discuss the merits of each of the suggestions.

Step 3   (open-ended)

Class discussion.

Questions for Discussion

1. What were the strengths and weaknesses of the brainstorming method?
2. In what kinds of situations would you use this method? In what kinds of situations would this method be inappropriate.
3. How did you feel during the process? Were you encouraged to participate? If not, what got in the way, and why? At any time, did you feel discounted? Why?
4. In what ways would you alter this process to make it more effective?

This exercise was written by Janet W. Wohlberg.

Desert Survival Situation

THE SITUATION

It is approximately 10 A.M. in mid-August and you have just crash landed in the Sonora Desert in the southwestern United States. The light twin engine plane, containing the bodies of the pilot and the co-pilot, has completely burned. Only the air frame remains. None of the rest of you has been injured.

The pilot was unable to notify anyone of your position before the crash. However, he had indicated before impact that you were 70 miles south-southwest from a mining camp which is the nearest known habitation, and that you were approximately 65 miles off the course that was filed in your VFR Flight Plan.

The immediate area is quite flat and, except for occasional barrel and saguaro cacti, appears to be rather barren. The last weather report indicated the temperature would reach 110° that day, which means that the temperature at ground level will be 130°. You are dressed in light weight clothing—short-sleeved shirts, pants, socks and street shoes. Everyone has a handkerchief. Collectively, your pockets contain $2.83 in change, $85.00 in bills, a pack of cigarettes, and a ballpoint pen.

THE CHALLENGE

Before the plane caught fire your group was able to salvage the 15 items listed below. Your task is to rank these items according to their importance to your survival, starting with "1" as the most important, to "15" as the least important.

You may assume—

1. the number of survivors is the same as the number on your team;
2. you are the actual people in the situation;
3. the team has agreed to stick together;
4. all items are in good condition.

Step 1

Each member of the team is to individually rank each item. Do not discuss the situation or survival items until each member has finished the individual ranking.

Developed by J. Clayton Lafferty, Ph.D., in consultation with Alonzo W. Pond, Survival Expert.

About the expert: Alonzo W. Pond, M.A., is the former chief of the Desert Branch of the Arctic, Desert, Tropic Information Center of the Air Force University at Maxwell Air Force Base. During World War II, Mr. Pond spent considerable time working with the Allied Forces in the Sahara on desert survival problems. He has traveled to deserts cross the country, living with people of nearly every desert in the world. Mr. Pond is the author of several books on survival training, including *Survival* and *Peoples of the Desert*.

Step 2

After everyone has finished the individual ranking, rank order the 15 items as a team. Once discussion begins, do not change your individual ranking. Your team will have until _____ o'clock to complete this step.

—Items—	**Step 1** Your Individual Ranking	**Step 2** The Team's Ranking	**Step 3** Survival Expert's Ranking	**Step 4** Difference Between Step 1 & 3	**Step 5** Difference Between Step 2 & 3
Flashlight (4 battery size)					
Jackknife					
Sectional Air Map of the Area					
Plastic Raincoat (large size)					
Magnetic Compass					
Compress Kit with Gauze					
.45 Caliber Pistol (loaded)					
Parachute (red and white)					
Bottle of Salt Tablets (1000 tablets)					
1 Quart of Water Per Person					
Book Entitled, *Edible Animals of the Desert*					
Pair of Sunglasses Per Person					
2 Quarts of 180 Proof Vodka					
1 Top Coat Per Person					
Cosmetic Mirror					
TOTALS (The lower the score the better)					

Your Score   Team Score
(Step 4)   (Step 5)

Please complete the following steps and insert the scores under your team's number.	Team Number					
	1	2	3	4	5	6
Step 6 Average Individual Score—Add up all the individual team member's scores (Step 4) and divide by the number on the team.						
Step 7 Team Score (Step 5 above)						
Step 8 Gain (Loss) Score—The difference between the Team Score and the Average Individual Score. If the Team Score is lower than Avg. Ind. Score, gain is "+"; if higher, gain is "–".						
Step 9 Percentage Change—Divide the gain (loss) by the Average Individual Score.						
Step 10 Lowest Individual Score—on the team						
Step 11 Number of Individual Scores—lower than the team score.						

Synergistic Decision Making

Process	Resources

People

Skills	Knowledge
	Facts and principles relating to the subject

Materials

Mammade	Natural
Tools, facilities, products, etc.	Plants, animals, the elements, terrain, raw materials, etc.

Interpersonal skills

The ability to work with people

Task Skills

The skills necessary to perform a specific job; specific survival skills (i.e., fire building, hunting, etc.)

Rational Skills

The ability to deal with the problem rationally

The Interpersonal Skills

Active Listening/Clarifying by:
Paying attention and responding to others' feelings and ideas
Not interrupting
Making open-ended inquiries
Not judging others
Summarizing and reflecting back others' ideas and feelings

Supporting/Building by:
Accepting what others have to say
Not debating, persuading, controlling or manipulating others
Speaking in friendly, warm terms
Creating opportunities for others to make their thoughts and feelings known
Assuming others have useful ideas, information, etc.

Building on others' ideas
Responding in an open, spontaneous way
Encouraging divergent points of view
Freely offering new ideas at appropriate times

Differing/Confronting by:
Continually focusing attention on the problem-solving process
Questioning own and others' assumptions in a non-threatening way
Dealing directly and specifically with apparent discrepancies
Reflecting on how the team is doing with regard to:
• progress
• personal relations
• time

The Rational Skills

Deciding on a Rational Process
What issues need to be dealt with, and in what sequence, in order to arrive at a rational decision?

Analyzing the Situation
Survivors' mental/physical condition
Materials on hand and their utilization
Location
Weather conditions
Surrounding environment
What are the teams' concerns?
How serious is each?

Setting Objectives
What are the *minimum* outcomes hoped for?
What are the best outcomes that can be reasonably hoped for?
What are the probable outcomes?

Developing Alternative Courses of Action
What actions could *possibly* be taken to achieve:
• the minimum outcomes?
• the best outcomes?

Identify Obstacles and Adverse Consequences
What would stand in the way of taking each course of action?
What would be the adverse consequences of each alternative?
How likely are they to occur?
How serious would it be if they did?

Deciding
Which alternative is most likely to achieve:
• the minimum outcomes?
• the best outcomes?
• the least adverse consequences?

This algorithm illustrates the skills and resources involved in Synergistic Decision Making, a method of utilizing the human resources available in a group. The results are a product of the available *resources* and the *process* by which those resources are used. Resources consist of all natural and manmade materials, as well as people's knowledge and skills. The Synergistic Decision Making Process encompasses these resources in conjunction with the three following skill areas: *Interpersonal Skills* (the skills of working with others cooperatively); *Rational Skills* (the skills necessary for dealing with a situation with systematic creativity); and *Task Skills* (skills necessary for implementing a specific course of action). These are described more fully in the above algorithm.

Dr. Watson Gets Published

Steiner Willhelm, president of the Regional University of the South, hit the buttons on his phone as if they were mini–punching bags.

"Bill," he shouted, when the phone on the other end was picked up, "you had better read the letter to the editor on page 31 of the *Tribune*, and then get on over here. We have to figure out who wrote it and how to deal with it."

In less than half an hour, Bill Bolles, dean of the Regional University's College of Business, and Henry Lessing, the university's academic vice-president, were sitting in President Willhelm's office, each with a copy of the *Tribune* in his hand.

"I knew," Bolles moaned, "that there was going to be some backlash when we instituted the new performance appraisal and reward system for the faculty. I never expected it to be open warfare."

"Whoever wrote this obviously is angry and wants to cause trouble," he added.

"If the economy had held up, it wouldn't have had to be this way," said Lessing. "But when we changed the emphasis of our goals, and money started to dry up at the same time, some of our best classroom teachers, particularly at the College of Business, actually had their salaries frozen. We have a real problem here, and we had better figure out how to handle it before the phone starts to ring."

THE LETTER

To The Editor:

I am writing this letter to inform the local taxpaying public concerning adverse changes which are taking place within the College of Business at the Regional University of the South. Because I am a professor at this college, I feel it would not be prudent to sign this letter.

As you are well aware, our state is experiencing a severe economic recession because of our overdependence on one declining industry. As this decline has severely reduced our tax base, the state legislature has been forced to make drastic cuts in funding for all state services, including higher education. At the same time that the Regional University of the South is experiencing another in the series of annual reductions in funding, this time 13 percent, the current university administration is changing the mission of our College of Business. For over 50 years, we have been viewed as a regional teaching institution in the second tier of universities within our state. We have attempted to provide excellence in classroom teaching as our primary goal. University and community service objectives were secondary, as was research. The dominant (first tier) state university is the one with doctoral programs and a corresponding emphasis on research.

This case was prepared by Roland B. Cousins of LaGrange College as the basis for class discussion (or other purpose), rather than to illustrate either effective or ineffective handling of a managerial situation. All names and other data presented in this case have been disguised. Used by permission.

Suddenly, the rules have changed. Research has become our primary objective. Over 50 percent of the salaries paid to some faculty members is compensation for research productivity. These faculty, who are the highest paid in the college, are teaching fewer courses and students. This is a gross misuse of what are already very limited state funds. You, the taxpayer, are supporting this institution for the purpose of providing an excellent undergraduate education for your sons and daughters. You are receiving zero return on your investment when your money is spent on the generation of articles which are published in obscure journals having very small circulations. The local and regional business community will never see any benefit from the esoteric kind of article being bought and paid for by you. At the same time, the cost of educating each undergraduate student is escalating because of this misuse of your hard-earned dollars.

I ask that you contact your legislator and/or President Willhelm of the Regional University of the South, and tell him/them what you want from your university. Do you want the best education for your children, or do you want articles generated just for the purpose of article generation?

Name and Address Withheld by Request

Questions for Discussion

1. Was it appropriate for Dr. Watson (the letter writer) to write this letter? Why?
2. Do you agree with Dr. Watson? Why?
3. What distinctions would you draw between the acceptable goals and purposes of a state college or university as opposed to a private college or university, if any?
4. What do you think the administrators should do now that this letter has been published?

Calendars and Clips

PROCEDURE

Step 1   (5 minutes)

Read the brief background of the situation at Calendars and Clips and consider what you would do if you were the manager or the salesperson. In addition, familiarize yourself with the areas for consideration in the Part I observer sheet.

Step 2   (10 minutes)

The facilitator will distribute Part 1, role 1 to half of the class and Part I, role 2 to the other half of the class. Read the role to which you have been assigned.

Step 3   (20–30 minutes)

Perform the role play. While doing so, stick to the facts that have been given, and stick closely to the role in an attempt to make the experience as realistic as possible. Try to reach a point at which there is mutual understanding of one another's position and further dialogue is possible. This exercise does not present a specific problem with a specific answer; rather, it requires the sharing of feelings in such a way that it is possible to preserve the relationship and to move ahead.

Step 4   (30 minutes)

Class discussion.

Step 5   (60–90 minutes)

Repeat the above steps with Part II of the exercise.

BACKGROUND

The setting is an independent business, Calendars and Clips, that deals in retail and quantity discount office and stationery items. It is wholly owned by role player 1, who employees five part-time clerks; a full-time assistant who handles stock, makes deliveries, and does odd jobs; and a full-time outside salesperson who receives a base salary and commissions.

The outside salesperson, role player 2, has been with the company for three years—since graduating from college. During this time, the personal service aspect of the company, selling to small local professional offices and businesses that have the products delivered, has grown from practically nothing to over $500,000 in gross receipts per year.

The owner and the salesperson have had a reasonably good working relationship. Today, the salesperson returns midway through the afternoon and announces across a

This exercise was written by Janet W. Wohlberg.

store full of people that the store's biggest customer, a first cousin of the owner's spouse, has switched to the competition. The salesperson then walks into the owner's office and slams the door.

Calendars and Clips
Part I Observer Sheet

Did the owner allow the salesperson to take the lead in the discussion, listen, and make an effort to understand what the salesperson's concerns were? What clues did you have that this was or was not happening?

_____

_____

_____

_____

_____

Did the owner encourage the salesperson to talk about the issue? How?

_____

_____

_____

_____

_____

Did the owner focus on the issue in order to resolve it, or did the owner become side-tracked by personality or behavior issues? Why or why not?

_____

_____

_____

_____

_____

Were there ideas and attitudes of the owner and the salesperson that got in the way of their ability to communicate? Describe them.

_____

_____

_____

_____

_____

Did the owner make a timely effort to discuss solutions for the problem and plan for a future opportunity to get together and explore ideas generated by this meeting? How was this done?

_____

_____

_____

_____

_____

Calendars and Clips
Part II Observer Sheet

In what ways did the owner try to set a relaxed and cooperative tone for the meeting?

_____

_____

_____

_____

In what way did the owner involve or fail to involve the salesperson in the performance appraisal process?

_____

_____

_____

_____

In areas in which there were problems, did the owner involve the salesperson in generating solutions? How?

_____

_____

_____

_____

Was the owner able to give negative as well as positive feedback in a way that the salesperson could understand?

_____

_____

_____

_____

Did the owner and the salesperson agree on an action plan? Was it realistic? Why? Why not?

_____

_____

_____

_____

Did they set a date for a future meeting? _____

If you were the owner, what would you have done differently?

_____

_____

_____

_____

Vegetable Management

Congratulations! You have been hired as a consultant by Pete Moss, an entrepreneur who has just built a 50,000-square-foot greenhouse and adjoining office building. Moss had a sudden flash of inspiration one day when he went to the grocery store produce section and saw a vegetable called broccoflower, a cross between broccoli and cauliflower.

Using some of the money he had inherited from his grandfather's multimillion-dollar estate, Moss hired a team of horticulturists who specialize in creating vegetable hybrids. The horticultural team was charged with creating similar hybrids to broccoflower, and they have made a number of suggestions: Spinlett, a cross of spinach and lettuce; Acorn Squips, a cross of Acorn Squash and Turnips; and Lepper, a yellow pepper with a sweet, lemony flavor. (Moss's marketing manager is still undecided about that last name.)

In the meantime, Moss is also using hydroponics to grow more traditional vegetables, and sales have been good. In fact, the business has been growing so rapidly that he has had little time to make some of the necessary decisions that go along with developing and structuring a company. Among the decisions that Moss faces are ones having to do with the span of worker responsibilities, quality of worklife issues for the employees, marketing and pricing strategies in a changing market, and corporate identity.

Moss is anxious to give his employees a feeling that they are really important. He wants to retain the feeling that the business is small, despite its rapid growth, by involving everyone in the business at every level. He has told you that he believes this is the best way to keep his people interested and motivated.

He shows you the agenda for his meeting with the horticulturists. These are Moss's notes covering the topics that he plans to take up in his meeting:

AGENDA FOR
MEETING ON THE 12th, 9 A.M.

1. During weekends, we will need to have a horticulturist on call and equipped with a cellular phone. This will give emergency expertise when faced with sudden wilting or dehydration. Decision to be made: Who should be on call, and what should the responsibilities include?
2. Our corporate color is green. Decision to be made: What shade(s) of green should be used in the new building for carpets, wallpaper, employee uniforms, and so forth?
3. We have some unique products, for which we have no competition, and some other more common products, for which we have lots of competition. Decision to be made: How should we price them?

Be sure to be on time; we need everyone's input.

This case was written by Scott Weighart.

Questions for Discussion

Consider each of the three business issues that Pete Moss wants to address at his meeting separately:

1. Are they all appropriate issues to raise at the planned meeting?
2. Why or why not?
3. What would you advise him to do instead?

PART IV

INTEGRATING INDIVIDUALS, GROUPS, AND ORGANIZATIONS

OVERVIEW

This section deals with organizational structure—that is, the ways in which organizations set up chains of command; the impact of the external environment on internal operations; the climate of internal operations, generally referred to as the corporate culture; and issues related to managing change.

Organizational Structure

Typically, the word *bureaucracy* is used negatively. Aspiring politicians attack "fat-cat bureaucrats" in federal government, lots of people complain about having to "cut through the red tape" at work, and college students often feel frustrated by being sent from department to department to achieve what seem like simple tasks, such as getting a student ID card or transcript.

A recent university graduate got a word-processing job at a European company that manufactured commercial boilers that supplied energy for developing areas in Asia and Africa. In addition to typing his manager's correspondence, the grad's main responsibility was to take the huge pile of mail and telexes that arrived each day and stamp each document with the date and with a stamp that listed twelve sets of officials. His boss would go through the pile and put little checkmarks next to some or all of the officials. All of the people whose names were checked would have to get copies of that piece of correspondence.

Basically the job was taking big mounds of paper, making them into bigger mounds of paper, and delivering them around so that everyone could have a bigger mound of paper. A veteran employee explained the system to him: "When the amount of paperwork is equal to the number of tons of water that the boiler can hold, then that job is finished." The grad wondered how many forests had been sacrificed to the insatiable appetite of the paperwork monster.

If everyone has had such negative experiences with large, impersonal bureaucracies, then why are they created? If they're so wasteful, why don't companies separate themselves into small independent units in the name of efficiency? What would seem to be almost counterintuitive is the fact that large corporations are generally more efficient than smaller ones. As frustrating as it is to follow the endless rules and procedures of a formalized, mechanistic bureaucracy, large corporations do provide goods and services more cheaply than their more informal counterparts.

Less formal, more organic structures—sometimes called adhocracies—may not be able to match the cost-efficient bureaucratic machine, but this looser structure encourages creativity and innovation. When people can basically create their own rules, the possibilities are numerous. In addition, adhocracies are more flexible than bureaucracies.

Today, some companies are moving in the direction of adhocracy by trying to become more decentralized and to *empower* their employees by giving them more decision-making responsibility. The rationale is that empowering individuals makes them more motivated and autonomous while helping them provide better, faster service to customers. In addition, many companies are encouraging cross-functional collaboration to give employees a greater sense of connectedness to the processes.

The External Environment

Forces outside of an organization can have dramatic impact on the success of a company's operations. Remember the pet rock craze of the 1970s? Let's imagine trying a similar entrepreneurial venture in the 1990s. We're going to buy twenty-five thousand large white button-up shirts, import a dozen baboons from Kenya, put the shirts on hangers, and run them down an assembly line, where the baboons will take brushes and spoons to randomly fling paint onto the shirts. Then we sell the shirts to schools so kids can wear them in art classes or when doing anything else in which they don't want to get their regular clothes dirty. We'll call our product the Pet Smock.

Numerous sectors of the external environment can have a substantial impact on such a venture.[1] Kenyan laws may only allow baboons to be exported to zoos. The Department of Labor may have baboon labor laws that deem such work inhumane or demand that we give our "workers" veterinary benefits. We will need to convince our target market that the Pet Smock is essential for peer-group acceptance, and to do so, we may need to run countless television commercials every Saturday morning.

In addition, if the country is struggling through a recession, parents across the country might be likely to ask, "You want a pet *what*?" and say "I'm not wasting my hard-earned money on a fifteen-minute fad." We'll also have to keep a watchful eye on other companies that might try to exploit our target market with something equally trendy and ridiculous.

Clearly, there are many external forces that will affect our Pet Smock venture. The main point, however, is that organizations cannot control everything that helps or hinders their business success. Accordingly, good managers have to effectively monitor the external environment to determine how best to utilize the resources that are within their control.

Corporate Culture

Managers may not consciously attempt to establish a particular organizational atmosphere, but one always develops. Corporate culture refers to the values, habits, and attitudes that are commonplace in a company, attributes that can be positive, negative, or both.

Imagine working for a computer company at which everyone is obsessed with developing a revolutionary new machine—the Over-Byte. For twelve months straight, the engineering team works roughly sixty hours a week on the project. In the summer, everyone comes to work in shorts and T-shirts, and pranks are pulled all the time. Upper management understands that this is a good release from the pressures of completing the machine; they encourage the engineers to have as much fun as they can.

Toward the end of the project, most group members are working seventy to eighty hours a week. They bring in sleeping bags and nap under their desks. When asked, one engineer can't recall the name of his baby daughter. When the project is completed, the whole team goes out to celebrate—and then comes to work the next day, completely depressed. No more pranks are played; the engineers start wearing ties again and working conventional hours. If you walked in, you would think that everything's going great, but actually, the engineers are nowhere near as productive as they had been during the

---

1. For additional information, see R. L. Daft, *Organization Theory and Design* (St. Paul, Minn.: West Publishing, 1983), 55 ff.

project. Before, they had agreed-upon norms, high cohesion, and a common goal. Now, the goal no longer is clear; there is no focal point for their efforts or their relationships.

Not all cultures are this strong. Have you ever had a job in which a powerful culture made you do things you wouldn't ordinarily do? When you tell people stories about a job that you had, what kind of culture are you describing?

Culture can also be revealed if you study symbolic gestures, official company functions and rituals, or the physical setting of the company: Some organizations have lush furniture and elaborate marble entrances. These may suggest that a company values prestige and money. Some companies will intentionally choose very nondescript offices to show its patrons that they are interested in value and conservation of resources.

Organizational Change

A large number of forces drive the need for change. These include changing needs and habits of a population; products or services becoming obsolete because the competition is making them faster, better, and cheaper; and rapidly changing technology that introduces more and better possibilities.

Just as people tend to avoid conflict, few people really enjoy the idea of change. David A. Nadler has identified six reasons that individuals resist change: habit, security, economic factors, fear of the unknown, lack of awareness, and social factors.[2] These reasons are not necessarily irrational: Often change does hurt. In terms of economic factors, for example, changing from manual systems to automated ones can make some jobs obsolete.

Organizations also resist change. Daniel Katz and Robert L. Kahn suggest six reasons why: overdetermination of job descriptions and employment systems; too narrow a focus for change with little regard for jobs, people, and so forth; group inertia; threat to the expertise of those individuals and groups knowledgeable about existing methods; threats to existing power bases; and concerns about changes in resource allocations.[3]

Nonetheless, change is inevitable. A few tools are available to managers to help in the implementation of change. Force field analysis, for example, is used to disaggregate problems of change into driving forces—things that push toward a needed change, and restraining forces—things that push back and create a stalemate.[4]

Let's say that the Oshkosh Dynamite Factory is having a problem with defects. Twelve percent of the dynamite produced is defective and frequently explodes during shipment. Generally this means that one of the eight Oshkosh trucks explodes each month.

The ideal situation for Oshkosh would be zero defects, and a number of factors drive the need to work toward that change. Certainly the loss of trucks and products are factors, as are concerns about product safety after delivery. In addition, the customer base is shrinking as Oshkosh is less able to meet orders due to the large losses, and the high level of defects is driving up the cost of production, which in turn pushes up the cost to the customer.

2. D. A. Nadler, "Concepts for the Management of Organizational Change," in J. R. Hackman, E. E. Lawler III, and L. W. Porter, eds., *Perspectives on Behavior in Organizations,* 2nd ed. (New York: McGraw-Hill, 1983), 551–561.
3 D. Katz and Robert I. Kahn, *The Social Psychology of Organizations,* 2nd ed. (New York: Wiley, 1978), 36–68.
4. K. Lewin and D. Cartwright, eds., *Field Theory in Social Science* (New York: Harper & Row, 1951).

However, some restraining forces make the necessary changes difficult. The plant is located in New Mexico, where temperatures often top 90 degrees. If the dynamite sits in the loading dock too long, it warms up and is more likely to explode when the trucks go over bumps or come to sudden stops. The cash bonus for defect-free work for employees is only $5; management claims it is meant to be a symbolic show of recognition. Given the amount of money that Oshkosh has had to spend on repairing trucks, they feel they can't afford bigger incentive bonuses for defect-free work. Also, the shipping clerks are inexperienced and carelessly toss the dynamite into the boxes, which loosens the caps.

With a force field analysis, it is possible to isolate those restraining forces that can be eliminated or diminished. Oshkosh may not be able to give the workers bigger bonuses, but perhaps it can educate the careless shipping clerks. It is unlikely that the plant can be easily moved, but better shipping controls can be instituted to avoid having the dynamite sit in the sun for extended periods of time.

Kurt Lewin also proposes a three-step model for managing change.[5] It begins with *unfreezing* the current situation, which involves breaking down resistance to change by explaining the need and the benefits to be derived. Secondly, the change is implemented. The third and final step, when the change is supported and reinforced, is called *refreezing*.

John P. Kotter and Leonard S. Schlesinger suggest six possible tactics for managing resistance to change: education and communication, useful when knowledge about a proposed change has been inadequate; participation and involvement, useful when employee commitment to the proposed change is necessary; facilitation and support, useful when employees feel personally threatened by a proposed change; negotiation and agreement, useful when resistance is a threat to the existing power structure; manipulation and cooptation, useful when the proposed change threatens resource allocations; and coercion, useful when all else fails or change must be made quickly.[6] The last two tactics can backfire; the first three are often the most effective, as they help people understand the change and have a say in how it happens.

---

5. Ibid.
6 J. P. Kotter and L. S. Schlesinger, "Choosing Strategies for Change," *Harvard Business Review*, March–April 1979, 106–114.

The Rise and Fall of Bruno Reilly

"People don't know what's good for them," Bruno Reilly muttered to himself. He hadn't been surprised when the newly elected school board of Marsh County informed him they would not be renewing his contract, effectively firing him after six years with the school system. This had been his fifth school superintendency in a twenty-six-year career; all had ended essentially the same way. Looking back, Reilly remained committed to both his educational tenets—returning public schools to traditional values and highly regimented systems—and to his methods for achieving these results—firing nonperformers, basing pay on merit, and keeping tight controls over personnel and students alike. Many parents virtually worshiped Reilly; most teachers and principals hated and feared him. In the end, it was the teachers and principals who brought him down.

BACKGROUND

Bruno Reilly, now fifty-five years old, received his undergraduate education from a midwestern university. His degree, in English literature, had led to a job teaching in a public school, a position he held while taking courses nights and summers to earn his master's degree and eventually his doctorate in education. After receiving his Ed.D., Reilly accepted a position as a principal at an inner-city high school in New Jersey. Almost immediately, he became known as a reformer. Within two years, absenteeism at the school had dropped by more than 30 percent, grades on standardized tests had improved, and the number of students enrolled in the college track had increased.

Four years later, Reilly left the principal's position to become superintendent of a small school system in Ohio. Many modern teaching methods had been instituted throughout this system, but something was clearly amiss. Student scores on standardized tests were the lowest in the state, and a high percentage of even the best students dropped out before high school graduation to take low-paying, dead-end factory jobs.

One of Reilly's first acts was to call the principals together and read them the proverbial riot act.

"You people," he told them, "are clearly not doing your jobs. Good students aren't graduating, virtually no one is college bound. You and you alone bear the responsibility for what is being allowed to happen here, and I'm going to hold you to that responsibility."

Reilly then gave orders to fire several teachers he considered inadequate, and he told three principals that they could consider themselves to be "on probation," saying that they too would be terminated if student performance at their schools did not markedly improve.

The meeting ended with the principals filing out of Reilly's office, one by one. No one looked up.

This case was written by Janet W. Wohlberg.

Student performance did improve, about 15 percent of the high school's graduates began to go on to college, and the students' scores on standardized tests rose from last in the state to the bottom half of the middle. Despite this, angry teachers and principals waged a devious war against Reilly. In parent-teacher conferences, in chats with their neighbors and friends, the teachers and principals complained that Reilly was standing in the way of real progress, was mishandling school funds, and that any improvements were being made in spite of him, not because of him. Two principals who had been demoted by Reilly ran for school board and won. Reilly's contract was not renewed. Five years later, performance within the system was virtually back to where it had been prior to Reilly's regime.

The stories of Reilly's subsequent jobs virtually paralleled that of his Ohio superintendency. Reilly came in, turned each system inside out, got rid of nonperformers, upped the standards, instituted stringent rules and regulations for principals and teachers as well as for students, and ultimately was forced out.

THE MARSH COUNTY SCHOOL SYSTEM

Ten days after moving into his office in Marsh County, Bruno Reilly summoned the system's principals into his office. Using overhead transparencies, Reilly proceeded to give a two-hour, fully illustrated talk on the problems in the schools. With charts and graphs, Reilly explained that student scores on standardized tests had been going down all over the district, and he outlined a ten-step improvement plan. Included was the development of a group of "magnet" schools that were to receive additional funding to support enrichment programs.

"We'll admit only the best students to the magnet schools," Reilly told the principals. "If you want good students, you're going to have to make your schools competitive."

"Otherwise," he added, "you'll just have to make do with the dregs."

Toward the end of his presentation, Reilly put an overhead on the screen that shocked everyone. In the left-hand column was a list of teachers whom Reilly had tagged for dismissal, transfer, or probation. On the right side of the graphic, Reilly had listed the names of those principals whose contracts would not be renewed or who were to be demoted.

"We're going to run this place like a business," Reilly said. "Anyone who can't cut it is out."

"You people," he went on, "have been getting away with too much for too long. I intend to hold you accountable for what happens to our students. If they don't make it, neither will you."

Over the next five years, Reilly froze salaries and continued to do what he referred to as "cleaning house"—that is, he fired teachers and administrators whose performance he judged to be less than optimal. He consolidated programs, instituted a merit pay system for teachers based on the performance of their students on standardized tests, and enforced strict rules of student discipline. From kindergarten through grade 12, students were required to walk single-file through hallways. Talking was not allowed. Students who arrived late found themselves locked out of classrooms, and parents were summoned immediately when students misbehaved. Teachers were ordered to double the amount of homework.

Reilly's aggressive tactics got results. Attendance improved; more students stayed on through graduation, with over 70 percent going on to college or to other forms of advanced education; and most striking, scores on standardized tests went from below average for the state to being near the top. By the end of Reilly's fifth year as superintendent, Marsh County was producing more Merit Scholars than any other county in the state. Reilly was named educator of the year by the governor and was honored in a special ceremony at the capitol, where he also received a letter of commendation from the president of the United States.

Despite the honors Reilly and his school system received, the relationship between Reilly and the teachers grew increasingly tense. On one occasion, Reilly had walked into a classroom to find a teacher napping while the students read to themselves at their desks. "Get your things and get out," Reilly had told the teacher. "Don't come back tomorrow." The teacher, who had considerable seniority, filed a union grievance and was ordered reinstated. After that, Reilly made a point to check on him virtually to the point of harassment. At least three to four times a month, at irregular intervals, Reilly walked into the teacher's classroom unannounced.

Helen Tedeschi

Helen Tedeschi had started as a teacher in the Marsh school system shortly after graduating from college. Over her thirty years in education, she had been promoted from teacher, to head teacher, to assistant principal, and ultimately had become principal of Marsh County's largest elementary school. She had served several terms as an elected member of the school committee and had spearheaded the introduction of drug and alcohol education and the enrichment of the county's science education programs. Prior to assuming her administrative duties, Tedeschi also had served two terms as president of the Teachers' Alliance, the largest teachers' union in the state.

Tedeschi's husband, a pediatrician, had a large private practice in addition to his work in the pediatric clinic of the county hospital. The couple lived in a seven-bedroom house with rolling lawns. Their three children had attended the local public schools, and each had gone on to a prestigious college or university.

Considered the "principal's principal," it was to Tedeschi that other principals in the system often turned for advice and support. Teachers also admired her; a position at her school was considered to be the best assignment a teacher could have within the entire Marsh system, so whenever she had an opening—which was rare—applications were plentiful. In addition to liking Tedeschi, teachers found the largely upper-middle-class students in her school to be easier to teach than the more socioeconomically diverse populations that existed elsewhere in the system.

Tedeschi set high standards. Any teacher who did not measure up would receive support and mentoring, but once Tedeschi concluded that it was useless, she would quietly fire the teacher and suggest that he or she find a different career.

Tedeschi encouraged her teachers to be innovative in the classroom and to share ideas with their colleagues. Each month, she gave an innovation award, and the recipient's photograph, along with a description of the innovation, was posted in a visible place in the school office.

Students at Tedeschi's school appeared, from all traditional measures, to be among the best prepared in Marsh County. Helen Tedeschi made a point of learning the students' names, and she maintained good relationships with their parents by keeping in regular touch through meetings, telephone calls, and a monthly newsletter. A number of the parents belonged to the same country club as Tedeschi and her husband.

Tedeschi and Reilly Go to War

Helen Tedeschi had disliked Bruno Reilly from the start. Based on stories she had heard about Reilly, she had advised her friends on the school committee not to hire him. His illustrated lecture had confirmed her feelings. Not only did she feel he was poor in handling personnel issues, she also believed that the improvements that were being made in the system had begun long before Reilly had appeared. In fact, Reilly had been brought in during the third year of a ten-year plan that had already included huge increases in the school budget; a teacher training program; better teacher salaries; the use of specialists in math, science, reading, and learning disabilities; and the introduction of Head Start—a pre–primary school readiness program that had been successful in many other systems.

"Some of the parents might think you're hot stuff," Tedeschi had yelled in exasperation at Reilly during one of their meetings, "but we know better. All you're doing," she said, "is taking credit for what we've already started. You think that by dividing us up and using scare tactics, you're protected. Well, you're not, and I intend to do something about it."

"You don't care about education," Reilly shot back. "All you care about is yourself and your power. If someone supports you, you don't care if they can't teach for beans or even if they fall asleep in class. You and your buddies in the union have gone out of your way to protect bad teachers. I could really clean this place up if it weren't for people like you.

"Besides, you let your teachers use their students as guinea pigs. All this new stuff you do just doesn't work. Since I've been here," he added, "the other schools in the system have improved a lot more than yours! You had better shape up, or you'll be out of here, too."

"I don't care about education???" Tedeschi fumed. "Since you got here, the only thing our students have learned is how to take tests. Your whole ego is tied up in how well our students do on math tests. You don't care if they understand what they're doing just so long as they can memorize it and spew it back.

"It's only a matter of time," she said. "It's only a matter of time before people figure out just what a phony you really are."

Epilogue

Six months after Tedeschi and Reilly's argument, elections were held in Marsh County. Helen Tedeschi and several of her friends ran on a slate for school committee and won. It was immediately after their first meeting that they informed Reilly that his contract would not be renewed.

Questions for Discussion

1. What sources of social power did Reilly and Tedeschi have and use? How? Do you consider their uses of power to have been appropriate? Why?
2. This case involves managing change. Suppose you're Reilly, and you're faced with some of the same challenges at your next job. What do you think you would do differently, how, and why?
3. The school board is essentially the equivalent of a corporate board of directors and has a fiduciary responsibility to represent the best interests of the organization. Did the new Marsh County school board act responsibly in removing Reilly from his job? Why?
4. Was Reilly successful? Why?

Playing Footsy with the Family Business

BACKGROUND

In 1990, Joseph Savenor, founder of a small shoe manufacturing company in North Deighton, Massachusetts, died at the age of ninety-six. Despite the fact that he had turned the day-to-day management of his business over to his son-in-law, Abe Seiler, ten years earlier, Joseph Savenor had continued to go to his office daily until just two weeks before his death. Savenor's strong hand and Old World management style were very much a part of the company culture. He knew all of the workers, some of whom represented second and third generations in the company; they considered him to be the grand old man, and indeed, Joseph had treated them with a firm hand but well. More than one told stories of his coming to their aid in times of sickness, helping them to educate their children, and supporting them as if they were family. The company had never had a strike, and notwithstanding attempts by the Shoe and Boot Workers Union to organize the Savenor employees, they had shown no interest. The company had always been profitable, and the Savenors had become one of the wealthiest families in the North Deighton area.

Beginning in 1980, Joseph had begun to gift shares of stock in the company to workers on their twentieth anniversary of employment. By the time he died, this amounted to about 20 percent of outstanding stock, largely held by employees who had retired or were nearing retirement. In his will, the old man left his remaining 80 percent stock interest in the company, as well as the other assets of his considerable estate, to his two daughters and two sons in equal shares.

One daughter, Eleanore, in her sixties and never married, worked for the company as head of sales. She managed seven people, who had been with the company an average of twenty-seven years. Their sales routes were well established and changed little. It had been more than five years since there had been any growth in the customer list, and sales were sluggish. The market for shoes had shifted largely to discounting, with domestic shoemakers having an increasingly hard time competing against foreign manufacturers.

Joseph's eldest son, Malcolm, was a busy and successful ophthalmologist in Manhattan. Malcolm had never had much interest in his father's business, considering it a "trade" that was far beneath him both socially and intellectually. Malcolm's wife, Anne, however, saw the words "my son the executive" written all over the inheritance. Here was a perfect opportunity to install Jeffrey, a thirty-year-old college dropout with a spotty work record, in an "appropriate" position.

Harold, the "baby" in the family, was a professor of sociology at Simmons College in Boston. Like his brother, he had little interest in the business. To him, the best thing he could do with his stock would be to sell it and use the proceeds to finance his studies of primitive tribes on remote Indonesian islands. Nonetheless, he had some sentimental feelings toward his father's company and especially toward the cutters and stitchers, who, when he was a small child, used to fashion playthings for him out of leather scraps and often sat him in their laps and let him pretend to run the huge machines.

This case was written by Janet W. Wohlberg.

The other daughter, Susanne, was married to Abe Seiler. She shared her father's loyalty to the family and had grown up with the feeling that the employees at Savenors were an extension of that family. Susanne and Abe had two sons and a daughter, all of whom had worked for the company for a number of summers, each coming on full-time after graduation from college.

THE PLAN

Abe Seiler had, for a long time, wanted to make radical changes in the company, moving it primarily into retail operations with a series of outlet stores. This would mean phasing out manufacturing and wholesale sales, and purchasing leather goods—shoes, belts, purses, and so forth—from abroad. He believed that the long-term future of the company depended on taking it in new directions, but he was also aware that this was not feasible during Joseph's lifetime. Quietly, and without discussion, Abe researched the possibilities, worked out a plan, and became increasingly convinced that the retail store concept would be enormously profitable and considerably enhance the value of the company's stock. He knew that he would have to get rid of the "dead wood" and bring in new, young, and dynamic leadership to execute the plan.

After Joseph's will had been probated, Abe moved quickly to try to buy out the others' shares. He had the business appraised and offered Harold just slightly more than the appraised value of his 20 percent. Harold gladly took the money. Eleanore and Malcolm weren't so easy. Indeed, Eleanore was adamant about retaining her stock, and Malcolm offered Abe a true Hobson's choice—either he would sell his shares to an outsider, or he would turn them over to Jeffrey—Abe could decide. Malcolm and Anne also wanted Abe to agree to make Jeffrey a vice-president. Personally, Abe believed he would have fewer problems with an outsider, but Susanne was uncompromising about wanting to keep her father's company within the family. For the sake of his marriage, and because his wife was both a stockholder and a director, Abe grudgingly agreed. Malcolm and Anne turned their stock interest over to Jeffrey, who also became vice-president for manufacturing. "At least," Abe thought to himself, "if all goes as planned, manufacturing and wholesale sales will be a thing of the past within two to four years, and this kid will have to find something else to do."

BOARD OF DIRECTORS

Prior to Joseph's death, the company's board of directors consisted of Joseph, who was chairman and CEO; Abe, who was president and chief operating officer; and each of the four children. The board met four times a year, received a brief report on operations and the latest company financial statement, and voted a dividend. Once a year, they went through the formality of reelecting the officers. Joseph used these meetings as opportunities to gather his family around him, and it was understood that the meetings were essentially ceremonial. No other meaningful business was transacted, as there was a tacit understanding and agreement that Joseph was in charge. Therefore, the board meetings, often scheduled around holidays, served as little more than joyous reunions for this close-knit family. Joseph had always been generous in gifting a portion of the dividends to his children; in the years following his wife's death in 1978, this portion had steadily increased.

After Joseph's death, Malcolm, Susanne, Harold, and Eleanore remained directors. Abe became CEO, the board was reduced in size to five, and the position of chairman went unfilled.

Abe

Abe Seiler was a high school physics teacher when he met and married Susanne Savenor. Susanne's father was openly critical of both his daughter's choice of spouse and Abe's choice of career. "He'll never be anything," Joseph had told his daughter on many occasions, "and just how happy are you going to be living on his salary when your hormones stop running your life?" Susanne knew that Abe was happy in his job, but after their second child was born, Susanne too began to worry about how they were going to survive.

After seven years of marriage, Abe went to work for his father-in-law in the purchasing department. Abe's style was abrasive, and it was only because of his concern for his daughter that Joseph intervened when Abe offended the workers by making what they considered to be unrealistic demands. After a while, the workers began to joke about Abe and essentially ignored him. Joseph, aware of the problems, nonetheless was insistent that Abe remain a part of the business. While it took pretty close to ten years, Abe finally began to like the business and actually got quite good at handling purchasing and finance, areas that did not bring him into close contact with the employees in manufacturing and sales. Later, despite his being second in command, he remained largely shielded from employee contact, those relationships being maintained by Joseph and Eleanore.

Eleanore

Eleanore Savenor had gone to work for her father immediately after graduating from Katherine Gibbs Secretarial School. Her whole life revolved around her family, and like her sister, she saw the employees at Savenors as family. Once a month, Eleanore and her sales staff would get together at Leonard's, a local restaurant, for lunch, and the group often entertained one another in their homes. Retired members remained very much a part of this network.

The Workers

Virtually all of the workers at Savenors lived in North Deighton, within a mile or two of the plant—it was rare, even for a retiree, to move away—and most of them belonged to a local Portuguese church. Turnover at the company was virtually nonexistent. Employees tended to join the company after high school, a few completed college, and most stayed until retirement. In many cases, husbands, wives, and children of the same family all worked at Savenors at the same time.

The company had been late in instituting a retirement plan; thus most of the retirees lived on their Social Security and welcomed the small dividends they received from their Savenor stock. When one of them ran into trouble, he or she would go to Joseph Savenor, who invariably reached into his own pocket to help them out.

Abe's Problem

Eight months have passed since Joseph's death, and Abe Seiler wants to move ahead with his plan to change the direction of the company. Deep down inside, Abe has a feeling that getting some of the members of the family and many of the employees to accept what he has to propose will not be easy. Not being a "people person," however, he really isn't sure why. He knows that his plan will make money and possibly even save the company from a severe downslide. But Abe has never taken courses on management, and he needs help to figure out how to get his plan accepted.

Does Abe Seiler have the power, insight, and ability to change radically his late father-in-law's company from a stagnating manufacturing operation to what he believes will be a more viable import/retail outlet operation with the potential for growth and expansion? Abe has limited power, as an outsider in a family-held business, and his credibility with at least some of the stakeholders is in question. To effect the change, Abe is going to have to do a meaningful stakeholder analysis and gain an understanding of how to convince at least some of those stakeholders that the move will benefit them without seriously damaging existing norms and interests.

What interests can Abe realistically meet in order to achieve his ultimate goal, and how can he best go about meeting them?

Questions for Discussion

1. Analyze the group dynamics at Savenor Shoe Company and the roles of the members within the various groups, being sure to identify and discuss the areas of group cohesion, norms, stages of group development, uses/abuses of power, potential for intergroup conflict, ethics, and leadership.
2. Identify the resistances to change that Abe is likely to encounter, and suggest some ways in which Abe can reduce these resistances to introduce and manage the change that he is proposing. A graphic depiction of a force field analysis might help Abe understand your suggestions.

PROCEDURE

Step 1   Draw a chronology of the events.

Step 2   Draw organizational charts of the board prior to 1990 and after 1990. It might also help to draw a chart of what is known of the present organizational chart at Savenor Shoe.

Step 3   Identify and analyze the relevant individuals and groups that are stakeholders who are likely to have an interest in the issue at hand. Explain why each of these stakeholders would resist and/or support the proposed changes.

Step 4   Do a force field analysis.

Step 5   Identify the macro and micro problems presented by the case.

Step 6   Give five to six recommendations for Abe to use in effecting the change.

The Construction of Star Station #32465

In February 1990, Roger Rookie took a position at Star Oil Corporation as a field engineer responsible for supervising the construction of convenience stores and gasoline stations. Rookie had earned his B.S. in Civil and Environmental Engineering from Clarkson University in 1988. Prior to taking the job with Star, he had been working as a design engineer for Parsons Brinckerhoff-FG, Inc., an international engineering firm specializing in highway and bridge design. At Parsons, he performed basic tasks associated with roadway design and worked on sophisticated computer-aided design and drafting (CADD) systems. Although he found some of the work interesting, Rookie had decided that he wanted to get out from behind the drafting board, escape from the endless number crunching, and pursue a job in construction management.

Rookie's initial interview for the position with Star had been with a headhunter through whom he had learned that the turnover rate for the position was extremely high. This, he was told, was partly because the job entailed continuous travel and partly because Pete Edwards, the manager of the construction division, was known to be difficult. Three days after Rookie's initial interview, he was asked to go to Star's corporate headquarters in Southbridge, New Jersey, to meet with Edwards.

Although it was a Saturday morning, Edwards conducted a highly formal and intense interview. From Edwards, Rookie learned that the Star Oil Corporation had just budgeted for the construction of a number of large (+/– 2,600 sq. ft.) convenience stores all along the east coast. Rookie's job would be to supervise the regional contractors who had successfully bid the job at each site and ensure that everything was built to Star Oil specifications. Edwards offered Rookie the job but also stated that the only reason he hired inexperienced people like Rookie, who were frequently "chewed up and spit out" by seasoned contractors, was because the "older guys" were all married and would not take jobs that kept them on the road. Rookie realized that Edwards would be tough to work for, but because the job was a field position, he would mainly be dealing with him by phone. However, the large salary increase and an attractive expense account led Rookie to accept the offer.

For the first week, Rookie reported to the main office in Southbridge and reviewed specifications and blueprints of current construction projects. Then he was sent to Binghamton, New York, to supervise his first job. The contractor at this site was Joe Olson and Sons Construction Company, a firm that had considerable experience with such commercial projects as Toys 'R' US and Grand Union.

Joe Olson

When he arrived in Binghamton, Rookie met with Joe Olson, the president of Olson and Sons; Jim Olson, Joe's son and vice-president; Mike Puffer, who was responsible for ordering materials; and Larry Starring, who would be Olson's on-site superintendent.

This case was written by Robert T. Schmitt. Used by permission.

About the author: Robert T. Schmitt is an assistant manager at Latimer & Buck, Inc., Pension Fund Real Estate Advisors in Philadelphia. He received his M.B.A. from Boston University's School of Management in 1991.

After the meeting, Rookie felt pretty confident that the job would progress smoothly. The contractors seemed sincere about using only the best subcontractors and construction materials, not only because they wanted to impress Star Oil (this was Olson's first job for Star), but also because they had a reputation for quality throughout the industry and intended to keep it. Despite Edward's advice never to trust a contractor, especially one who hadn't been subjected to Star's standards before, Rookie decided he liked this contractor. Furthermore, the Olsons had offered to take him golfing at the local private country club at which they were members.

Joe was a "townie" who had made good. He had started his own highly successful business, drove a new sports car, wore gold chains, and carried wads of cash in his pocket at all times. He also owned an extremely successful donut franchise operation in Binghamton that provided him with a substantial second income. Rookie realized that "Big Joe" talked a good game, but he also felt that he was a solid and knowledgeable businessman. The many Olson projects in the area were extremely impressive looking and, according to various code enforcement officers and town officials, had, for the most part, been completed on time and within budget. Furthermore, many of the subcontractors said that they really liked working for Olson and usually bid any job he put out.

Either Joe or Jim personally visited the site at least once every day. After two weeks of construction, the project was ahead of schedule. Under the experienced leadership of the site superintendent, Larry Starring, and with the use of skilled union masons, heavy equipment operators, and Olson's diligent laborers, the building was projected to be completed in three months, well ahead of the four-month average for construction of stores the same size.

Larry Starring and Jim Olson

Starring was a thirty-year-old bachelor who took a job with Olson Construction right after graduating from high school thirteen years ago. Joe Olson's son, Jim, had been in his same high school class. Though Starring's title was superintendent, he clearly enjoyed doing the manual work. It did not take Rookie long to realize that Starring spent more time banging nails than supervising his workers. The job was going well, however, and Rookie felt that maybe the workers did not need that much direction.

On several occasions, Starring invited Rookie out for drinks with the crew after work. Although he felt it might be fun, Rookie refused, remembering Edwards's warnings that the workers would lose respect for him if he fraternized with them.

Tom Verderame

During the first weeks on the job, Rookie's progress at the construction site was monitored by Tom Verderame, a Star Oil engineer who had been overseeing gasoline station construction for several years. Verderame would visit the site for a couple of days each week, never announcing his arrivals. He constantly preached to Rookie on the importance of being tough on the workers, especially early in the job, so that they would learn Star standards and provide the quality desired.

After his first visit to the site, Verderame took Rookie out to dinner. Rookie learned that Verderame was shuffling between three jobs, including the one in Binghamton. The other two, one in Reading, Pennsylvania, and one in East Brunswick, New Jersey, also were being supervised by two newly hired engineers with limited construction management experience. During dinner, Verderame talked only about business, and he expressed some reservations about Starring's abilities. "He does not seem very bright," Verderame told Rookie, "and he never knows what's going on."

When Rookie entered the job trailer the next morning at 6:30, he found Verderame on the phone with Edwards. When he became aware of Rookie's presence, Verderame seemed to end his conversation abruptly and hang up. It was not until later in the day, after Verderame had left the site, that Rookie checked in with Edwards.

"I hear things aren't going too well up there," Edwards said. "You've got a second-rate superintendent giving you second-rate work, and apparently you're not doing anything about it. Speed," he added, "is not a substitute for quality."

While Rookie really believed that the workers weren't taking advantage of him, he suddenly felt far less certain that he was getting top-quality work. When Joe Olson showed up on the site that afternoon, Rookie told him of his concern. Joe assured him that the craftsmanship was superb and that Starring was one of the best "field" men in the area. "How can Edwards say I'm not giving him my best when he's never seen the work?" he asked. "Frankly, Rookie, if you went golfing every day, I would still give Star the best-built convenience store in the state."

A week later, Verderame paid another visit to the site. This time Rookie was forewarned. He had contacted the two engineers on the job sites in New Jersey and Pennsylvania, and they had established a phone "radar" network to keep tabs on the boss's second in command. Rookie had been working closely with Starring and the subcontractors since Verderame's previous visit, and he was confident that all of the new work was top quality and met Star's highest standards. He had been putting in a lot of time with the foreman of the union masons because the white finish brickwork was one of the most important phases of the job. Through conversations with Edwards, he had learned that dirty white mortar joints, stained by tools used to place the gray mortar joints, were a common target of the complaints of nitpicky vice-presidents at inspection time. To prevent this, Rookie had persuaded the mason foreman to purchase special plastic joint tools that would be used for the white brickwork only. Considering that he was dealing with a union which usually had a "never do more than is required" attitude, he felt this was quite an accomplishment. Rookie sensed that the men were annoyed with his seemingly petty concerns, but in cooperating, they were demonstrating loyalty and respect.

Verderame pulled up to the site in the late afternoon, and even before greeting Rookie, he began to inspect the brickwork. When he had finished, he walked up to Rookie and declared that the brickwork was unsatisfactory and that Rookie should call Joe Olson and get something done about it.

Within half an hour, Rookie, Joe and Jim Olson, Starring, and the mason foreman were gathered in front of the brick wall listening to Verderame lecturing that the masonry joints were not straight enough and that the wall should come down. The argument that ensued lasted half an hour, at which point all of the contractors and the Olsons stormed off the job. Just before leaving, Joe Olson declared that he would take all of his men off the job if the wall was to come down.

Verderame's Rationale

At dinner that evening, Rookie told Verderame that he was both angry and confused. He had thoroughly expected Verderame to compliment the brickwork, and even if there had been flaws, he had at least expected Verderame to approach him about it first, rather than undermining his authority with the contractors and the workers. In response to Rookie's distress, Verderame acknowledged that the brickwork was about the same quality as a couple of other jobs he had supervised. He said, however, that he felt the workers didn't have enough respect for Rookie and therefore might be trying to take shortcuts in other aspects of the job; he admitted that he had no specifics. By being tough on Olson, Verderame felt the contractor would work harder on the more crucial details that would come up as the project neared completion.

Rookie's Dilemma

Driving to the construction site the next morning, Rookie contemplated the decision he would soon have to make. Before Verderame had left, he had told Rookie that, since he was with the men on a daily basis, it was up to him to decide what to do about the wall. It was clear, however, that Verderame wanted the wall torn down. Although he was still angry about the way it was handled, Rookie wondered whether setting a tough standard might benefit Star in the future. He also realized that if Verderame wanted the wall torn down, Edwards would want it torn down as well.

Rookie realized that ordering the wall torn down might very well result in Olson pulling his men off the job, a consequence that would benefit no one. He also considered the relationship he had developed with the workers. He had been a nuisance to the masons, but they had performed well; Rookie had made a point of complimenting them on their work. How could he tell them, the day after the visit from his supervisor, that the wall should come down, especially since all parties concerned, even Verderame, knew the workmanship was fine?

The Construction of Star Station #32465

Chain of Command

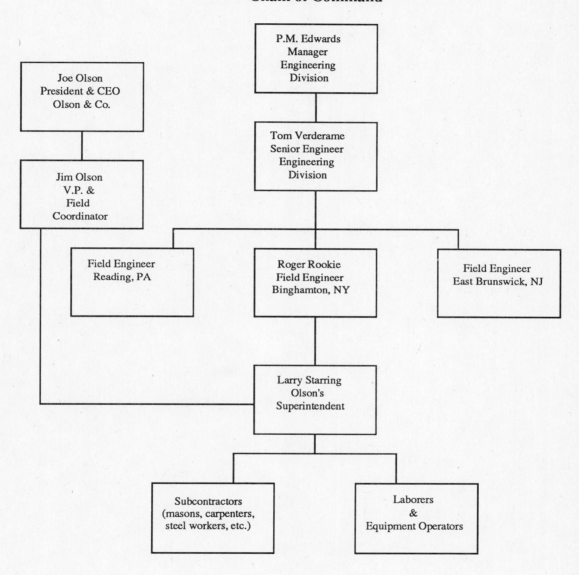

The Bureaucracy Game

PROCEDURE

Step 1 (20–30 minutes)

You will be assigned to one of the following groups: Research and Development Department (up to six people); Production Department (up to six people); Marketing Department (up to six people); Finance Department (up to six people); Task Team (three to six people); Executive Board (two to three people).

   After receiving your assignment, read the background sheet, which also gives the rules of the game. In addition, you will receive a sheet with job descriptions for the people in your department. Assign the roles and discuss both the roles and the background information to be sure there is mutual understanding of the assigned tasks.

Step 2 (45–60 minutes)

Following the directions given on the background and role sheets, and any oral instructions that may be given, develop a project proposal that is acceptable to everyone involved. If no agreement is reached, the game will be stopped at the end of one hour, and the participants will be debriefed. No proposal will be considered to be acceptable until signed off on (use the Proposal Sheet) by the managers of every department as well as by the Executive Board.

   Be sure that all rules are followed—for example, everything should be in writing—unless rule changes are agreed to according to the protocol given.

   During the game, observe the following:

- What effects does bureaucracy have on productivity, morale, and decision quality?
- What tactics did the task team attempt to use to get the proposal approved (i.e., persuasion, logic, threats, compliance with rules—no matter how absurd)? What tactics worked best?

Step 3 (open-ended)

Class Discussion

BACKGROUND

The Wildcat Compact Disc Company has just started operations, but upper management is already thinking big. They have discovered a new music group called Nuclear Lunchbox, who, they believe, will become the hottest group of the decade. The Nuclear Lunchbox sound combines elements of punk rock and rap music, but the band members play nothing but classical instruments.

This exercise was written by Scott Weighart.

You work for the Wildcat Compact Disc Company. Soon you will learn what your job will be. For now, all you know is that a task team has been formed. Its job will be to consult with all departments to work out all of the many specific details for the forthcoming Nuclear Lunchbox CD. Decisions will have to be made regarding each of the following:

- Color of compact disc label: Some companies produce nothing but the basic silver CDs, while others use various colors. What will Wildcat do?
- Production cost: Most CDs retail from $11.99 to $14.99. Obviously, production cost must be much less than that to make a profit, but the costs of ensuring a top-quality product are generally high.
- Packaging: Some CDs are boxed in cardboard, while others are packaged in inexpensive polymerized plastic. Still others are wrapped in more expensive but recyclable fritillated plastic. Which of these three options should the company choose?
- Running time of CD: Since all of Nuclear Lunchbox's songs are equally good (or equally bad, depending on how you look at it), the band's manager has stated that they have as much material as you want to use. The average CD runs about forty minutes, although seventy-five to eighty minutes is possible with the latest technology. How long should this compact disc be?

Each of the various departments at The Wildcat Compact Disc Company has strong opinions regarding the issues raised above. Wildcat's president hopes that the appointed task team will be effective as a liaison that can then, having gathered all of the vital input, make the best decisions.

At times there may be unsolvable conflicts between departments. If this occurs, the task team is allowed to submit a written memo to the executive board. If the board's members decide a rule change should take place, they will send a memo notifying all department heads. This memo must then be initialed by two members of each department.

Important Note: Regardless of what any task team member may say, all rules must be followed unless countermanded by a duly signed written memo from the executive board.

The Bureaucracy Game

PRODUCT PROPOSAL

We, the Task Team, hereby submit our product proposals in order to ain the approval of all concerned parties. We wish to produce a CD that has the following characteristics:

Color of CD label: _____

Production cost: _____

Packaging material: _____

Running time of CD: _____

Approved by Research & Development: _____

Approved by Finance Department: _____

Approved by Marketing Department: _____

Approved by Production Department: _____

Approved by Executive Board: _____

The Codfish Company

PART I (45–60 minutes)

You and four of your classmates have been given a group project to do that requires each of you to carry out at least one face-to-face interview with a manager at a company of the group's choosing. After you have completed these interviews, you and your groupmates must then get together, compare interview results, and compose a single fifteen- to twenty-page paper on the job of a manager—for which you will all get the same grade. You must also do a twenty-minute presentation to your other classmates on your findings.

Your group has decided to interview managers at the Codfish Company, producers of high-quality marine hardware. All of your group's members agree that the product area is one that interests them. The project must be completed and turned in exactly six weeks from today; the oral presentation is to be delivered exactly one week later.

You realize that the best way to avoid last-minute chaos is to do some planning now. This will include selecting a leader, dividing the task into manageable pieces, and establishing a schedule. All of the following must be completed; they need not be done in order.

A. In discussion with the other members, decide on a name for your group that you feel best describes what your group stands for.

_____

B. Select a leader, and list below four to six of the duties you would like your leader to perform.

Leader's Name _____

1. _____
2. _____
3. _____
4. _____
5. _____
6. _____

C. Discuss what you believe the central (superordinate) goal of your group should be, and briefly but clearly state it below:

_____
_____
_____
_____

_____

This exercise was written by Bruce Leblang. Used by permission.

D. Discuss the other goals and values shared by the group (e.g., making the most out of a learning experience, doing the least amount of work possible, being professional, etc.), and list at least three below:

1. _____
2. _____
3. _____
4. _____
5. _____

E. Divide the job that must be done into at least six to eight component parts/jobs, and list them below. Be sure to include such jobs as typing the paper, proofreading, data gathering, organizing the oral presentation, and so forth. Assign each part/job to one or more person(s) in your group, and list that person's name next to the job.

Part/Job	Assigned to
1._____	_____
2._____	_____
3._____	_____
4._____	_____
5._____	_____
6._____	_____
7._____	_____
8._____	_____
9._____	_____

F. Develop a time line or schedule to indicate by what date each component of your project should completed. Draw the time line below.

G. Assume that you have been given the right to fire a fellow student; under what circumstances would you do so? List the reasons below, and then develop a firing policy which is agreed to and signed by all members of the group.

    The policy should include provisions for serving notice on the individual to be fired and a list of the circumstances under which that individual can make amends and preserve his/her position in the group.

1. Reasons:

_____
_____
_____
_____
_____
_____

2. Statement:

_____
_____
_____
_____
_____

PART II (20–30 minutes)

By your set due-date for completion of all interviews, two of the members have not yet held them.

A. Knowing what you do about motivation, how can you convince the two who haven't completed their interviews to do so?

_____
_____
_____

B. What should you do if you are unable to convince the others to complete their interviews? What should the role of your leader be in dealing with this problem?

_____
_____
_____
_____
_____

C. The two members who had not done their interviews on time finally hand them in. You realize that the two have made the interviews up and haven't actually done them. The paper is due in two days. What should you do?

_____

_____

_____

_____

D. In what ways is your method for dealing with this problem consistent or inconsistent with your group's stated goals and values? Are you comfortable or uncomfortable with your goals and policies and the way in which they address your group's needs in dealing with a problem such as this? Why or why not?

   What changes, if any, would you like to make to your statements of goals and policies to better meet such problems?

_____

_____

_____

_____

E. Your group finished the project and got an A– (with two faked interviews). Was your **group** successful? Why or why not?

_____

_____

_____

_____

The Florida Sunshiners Baseball Club

The Seattle Salts Baseball Team, plagued by poor attendance, community disinterest, and the lack of a lucrative TV contract, have decided to move to a new domed stadium in the Tampa–St. Petersburg area of Florida. To attract the area's numerous senior citizens to the games, team officials have selected an appropriate new name: the Florida Sunshiners.

News of the proposed move has caused considerable concern to the players, coaches, and organizational personnel. For many reasons, they are reluctant to disrupt their lives by moving: They will have to either uproot children from schools when the season starts or live apart from their families until school ends in mid-June. No one is looking forward to leaving friends behind. Then there's the hassle and expense of moving from the Seattle area to Florida, not to mention the emotional and logistical issues of hunting for new homes in Florida.

The owner of the franchise doesn't want team morale to be affected by the move. He feels there are many things that make the change a positive one for all parties. The stadium is brand new; the locker room facilities are exceptionally good. He also feels that once the players find out about the high quality of the school systems in Florida and the reasonable prices of homes, they will warm up to the move. And speaking of warming up, the excellent weather in Florida will likely be more popular with the players and their families.

Questions for Discussion

1. Given what you've learned about managing change (freezing/unfreezing, force field analysis, etc.), analyze the above situation in theoretical terms.
2. Many techniques of change are possible: Which tactics would you use? Why? What are some techniques that could backfire? Explain.

This case was written by Scott Weighart.

The Deep-Water Harbor

BACKGROUND

Your community of about 750,000 citizens has recently voted to deep-dredge the natural harbor on which your town is located. Just under $1.2 million has been allocated for completing the project, which the town hopes to raise through a bond issue. Any need for additional funding would have to be brought back to the town government for approval.

The dredging is part of a plan to develop a deep-water shipping port to meet the needs of the fish-packing plant at which many of your town's residents are employed. Without the ability to bring larger boats into the harbor, the owners of the plant say they will have to move their operations to a more favorable location.

Loss of the fish-packing plant could be an economic disaster for your community, which is already in severe financial decline. At one time, the town was a center for the timber industry, but environmental concerns have brought that industry virtually to a halt, and the sawmills have all been shut down. The rail lines that were used by the timber industry are still accessible and make the proposed deep-water harbor extremely desirable. Container ships could be unloaded in the harbor and the containers then moved by rail across the country.

Your town is also a summer haven for vacationers, sailors, and tourists. The population very nearly doubles during July and August. Families come from surrounding states to enjoy the pristine beauty of the harbor, the surrounding mountains, and the woods.

You have been asked to serve on a special committee to plan and implement the deep-water harbor plan. You know there is both a need for the dredging as well as considerable resistance to it—some of which may be yours—but there is now a mandate that must be carried out.

PROCEDURE

Step 1 (5 minutes)

Read the role you have been given and consider what your position should be with regard to the proposed plan.

Step 2 (5–10 minutes)

Working in groups of six, introduce yourself (in your role) to the others. Consider that you and they are members of the committee. Explain what your position is with regard to the proposed plan.

This exercise was written by Janet W. Wohlberg.

Step 3   (15–20 minutes)

Identify the driving and restraining forces involved in making this change, and illustrate them in a graphic force field analysis. Propose a plan for implementing the required change, given what you have identified in your force field analysis. The fish-packing plant is also faced with a potential change—to move to a new location. You may want to do a force field analysis of the driving and restraining forces for the plant move as a way to further clarify where you can best place your efforts in managing the proposed change for your town.

Step 4   (open-ended)

When you have completed your force field analysis and your plan, present it to the members of your class. In class discussion, consider the ways in which your force field analysis helped you to identify the resistances to the proposed change as well as the driving forces favoring it. In what ways did disaggregating this problem help you in developing solutions?

The Deep-Water Harbor
Force Field Analysis

Goal: To develop a deep-water shipping port

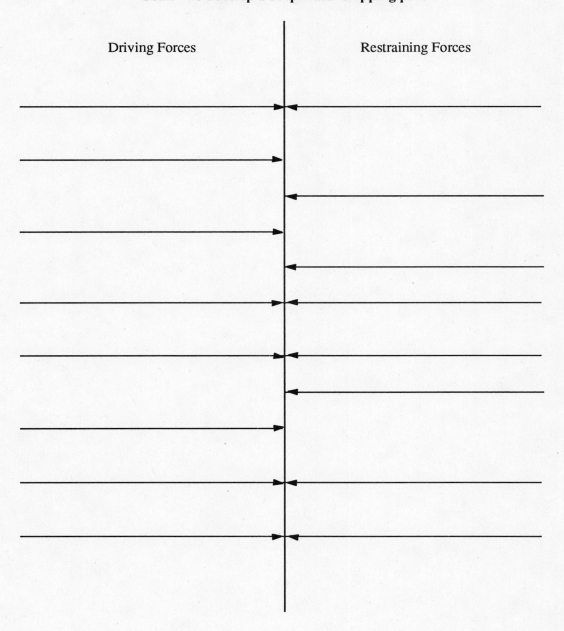

Driving Forces   Restraining Forces

Add more arrows as necessary.

Issuing a Blanket Statement

THE FIRE

At 11 P.M. on a cold Saturday in February, fire engines screamed toward campus as frightened students fled, some clad only in nightclothes, from Thompson Hall. Gathering in the parking lot, the shocked students watched in horror and amazement as flames shot out of the third-floor windows.

The commotion drew students from all over the small midwestern college campus, and soon the residence hall staff, comprised mostly of doctoral students, had all they could do to keep the growing numbers of students calm and away from the burning building.

"That's my room, that's my stuff!" Mark, a senior hockey player, bellowed. "I have to get my stuff!"

As he ran toward the building, Mark was intercepted by the resident director of Thompson Hall, Rob Martin.

"You can't go in there," Rob told Mark, as he grabbed him by the arm. "Look at it—my stuff's in there, too. Come on."

The entire staff of resident directors (RDs) worked quickly and efficiently throughout the night to ensure that the distressed students were safe. They escorted some to temporary quarters at a nearby hotel; others went to join friends in other dorms.

By 5 A.M., the weary staff was able to get a glimpse of the extent of the damage—the roof on the east side of the building was gone, three rooms on the third floor were completely destroyed by the fire, and many others throughout the building had been badly damaged by the smoke and water. Firemen threw charred bed frames and water-soaked mattresses out of the windows.

By midmorning, word had come from the fire chief that the fire, which had started in a third-floor room, had been caused by a faulty electric blanket that had been left turned on and crumpled at the end of a student's bed. The chief ordered the lower floors of the building closed until renovations and safety inspections, expected to take about a week, were complete. The upper floors were to be closed for much longer. That afternoon, residents of Thompson Hall, escorted by an RD, were allowed to enter the building, one at a time, to collect what remained of their clothes and other "necessary" belongings. Some students were relieved to find only very minimal damage to their belongings; others weren't so lucky.

"My shirt, where's my hockey shirt? It was right there, on the wall . . . ," whispered Mark, as he stared into the black hole that had been his room.

"It's gone, Mark," Rob told him. "I'm sorry, but everything is gone."

"But it can't be gone—it, it was my dad's—he played for the Northstars—he wore it in his last game. I have to find my shirt."

This case was written by Sandra L. Deacon. Used by permission.

Sandi Deacon has taught organizational behavior at Boston University's School of Management and at Northeastern University. She is a doctoral student in counseling psychology.

WHEN THE SMOKE HAD CLEARED

At 8 A.M. Monday morning, four exhausted RDs gathered for their weekly staff meeting with their supervisor, Susan Howell, Director of residence life.

"Where's Susan?" asked Lisa, the RD of Drake Hall, the only all-female residence hall on campus. "She's late. How are you doing this morning, Rob? Have you been able to get any sleep?"

"Not much, thanks, and you?"

"Sorry I'm late, guys," Susan said, as she entered the conference room. "How's everybody surviving? The first thing I want to say is that you all did an incredible job handling the crisis this weekend. I couldn't have asked for anything more—from any of you! None of us has gotten much, if any, sleep these past two days. I hope you're all holding up. You guys are great!"

"I was just in meeting with President Dickerson. He was not happy. It seems that he heard from the fire chief; according to the chief, that building was a fire waiting to happen. When the firemen investigated the building, they found candles stuck in beer bottles and tapestries hung on the ceilings to cover bare light bulbs. Not only that, but they also found microwaves, toaster ovens, minirefrigerators, and coffeepots. The building isn't under code to allow appliances in students' rooms."

"President Dickerson," she continued, "is furious. He asked why we don't have a rule banning appliances. I explained that we do have one—it's in the student handbook—but it hasn't been enforced. I tried to tell him how hard it is to enforce the rule without turning the residence halls into police states, but he's insistent. He wants all appliances removed from every room in every residence hall within one week."

"You're kidding."

"But I thought we had agreed not to go looking for that stuff or even enforce the policy when we came across something. It's a privacy issue."

"Yeah, the students already feel that we're on their backs because they're not allowed to drink in their rooms—we can't go and tell them that they can't eat either. They already think we treat them like kids."

"It's not that they can't eat; they just can't cook."

"But the cafeteria is only open until 7 at night, and most of the athletes don't finish practice until 7:30 or 8. I have a lot of athletes in my building. How can they eat?"

"Besides, it was a blanket that caused the problem—not a microwave."

Susan listened intently to the discussion. "I know," she said, "you have some good points, but President Dickerson gave the order—all appliances have to be out of the rooms in one week—they can either ship them home or take them home, but we have to do inspections in one week, and anything we find we have to confiscate."

"One week? This is incredible. The students don't like us much as it is. I can hardly wait to see what happens when we start taking away their toasters."

Rob had been sitting quietly throughout most of the discussion.

"You know," he said at last, "I agree with what you're all saying. But maybe it won't be as bad as we think. Most of the students were on campus to see the fire—and those who didn't actually see it burning can see the damage. We were really lucky that it happened when it did. Someone might have gotten hurt if it had been at 4 A.M. on a weekday. I think we need to give the students some credit; seeing all the damage, they just might understand why we have to do this."

"Maybe Rob's right," Lisa responded. "I guess they would be crazy not to agree with the policy. It's for their own safety."

"And ours," added Rob. "I don't want to be in a situation like that again, or lose everything like Mark."

"Speaking of Mark, how is he doing?"

"He's still very upset. He lost some pretty important things in the fire. But I've been talking with him about it. He'll be all right."

"I think we'll need to meet again this week," Susan told the group, "just to check in to see how everyone is holding up. If you can all meet with your students before Wednesday, we'll have another staff meeting that day to talk about what we need to do next. Thanks."

THE WINDS OF WAR

"By the looks on your faces," Susan began, "I'm not sure I want to know how things went with the students. Lisa, why don't you start?"

"Yeah, sure. My floor meeting was awful—all they did was complain. They brought up everything, 'What do you mean we can't even make coffee in the morning?' 'We're not two year olds.' 'Why did you ever let us have the appliances in our rooms in the first place?' 'How can we eat? The cafeteria food is lousy!' Shall I go on?" asked Lisa, exasperated.

"My floor meeting wasn't much different," said Pat. "The athletes, in particular, are really upset. Even the snack bar is only open until 10. They can't afford to order pizza or take-out every night after practice. They wanted to know why they were being punished for someone else's stupidity."

"I thought the snack bar closed at one in the morning," Susan said.

"It used to, but the students responsible for the late shift hardly ever showed up, so the manager just decided to cut out that shift altogether and close at 10."

"Susan, I tried to reason with them," Lisa insisted, "I really did. I told them that the fire could have been in Drake Hall just as easily as Thompson, but they wouldn't listen. I told them that the rule hadn't changed; it was always there in the student handbook, but now it was going to have to be enforced."

"Ditto," said Eric. "I had the same reactions in my hall."

"Rob, you've been pretty quiet. What happened in your meeting?" asked Susan.

"I'm kind of surprised that you all had such a rough time," Rob told the group. "My meeting went pretty well in comparison. I got all the guys together at the hotel and told everyone about the change. A few people started to complain, but then Mark spoke up. He said that he agreed with the policy and that it might help prevent something like this from happening again. I think a lot of the guys look up to Mark, and they're pretty sympathetic toward him, too—his father having died and all—and toward some of the others who lost so much. They seemed to agree with him. At least no one said much of anything after that."

EPILOGUE

After spending a week trying to explain the reasons for the no-appliance mandate to the students, the RDs were thoroughly frustrated. On inspection day, they found themselves confiscating truckloads of toaster ovens, hot pots, and other appliances.

Even Rob, whose students had initially agreed to removing their appliances, found that they seemed to have changed their minds once they had moved back to Thompson Hall. He, too, had to confiscate his share of microwaves and minirefrigerators.

Questions for Discussion

1. Why are the students resisting the change to enforcement of the no-appliance rule, despite the clear dangers of keeping appliances in their rooms?
2. Using a force field analysis, identify the forces driving and resisting the change. Which of the forces resisting the change do you believe could be reduced? How and why?
3. If you were a member of the residence staff and had this change to manage, what would you have done differently to reduce the resistance of the students? Why? Be specific.

Issuing a Blanket Statement
Force Field Analysis

Goal: To remove appliances from students' rooms

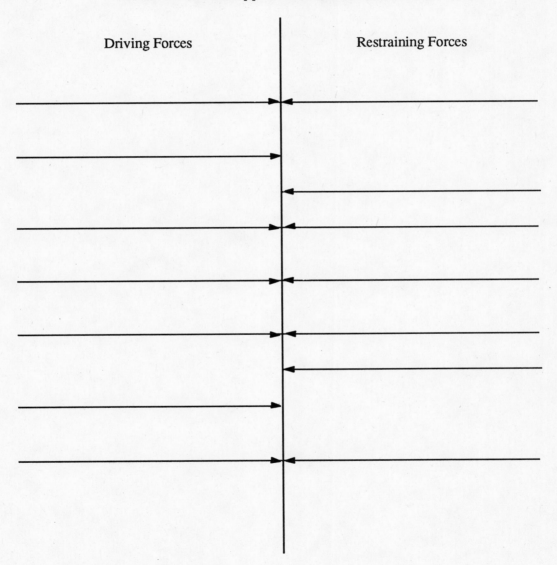

Driving Forces   Restraining Forces

Add more arrows as necessary.

PART V

NEGOTIATION

Morris Raker, J.D.

OVERVIEW

Many people feel inexperienced and uncomfortable with the prospect of negotiating an agreement. Indeed, a surprisingly large number willingly forfeit valuable opportunities, such as negotiating with the boss for a raise, out of fear of the unknown.

Americans have grown up with one-price stores, where you either pay the fixed price or take your business elsewhere. In contrast to persons from other parts of the world, where every purchase involves a negotiation over price, Americans often fear that their lack of familiarity with the process of bargaining will lead to failure.

In fact, most Americans have far more negotiating experience than they realize. Even in the United States, bargaining is not confined to big ticket items such as a car or house. Negotiations are involved every time you and family or friends reach a compromise on which restaurant to eat at or which movie to attend. Think of the protracted negotiations between teenagers and parents for use of the family car, the right to watch television on school nights, or the deadline for returning home from a Saturday night date.

For most individuals, negotiations fall broadly into two categories. First, there are negotiations with strangers, persons with whom you do not expect to have an ongoing relationship. Typical examples would be negotiations over the price of a car or condominium. These are the kinds of transactions that most people identify as involving negotiations.

The other category covers negotiations in the context of ongoing relationships, such as negotiations with family members, friends, teachers, or co-workers. In these situations, it is the relationship that gives rise to the negotiation and disciplines the parties to act reasonably and in good faith.

Managers must be skilled in both types of negotiations. They are called upon to negotiate contracts not only with persons or companies outside the organization, but also with their co-workers in the context of a wide variety of events within the organization.[1]

Although the contexts may seem very different, the same principles and techniques apply to both categories of negotiation. The basic principle is that you should not enter an agreement which, from your perspective, places you in a worse position than if no agreement were reached.

This doesn't mean that for an agreement to be acceptable it must give you exactly what you want. By its nature, negotiation involves compromise, and it is often desirable to pay more or accept less than had been your goal, so long as the agreement reached continues to be in your best interest.

This means that you should never enter a negotiation unprepared. At the very least, you must decide, before the bargaining begins, the most you would be willing to give up,

---

This overview was written by Morris Raker. Used by permission.

Morris Raker, J.D. is a lawyer/consultant who specializes in Litigation Cost Containment™ and is CEO of TreeAge Software, Inc.

1. David A. Lax and James K. Sebenius, authors of *The Manager as Negotiator* (New York: The Free Press, 1986), note that negotiations are likely to be involved whenever a manager requires the approval of his or her superior. They are involved each time a manager must seek the cooperation of peers or others, either within or without the organization, who do not fall within the manager's chain of command. Negotiations are even involved in securing the support of subordinates within the organization whenever the use of raw command is either impossible or undesirable. Lax and Sebenius's book is highly recommended for those who wish to further explore negotiation and specifically intraorganizational negotiation.

or the least you would be willing to accept, depending on your role in the negotiation.[2] This outside figure constitutes your "reservation price." It is based on an appraisal of what you understand your alternatives to be. You identify and evaluate your best alternative—that is, the one you would choose if the negotiation at hand fails to reach an agreement; this is known as your "no-agreement alternative."

Let's say you are in the market for a used car and have a particular model in mind. Yesterday, you saw one that was nice but not exactly what you are looking for. Some desirable options are missing; the color is OK, but it's not your favorite, and the general condition is about average for a car of this age. On the other hand, the owner appeared very anxious to sell and seems willing to settle for as little as $4,000.

Later this afternoon, you plan to return to a dealer who recently took in trade exactly the car that you want. It has all the desired options, it's your favorite color, and it is in impeccable condition. The problem is that the dealer has been holding out for $5,600. You believe there is still some bargaining room.

Your budget would permit you to spend as much as $6,000 for a car, so even the $5,600 price is possible should the dealer hold firm. On the other hand, you realize that your excitement over the car could cause you to bargain badly and overpay. Furthermore, if you can save enough out of your $6,000 budget, it would be possible for you to take the new car on a long awaited vacation.

The answer to your quandary lies in doing adequate preparation before entering the negotiation. Without realizing it, you've already obtained most of the information that you need. You know that your best alternative to reaching agreement with the dealer would be to buy the car you saw yesterday for $4,000. This option constitutes your "no-agreement alternative" and is used to determine your reservation price, the maximum amount that you should agree to pay in this afternoon's negotiation.[3]

Since the two cars are not identical, and one clearly is worth more to you than the other, your reservation price is greater than $4,000. Just how much greater depends on the value differential from your perspective.

You must decide, in advance of the negotiation, the maximum amount you would be willing to pay over $4,000 for the more desirable features. Publicly available data will give you a pretty good idea of the difference in resale value created by the additional options and better condition. You can probably justify a greater differential for a variety of reasons, such as having more pleasure from owning the car of your dreams, or because you would feel compelled to do restoration work and add options to the $4,000 model, and these would run much more than the difference in resale value. On the other hand, if you could live with either car as is, you might conclude that the resale differential exceeds the present value to you of the added features.

---

2. The benefits from reaching an agreement are not always confined to money or tangibles. For example, parties to a negotiation among family members or coworkers in a business will often attribute value to the maintenance of a harmonious relationship and will be willing to forego options otherwise more valuable to achieve that goal. There are even situations where the process of negotiation itself is regarded as a benefit. Thus, an individual might balk at an order to undertake a disagreeable task, yet might voluntarily agree to the assignment in the context of a negotiation with his or her boss which permitted a full expression of views.

3. In many situations, you will not have an alternative immediately available to you; nevertheless, it should still be possible to identify and assess the value of your no agreement alternative. Let's say you want to sell your stereo and have posted a notice asking for $600, hoping to get at least $500. An acquaintance sold an outfit almost identical to yours for $550. However, that was four months ago and now it is only three weeks until the end of the school year. Your notice was posted five days ago, and the first caller is on her way over. In this case, you must assess the probabilities of receiving offers at various levels over the next three weeks. The expected value of this lottery is the value of your no agreement alternative.

In any event, once you have determined your reservation price, it is important that you stick to it, unless you obtain information (such as learning that the second car has been sold) which changes the consequences of failing to reach agreement with the auto dealer. Since the reservation price will be based on your no-agreement alternative, it follows that going above it would be worse than failing to reach agreement, and, surely, it wouldn't make sense voluntarily to accept an agreement that hurts rather than helps you.

This hypothetical negotiation is an example of distributive bargaining. The only issue to be negotiated is the number of dollars to be paid for the car. Your objective would be to pay as few dollars as possible (in no event more than your reservation price), while the dealer wants as many dollars as possible (in no event less than his reservation price). So long as your reservation price is greater than the dealer's, a zone of agreement exists; the zone of agreement being the range between the two reservation prices provided that the buyer's reservation price is greater than the seller's. When a zone of agreement exists, it should be possible to strike a deal. If the opposite is true—the most you are willing to pay is less than the least the dealer is willing to accept—no zone of agreement exists, and no agreement is possible.

Prior to beginning negotiations, it is possible for the parties to predict, but not to know with certainty, whether a zone of agreement exists—that is, whether the buyer's reservation price exceeds the seller's.[4] Distributive bargaining involves the use of offer and counteroffer to influence perceptions of value and to make it appear that one's reservation price is much lower (or higher, in the case of the seller) than it actually is. This type of bluffing, if viewed as crossing the ethical boundaries, can lead to accusations of dishonesty and loss of credibility in the business community. These boundaries will vary depending on cultural and other factors, and it is critical that negotiators be aware of them.

Many negotiations are not limited to an exchange of dollars (from the buyer) for property, goods or services (from the seller). These more complex transactions usually provide an opportunity for integrative bargaining, commonly known as "win–win" negotiations, rather than distributive, "win–lose" negotiations.

In integrative bargaining, the goal is to create value—often referred to as "expanding the pie"—so that each party to the negotiation can do better than in a purely distributive setting. This value creation is accomplished by identifying and taking advantage of the opportunities provided by the parties' different outlooks and interests.

Two hardware stores sell the same brand of paint. One store is located on Cape Cod, and the other in a suburb of Boston. In both areas, black and dark green have been the most popular colors for painting exterior doors, shutters, and window trim, with sales split about evenly between the two. However, over the past year, black has become increasingly popular on Cape Cod, while green has become the big seller in the Boston area.

This situation has left the Cape Cod store overstocked with green paint, while the Boston store has far too much black. The paint manufacturer does not accept returns, and a liquidator of excess merchandise will pay less than half the wholesale price.

---

4. In the hypothetical negotiation described in the text, the dealer's opening offer is the sticker price. If it is below the purchaser's reservation price, the purchaser is aware from the outset that a zone of agreement exists. The dealer will not learn this until the purchaser offers a price that exceeds the dealer's Reservation Price. This may occur with the purchaser's first counteroffer or, possibly, not until a series of offers and counteroffers will have brought the parties closer together.

The Cape Cod shopkeeper, who we will call Harry, is unaware that John, the owner of the Boston area store, is overstocked with black paint, but he decides to telephone to see if John would be willing to purchase his excess green paint.

Harry candidly explains his predicament, saying that he would be willing to sell seventy-five gallons of green-trim paint at 20 percent off the wholesale price because he needs to raise money to be able to place an order for black paint with the manufacturer. Harry's candor offers a valuable opportunity for joint gain. It also runs the risk that John will use this information about Harry's true interest in the negotiation to Harry's disadvantage.

John has the option of being equally candid concerning his need for green paint and his desire to unload his extra seventy-five gallons of black. If he took this option, John and Harry would probably agree to swap green for black, leaving both of them in better positions than prior to the negotiation. Joint gains are possible because Harry values a gallon of black paint more than a gallon of green, while the opposite is true for John. In other words, each is giving up a commodity that he values at less than X in return for a commodity worth X.

Alternatively, John might decide to take advantage of Harry's candor. He might say that he wants to help out his buddy, Harry, but he is short of cash and doesn't really need anything close to seventy-five gallons of green paint. On the other hand, he does have thirty-five or forty gallons of black paint that he could spare if Harry were willing to swap on a 2 for 1 basis. That may not be as good a deal as Harry was hoping to get, but it is better than going to a liquidator.

If John pulls off this deal, or something like it, he will do far better than if he had accepted Harry's proposal for a straight distributive bargain, as well as much better than if he had reciprocated Harry's candor. Of course, John runs the risk of being found out, and most (but, certainly, not all) businesspeople are increasingly aware of the importance of building a reputation for honest, ethical behavior.

It is the fear of being taken advantage of that leads most individuals to bargain on the basis of positions, holding back information on underlying interests. This is so even though the sharing of this information is critically important to generating mutually beneficial, joint gains.

In light of this reticence, it is often possible for both parties to a negotiation to benefit materially when a mediator or other neutral third party is employed to aid them in reaching agreement. Aware that the mediator is both neutral and bound to preserve confidences, parties are usually willing to share with the mediator information deemed too sensitive to tell the other side.[5] This permits the mediator to help the parties reach an agreement which is better for both than the best that might have been achieved by the parties alone.

In the following pages, you will find exercises to help you better understand the principles and practices of distributive and integrative bargaining. As you prepare for each negotiation, use the negotiator's worksheet to record the information necessary for arriving at the best possible outcome. Please feel free to photocopy the worksheet for use in future negotiations in your business and personal negotiations.

---

5. An experienced mediator can also be instrumental in helping the parties to shape more realistic goals and to understand better where their true interests lie.

Rabbit Fever

PROCEDURE

Step 1   (20 minutes)

Read both the General Information and either the Buyer's or Seller's Confidential Information, depending on which role you have been assigned. Identify your no-agreement alternative, and determine both your reservation price (based on your no-agreement alternative) and your target price. Prepare your negotiating strategy, which should include, if you are the buyer, your opening counter to the seller's advertised asking price.

Step 2   (30–40 minutes)

Meet with the other party in an attempt to negotiate a mutually acceptable price for the used Rabbit Convertible. By the end of the time period, you should have reached agreement on a price or concluded that it is not possible for the two of you to agree on a price.

Step 3   (open-ended)

Participate in class discussion regarding the negotiation. Topics for discussion may include the specifics of any agreement reached; your reservation price and the basis on which it was determined; your negotiating strategy and why it was or wasn't successful; whether you or the other party departed from the facts contained in the confidential instructions; whether you are happy with the process; and whether you are happy with the substantive outcome of the negotiation.

GENERAL INFORMATION

You and another individual will negotiate concerning the purchase and sale of a used car. The locale is Boston, during the second week of December, 1990.

The vehicle in question is a 1982 Volkswagen Rabbit convertible with the following features:

- The body is yellow and in excellent condition. The vehicle had been rust-proofed when new. The seller is the original owner, and the car appears to have been well-maintained and garaged overnight.
- The fully-lined, black canvas top is in excellent condition. The boot (a separate lined, black canvas piece used to cover the top when it is down) is missing.
- The interior is clean. The fabric-covered sports seats show only modest wear.
- The odometer reads 53,783 miles.

This exercise was written by Morris Raker. Used by permission.

- Replacement radial tires are in good condition, with about 15,000 miles of wear.
- The AM/FM radio works fine; however, the tape player is not functioning.
- The vehicle has been advertised for sale in the newspaper at $4,900.

In addition to these general instructions, you will also receive confidential, personal instructions.

You will have 15 minutes to develop your strategy and tactics. Make some notes below on your ideas and plans about how to bargain:

1. What is your goal?

    _____

    _____

2. What is your reservation price?

    _____

    _____

3. What are your opponent's likely goal and reservation price, and how will you attempt to learn more about them?

    _____

    _____

4. Strategically, how will you seek to persuade your opponent?

    _____

    _____

5. What will be your tactical moves?

    _____

    _____

Rabbit Fever
Negotiator's Worksheet and Checklist

The following worksheet sets out the critical areas for planning for and carrying out a negotiation.

1. Describe your best no-agreement alternative and set your reservation price.

   _____

   _____

2. Describe the actions that you think you can take to improve your no-agreement alternative.

   _____

   _____

3. List what you know about your opponent that could possibly be helpful in your negotiation, including possible interests and available alternatives. Describe what you believe his or her negotiating style is like.

   _____

   _____

   _____

4. List ways and sources for learning more about your opponent.

   _____

   _____

   _____

   _____

5. Briefly describe what you believe your opponent's best no-agreement alternative is. Estimate what you believe his or her reservation price is.

   _____

   _____

   _____

   _____

6. Identify ways in which you can worsen your opponent's no-agreement alternative.

   _____

   _____

   _____

   _____

7. Describe your underlying interests.

   _____

   _____

8. Describe what you believe are your opponent's underlying interests.

   _____

   _____

9. In integrative bargaining situations, identify areas of potential joint gain. This includes identifying and analyzing the differences between you and your opponent (in relative valuation, forecasts, risk aversion, time preferences, etc.), the possibility that you share certain interests, and the potential for using economies of scale.

   _____

   _____

   _____

   _____

   _____

   _____

   _____

   _____

10. Identify ways you believe would make it possible to satisfy the interests of both parties.

    _____

    _____

    _____

11. Identify the various arguments which you or your opponent might use to support the fairness of your respective bargaining positions. Prepare to use the ones which best support your position. Prepare arguments against those you think your opponent will use.

    _____

    _____

    _____

    _____

    _____

    _____

    _____

    _____

12. Use the early stages of the negotiation to learn more about your opponent's interests and style, and to set a favorable tone. The object is to cultivate opportunities for cooperation and creativity, and to reduce the potential for conflict. Focus on a joint effort to find a solution to what is seen as a common problem. Avoid using threats and otherwise personalizing the problem. Make it possible for your opponent to accept your position without loss of face.

_____

_____

_____

_____

_____

_____

_____

_____

Lakeview Towers

PROCEDURE

Step 1 (30 minutes)

Read both the General Information and either the Buyer's or Seller's Confidential Information, depending on which role you have been assigned. Identify your no-agreement alternative, and determine both your reservation price (based on your no-agreement alternative) and your target price.

Step 2 (30 minutes)

Caucus with other members of the class who have been assigned the same role in the negotiation. The purpose of this is not to assure a common negotiating strategy, but to provide the opportunity for cross-fertilization of ideas. Successful integrative bargaining entails the generation of joint gains, which, in turn, relies on creative problem solving. This session offers a good opportunity to apply brainstorming and other techniques studied earlier in this course.

Step 3 (30–45 minutes)

Meet with the other party in an attempt to negotiate a mutually acceptable closing date for sale of the condominium.

Step 4 (open-ended)

Participate in class discussion regarding the negotiation. Areas for discussion may include the specifics of any agreement reached; your reservation price and the basis on which it was determined; your negotiating strategy; whether you shared information; whether you told the other party of your true interests; whether the other party took advantage of your candor; whether you or the other party departed from the facts contained in the confidential instructions; whether the prenegotiation caucus was helpful; and whether you are satisfied with the result.

GENERAL INFORMATION

Jim and Peg Hurley have lived in Oak Park, a suburb of Chicago, for almost twenty years. Thirty months ago, with their youngest daughter going into her sophomore year in college, they decided to sell their big house and purchase a condominium in Chicago, much closer to their jobs.

It didn't take long for them to decide that a new project overlooking Lake Michigan on Lakeshore Drive offered the amenities and location they were looking for.

This exercise was written by Morris Raker. Used by permission.

Construction had just begun, and the developer, Lakeview Properties, was offering a handsome discount to early purchasers.

Although occupancy would have to be delayed until construction was complete, in about two years, this wasn't a problem for the Hurleys. They planned to use the proceeds from the sale of their suburban home to cover the cost of the condominium, and the delay would give them plenty of time, they thought, to sell their place before having to come up with the money for the new one.

Jim and Peg selected their unit, one of the few with a large terrace overlooking the lake. The agreed price was $490,000. Under the contract for purchase, the buyers were required to make a ten percent cash down payment. This amount would be held in a special bank account and applied, together with interest, against the purchase price at the closing of the purchase and sale. However, if the buyer defaulted and failed to close within the specified time frame, the Hurleys would lose their deposit which would be paid to the developer as damages.

The closing date specified in the purchase agreement is only forty-five days away. Under the agreement, the Hurleys have the right to postpone the closing date for up to sixty days but must give notice of postponement at least thirty days before the specified closing date. Yesterday, Jim Hurley telephoned the developer's sales office to request a meeting with Ted Roberts, the president of Lakeview Properties. The meeting is scheduled for tomorrow at 10 A.M.

Lakeview Towers
Negotiator's Worksheet and Checklist

The following worksheet sets out the critical areas for planning for and carrying out a negotiation.

1. Describe your best no-agreement alternative and set your reservation price.

   _____

   _____

2. Describe the actions that you think you can take to improve your no-agreement alternative.

   _____

   _____

3. List what you know about your opponent that could possibly be helpful in your negotiation, including possible interests and available alternatives. Describe what you believe his or her negotiating style is like.

   _____

   _____

   _____

4. List ways and sources for learning more about your opponent.

   _____

   _____

   _____

   _____

5. Briefly describe what you believe your opponent's best no-agreement alternative is. Estimate what you believe his or her reservation price is.

   _____

   _____

   _____

   _____

6. Identify ways in which you can worsen your opponent's no-agreement alternative.

   _____

   _____

   _____

7. Describe your underlying interests.

   _____

   _____

8. Describe what you believe are your opponent's underlying interests.

   _____

   _____

9. In integrative bargaining situations, identify areas of potential joint gain. This includes identifying and analyzing the differences between you and your opponent (in relative valuation, forecasts, risk aversion, time preferences, etc.), the possibility that you share certain interests, and the potential for using economies of scale.

   _____

   _____

   _____

   _____

   _____

   _____

   _____

   _____

10. Identify ways you believe would make it possible to satisfy the interests of both parties.

    _____

    _____

    _____

11. Identify the various arguments which you or your opponent might use to support the fairness of your respective bargaining positions. Prepare to use the ones which best support your position. Prepare arguments against those you think your opponent will use.

    _____

    _____

    _____

    _____

    _____

    _____

    _____

12. Use the early stages of the negotiation to learn more about your opponent's interests and style, and to set a favorable tone. The object is to cultivate opportunities for cooperation and creativity, and to reduce the potential for conflict. Focus on a joint effort to find a solution to what is seen as a common problem. Avoid using threats and otherwise personalizing the problem. Make it possible for your opponent to accept your position without loss of face.

    _____

    _____

    _____

    _____

    _____

    _____

PART VI

DYNAMICS OF FAMILY BUSINESS

Wendy C. Handler, M.B.A., D.B.A.

OVERVIEW

Whether you are the potential heir to a family business, are thinking about going to work as an outsider in a family-held business, or might have any dealings with such a business, understanding the dynamics peculiar to entrepreneurial enterprises will be helpful in your ability to interact with the various individuals involved.

Surprisingly, only 30 percent of the family firms in the United States survive the transition to the second generation, and only 10 percent make it to the third generation (Beckhard and Dyer, 1983). Many of the reasons for the failures of family businesses are directly related to the problems that business founders have with planning for and allowing for someone to take over, known as "succession."

Succession

Various research studies have suggested that succession problems are tied to the psychological elements that originally motivated the founder to start a business. Collins, Moore, and Unwalla (1964) discovered a significant similarity in the backgrounds and childhood experiences of many entrepreneurs. "Themes such as 'the escape from poverty,' 'the escape from insecurity,' 'death and sudden death,' [and] 'the parents that went away,' . . . occurred repeatedly. They seemed part of the entrepreneurial 'family romance' " (Zaleznik and Kets de Vries 1985, p. 221). To the entrepreneur, the business becomes his link to reality and his way of dealing with conflicts of identification developed during childhood.[1]

Levinson (1971) argues that the firm can give the founder meaning in three important ways. First, since the entrepreneur can have unresolved conflicts with his father, he starts the business to escape the authority of a powerful figure (Collins, Moore, and Unwalla 1964). In other words, the entrepreneur aspires to run his own empire as a result of his ongoing "need for control" (Collins, Moore, and Unwalla 1964, p. 161), a need evidenced by the serious difficulty that he has addressing issues of dominance, submission, and suspicion about "authority" (Kets de Vries 1985, p. 161). Second, because the business can represent the "baby" as well as the "mistress" for the entrepreneur, it is an intense source of energy and interest. Those who work for the entrepreneur are therefore seen as tools for shaping the company, and they are denied power.

Third, the business can represent an extension of the entrepreneur, and therefore succession issues get mixed up with the founder's "desire for applause" (Kets de Vries 1985, p. 163) and his own personal concern about the monument that he will leave behind. Given the meaningful relationship that develops between the business and the founder, it is not surprising that "it is in the nature of founders/entrepreneurs to have difficulty giving up what they have created" (Schein 1985, p. 275).

A fourth element should be added to the list of psychological elements that reinforce the founder's bond with the business, namely his resistance to facing the thought of

---

This overview was written by Wendy C. Handler, M.B.A., D.B.A.

Dr. Handler teaches family business management at Babson College and conducts research on succession in family firms from the perspective of next-generation family members.

1. Editor's note: Since the vast majority of family businesses that have now reached successor stages were started by men, the author generally refers to the founders by masculine pronouns. As more and more women are becoming entrepreneurs, this will clearly begin to change. In addition, more daughters are now being seen as viable successors in family firms (Gabriella Stern, "More Daughters Take the Reins at Family Businesses, *Wall Street Journal*, 12 June 1991, B1).

aging, dying, or being incapacitated (Lansberg 1988). The reluctance to face mortality is most easily maintained when the founder is in good health.

The degree of resistance that a founder has to planning for his succession will be influenced by the interaction between individual characteristics (for example, the reluctance of the founder to face aging, retirement, and death) and situational variables. Health, particularly poor health, has been found to be one of the most important factors causing early retirement in the general population. In family firms, a major health crisis can move a founder and his family to confront succession (Bork 1986; Lansberg 1988). Also, resistance to succession can be minimized if the founder has other interests that he wants to pursue after retirement (Walker and Lazer 1978).

The founder's resistance to planning for succession is related to the founder's inability to dissociate himself from the firm by spending time away from the business (Crane 1982) and by not being willing or able to delegate responsibility to others. Retirement is threatening because it represents a change from the continuity of one's daily routine. For the entrepreneur, barriers to retirement and succession also include the loss of heroic stature and mission (Sonnenfeld 1988). If the founder can conceive of his retirement as a beginning, with opportunities for new "life and career planning" (Bridges 1986), he may be more willing to face succession issues. Moreover, the founder's capacity for self-reflection or raised awareness (Lansberg 1988) around the issue of "letting go" (Osherson 1980) may reduce the degree of tension and loss felt during the succession process.

Problems with succession also may take place at interpersonal and group levels. If an owner's decision to retire cannot be juxtaposed with an heir's appropriateness and readiness to take over, succession may not occur, even under the best possible conditions (Barnes and Hershon 1976; Churchill and Hatten 1987; Stern 1986). Also, most founders have certain preconceived ideas concerning the age, gender, family affiliation, and education of their successors. A potential heir who does not fulfill all the "necessary" requirements may be denied the mentoring that he or she requires to take over the business. The founder may also simply prefer a particular successor, who is not necessarily the "best" one for the business's future. Finally, the succession process can be sabotaged when power imbalances and conflicts within the family (Levinson 1971; Stern 1986) permeate the business. Such conflicts can create a dynamic that makes the choice of a successor difficult or impossible (Bork 1986) and ultimately result in the sale or downfall of the business (Jones 1986). Systemic resistance to succession is minimized when there is only one child to whom the business can pass (Bork 1986).

The Owner/Entrepreneur's Role Adjustment

The owner's role adjustment to retirement, defined in terms of a diminishing level of involvement in the family firm, has been found to be integral to succession and central to the next-generation family member's experience. Successors indicate that their own roles in their family businesses are shaped by the roles of their predecessors. Specifically, the entrepreneur seems to progress through various distinguishable phases of lessening involvement in the business over time, while the next-generation family member(s) move through phases of increasing involvement.

For the owner, the diminishing level of involvement and authority in the organization may come about as a response to personal issues (health, age, and other interests) organizational factors (growth, need for change, technological innovations); environmental pressures (turbulence, uncertainty [Pfeffer and Salancik 1978]); and/or to accommodate the next-generation family member. The role adjustment is typically a slow and subtle process, which can be thought of as a succession "dance." Central to the progression of this dance is the transferral of leadership experience, authority, decision-making power, and equity. The ongoing evolution of this role transition is critical to the effectiveness of succession in family businesses.

Joining the Family Business

Next-generation family members join family businesses for many reasons: (1) to meet their career interests; (2) to develop their personal identities; and (3) to satisfy their needs associated with their life stages in the context of the family firm.

In this regard, individuals in their early twenties are concerned with exploration of life's options, while advancement is critical in one's late twenties and thirties. Balance between work and other activities is the concern for individuals in their forties. The degree to which each of these life-stage needs can be met in the context of the family firm is critical to the quality of the individual's experience.

The nature of involvement of family members can be distinguished in terms of three categories:

- *Helper.* The helper joins to help the family in the organization for an uncertain period of time. Often the helper joins at the early stages of the firm's development, when family members may need to be relied on for flexible work hours and pay. The helper may stay to learn the business "from the bottom up"; in this case, he or she usually does not have a regular title or position but is expected to do all kinds of work.

  For the helper, the family firm may serve as a safety net and security blanket. If the helper is a son, daughter, or other relative, he or she may have some limitations—for example, timidness; lack of confidence to seek work beyond the protective cover of the family; sheer lack of business power, creativity, and talent; or lack of ambition. The individual may choose to enter and remain in the family firm because of the security as well as potential shelter it provides from having to address personal weaknesses. This is a harsh reality that is often among the hardest things for parents, sisters, brothers, aunts, and uncles to face.
- *Apprentice.* Some individuals use the family firm as a stepping stone on a career path. They are interested in it as a convenient career opportunity—a launching pad to other job choices.
- *Socialized successor.* This individual joins and becomes socialized into the family business with the strong likelihood of becoming the next-generation president.

Gaining Credibility

For the potential heirs to a family business, gaining credibility can be a unique problem. Founding parents often have difficulty believing that their children ever grow up. They may push their children to enter the business but then fail to give them responsibility or encouragement. Few next-generation family members, for example, appear to be given direct positive feedback about their performance. Often they must find out from others if the parent thinks they are doing a good job.

Gaining credibility is typically slow and gradual between parent and child. Generally, the parent (particularly the founder) has worked hard and expects the child to do the same. Families often have high expectations of family members in the firm, with one implication being that *because* they are family, they do not have to be praised.

Alternatively, there can also be "credibility inflation" or overkill with a "pet child" or other family member who "can do no wrong." A family or parental myopia contributes to a grossly exaggerated level of credit and praise for the family member, which can be demoralizing to other high-performing family members as well as to nonfamily members.

Family Dynamics

In addition to the psychological elements of the founder, the motivations of the potential successors, and problems with credibility, family dynamics present unique problems in family firms. When there are no boundaries between family life and the business, tensions from one may spill over into the other. Family strains occur when the issues concerning the business pervade family discussions and interactions outside the business. Business strains occur due to excessive family emotionality, conflict, unrealistic expectations, and arbitrary policies for family members within the context of the business.

For example, in the case of siblings and relatives—especially if they are close in age and of the same gender—rivalry and jealousy may crop up if the relationship is not carefully managed. In addition, the relationship between predecessor and next-generation family member can have a critical effect within the business.

Managing the Family in the Family Business

While there are no absolute prescriptions, four strategies can help in the ascendance of a successor in a family business:

- *Expression of interest.* As a next-generation family member, it is important to express interest in the family business and to discuss goals if one is interested. Next-generation family members should be direct and forthright about the responsibility they want and feel capable of taking on.
- *Acquisition of experience.* A family member should acquire practical business experience outside the family business, particularly if one is uncertain about a career in the family business. This helps increase knowledge, experience, and confidence. It is also the single most effective way to enhance credibility with employees in a family business who may be skeptical about the qualifications of family members.
- *Acceptance of responsibility.* Family members should take responsibility for their own development and consider how—or if—personal goals are to be met by the family business. In addition, individuals who hope to become head of the business should learn as much about the business as they can.
- *Establishment of networks.* Next-generation individuals should cultivate relationships with mentors, peers, and family members who can act as coaches, protectors, role models, counselors, or friends. It may be unwise to turn to parents for mentoring because of the possible inherent conflict of interest. Looking to respected individuals outside the family for counseling and long-term development support is a good strategy. Becoming involved in a peer network is also highly recommended.

The following three strategies can improve family dynamics and help prevent conflict in family firms.

- *Definition of responsibility.* Responsibilities should be clearly based on personal capabilities and interests. In family businesses plagued by conflict, siblings typically perform similar jobs, competing with each other and vying for attention from parents and other family members.

- *Emphasis on issues.* Family members, if they fight, should fight over issues, not emotions.
- *Establishment of mechanisms.* Establishing mechanisms, such as a family council or regular meetings, can enhance communication, understanding, and trust, and allow the airing of problems or differences that might otherwise be ignored—but that will not go away.

Understanding the dynamics of family firms makes maneuvering within family systems more workable and enhances the likelihood of a firm's survival beyond the founder's generation.

References

Barnes, L. B., and Hershon, S. A., 1976. Transferring power in the family business. *Harvard Business Review* 54 (4): 105–114.

Beckhard, R., and Dyer, W. G., Jr. 1983. Managing continuity in the family-owned business. *Organizational Dynamics* 12 (1): 5–12.

Bork, D. 1986. *Family business, risky business: How to make it work.* New York: AMACOM.

Bridges, W. 1986. Managing organizational transitions. *Organizational Dynamics* 15 (1): 24–34.

Churchill, N. C., and Hatten, K. J. 1987. Non-market-based transfers of wealth and power: A research framework for family businesses. *American Journal of Small Business* 11 (3): 51–64.

Collins, O., Moore, D., and Unwalla, D. 1964. *The enterprising man.* East Lansing: Bureau of Business Research, Michigan State University.

Crane, M. A. 1982. How to keep families from feuding. *Inc.* 4 (2): 73–74, 78–79.

Jones, A. S. 1986. The fall of the house of Bingham. *New York Times*, 19 January 1986, 1F.

Kets de Vries, M. 1985. "The dark side of entrepreneurship." *Harvard Business Review* 63 (6): 160–167.

Lansberg, I. S. 1988. The succession conspiracy. *Family Business Review* 1 (2): 119–143.

Levinson, H. 1971. Conflicts that plague family business. *Harvard Business Review* 49 (2): 90–98.

Osherson, S. 1980. *Holding on or letting go: Men and career change at midlife.* New York: Free Press.

Pfeffer, J., and Salancik, G. R. 1978. *The external control of organizations.* New York: Harper & Row.

Schein, E. H. 1985. *Organizational culture and leadership: A dynamic view.* San Francisco: Jossey-Bass.

Sonnenfeld, J. 1988. *The Hero's farewell: What happens when CEOs retire.* New York: Oxford University Press.

Stern, M. H. 1986. *Inside the family-held business: A practical guide for entrepreneurs and their advisors.* New York: Harcourt Brace Jovanovich.

Walker, J. W., and Lazer, H. L. 1978. *The end of mandatory retirement: Implications for management.* New York: Wiley.

Zaleznik, A., and Kets de Vries, M. F. 1985. *Power and the corporate mind.* Chicago: Bonus Books.

Twelve Commandments for the Son/Daughter in the Family Business

1. Thou shalt continue the dream of the family business if thou art interested. (Otherwise, thou shalt allow thyself to pursue thy own dream.)
2. Thou shalt be involved in developing a workable organization and making it visible on a chart.
3. Thou shalt continue to gain credibility by improving thy knowledge of all aspects of the business.
4. Thou shalt be involved in developing an accepted accounting system and making available the data therefrom to thy managers, advisors, and directors.
5. Thou shalt be involved in developing a council of competent advisors.
6. Thou shalt be involved in developing a performance review system: Even those at the top should be subject to review.
7. Thou shalt work with others in the business to minimize the negative effects of nepotism so as to make the business attractive to nonfamily members.
8. Thou shalt express interest and dedication as the successor or help in the determination of a successor in a timely fashion.
9. Thou shalt be in charge of thy own learning as successor by actively participating in choosing and working with a mentor.
10. Thou shalt actively involve thyself in an interested and supportive way in the estate plans of thy parents.
11. Thou shalt advocate family meetings or forums as a way of facilitating communication concerning the family and the business.
12. Thou shalt apportion thy time to see that these commandments be kept.

These commandments have been adapted by Wendy C. Handler, in part (#2, 4, 5, 12) from L. Danco, *Inside the Family Business* (Cleveland, Ohio: University Press, 1980), inside back cover. Danco presents his "Twelve Commandments for the Business Owner" as advice for the head of the family business. The commandments presented above are given as advice for the successor generation.

HINTS FOR A SUCCESSFUL SUCCESSION

We've all heard stories about family businesses that have "gone under" because of mismanagement or family conflicts. We also have heard stories about how family firms have been "run into the ground" by the children of an entrepreneur who has retired.

These stories are all too commonplace; in fact, according to statistics, only three out of ten family businesses survive into the second generation, and only one out of ten survive into the third generation. Listed here are ten hints for the owner and ten hints for likely heirs that may ultimately help ensure a smoother and more successful succession.

TEN HINTS FOR THE OWNER

Hint 1: Seek Out Advisors

Succession is a difficult and complicated issue. It involves making plans for retirement, the future of the family, and the business. It therefore is much more difficult to plan for if done single-handedly. As an owner, you should actively seek out a lawyer who specializes in estate planning, a business consultant, and if necessary, a personal counselor. Ideally, the lawyer should be knowledgeable about the tax ramifications of estate planning for closely held corporations; the consultant should be experienced with small and/or family firms, and the personal counselor should have family therapy training. Other owners of family firms can also serve as important sources of support and advice.

Hint 2: Set Up an Advisory Board of Directors

If you do not already have one, now is a good time to assemble a board that can counsel you on succession. You should specifically consider setting up an advisory board—one made up of both outside people as well as family members—that will advise you on various issues (rather than simply function as a "paper board"). Outside advisors should include others beyond the family banker or lawyer. Local university professors and other respected members of the community are excellent choices. (See L. Danco and D. Jonovic, *Outside Directors in the Family-Owned Business* [Cleveland: University Press, 1981] for more information.)

Hint 3: Analyze Yourself and Your Role in the Business

Allow yourself the opportunity to think about yourself and your role in the business. Think also about the past, present, and future of your organization. Realize that while you may be indispensable to the business now, it can't be that way forever. And the only way

---

These hints were written by Wendy C. Handler. Used by permission.

to ensure that your business will have a long life is to plan for succession now. Finally, consider what you would like to do in the future by contemplating new life and career plans.

Hint 4: Make Sure Children Are Invited but Not Pushed into the Business

You should make sure that your children understand they are welcome but not expected or under pressure to join the firm. Also, make sure they are aware that it can be a good idea to work for another firm before joining the family business.

Hint 5: Create a Forum to Openly Discuss Family and Business Issues

Open, honest discussion concerning the family and business is critical to the future of both parties. One way to stimulate this discussion is to plan family meetings at which ideas and plans for the family and the firm can be presented and discussed openly. This should be a forum held for all interested family members, at which leadership of the meeting is rotated, and for which responsibilities are shared. It should be held at a regular, previously determined, and agreed-upon time—possibly once a month or even once every two months. These meetings should not be held during business hours or around the dinner table. The determination of a family plan, a business philosophy, and an executive succession plan are several of the possible objectives for these meetings. (See J. Ward, *Keeping the Family Business Healthy* [San Francisco: Jossey-Bass, 1987] for more information.)

Hint 6: Delegate Responsibilities to Others

Once the firm grows in size, it becomes necessary to let others perform and manage the day-to-day tasks of the organization. Your time needs to be devoted to strategic planning and the determination of future goals and objectives. Delegating responsibilities to others is therefore one of the first steps toward preparing for succession. Make sure that the tasks that are delegated are challenging and meaningful, particularly to those subordinates who are capable and interested in learning. A good test is to mentally put yourself in that person's shoes.

Hint 7: Establish Mentors to Train Potential Heirs

An integral part of the succession process is the training and development of potential heirs. It is advised that more than one heir be trained, if possible, to ensure the future of the firm. In-laws and daughters should be welcomed into the business. A mentor should never be assigned, but rather jointly selected with the heir to be trained.

Hint 8: Provide Constructive Feedback to Family Members Involved in the Firm

Owners of family businesses have been accused of being tougher on their own family than on non-family members. It therefore is important to remember that family members deserve positive as well as negative feedback. After all, family members are especially sensitive to too much criticism because they are family. They also may decide to leave the business if they feel they are not appreciated.

Hint 9: Avoid Bringing Family Conflicts into the Business / Avoid Letting Business Issues Dominate at Home

There should be a rule that personal family conflicts should not be brought into the business. There is nothing productive about family feuds on company time. Find a time outside the family business to discuss problems and differences. Similarly, business issues should not be the main topic of conversations for families at home (that means limiting conversation around these issues at the dinner table). Also, the family should be able to pursue activities outside the business that are enjoyable and non–business related (like baseball games, the movies, etc.).

Hint 10: Start the Planning Process Early and Take It Incrementally

Succession planning really involves three distinct types of planning (often lumped together under the term *executive succession planning*):

1. Training and development of successor(s)
2. Financial/estate planning
3. Personal retirement planning

Since planning in these three areas is necessary and time consuming, it should begin early enough (some say seven to eight years before the owner's planned retirement) and taken incrementally. This is the only way to be sure that the succession process will be ultimately smooth and successful.

TEN HINTS FOR POTENTIAL HEIRS

Hint 1: Express Interest in the Business

If you are thinking about going into the family business, the first step is to show interest in it. This sounds very obvious, but you would be amazed at how many heirs don't say anything. This leaves your parents in a situation of having to guess whether you may want to be a successor.

This works the other way as well—if you are not interested, make clear that you are not. It's much easier than playing a guessing game.

Hint 2: Be Committed and Involved in the Business

If you are an heir who is considering a future as successor in the family business, then you are going to have to prove yourself. This means commitment and involvement. What is ironic is that often friends of possible heirs to family businesses will tell them that "they have it easy." The truth is that they don't! Your parents actually expect more from you than another employer would. You really have no choice but to show your dedication or find a new job.

Hint 3: Be Patient and Respectful

Keep in mind how hard your parents have worked to make this business a reality. It is by being patient and respecting the hard work your parents have put into the business that the business may eventually be yours.

Hint 4: Gain as Much Information as You Can

You can never know too much about the business. Nor can you know too much about the industry, its suppliers, competitors, customers, and so forth. Be in charge of your own learning, and continually ask yourself if you are finding out what you need to know. Also, work with your parents to find an appropriate mentor in the business who can coach and instruct you.

Hint 5: Express Your Hopes and Concerns About the Future

Even though your parents may not ask, they are probably very interested in some of your hopes and concerns about the future of the business and your role in the business. If you are being trained as a successor, you should let them know how you feel about entering that role. This might be most natural during a family meeting, where the topic is "a frank discussion on succession." The idea is for each family member to discuss his or her hopes and issues honestly, with all family members listening carefully and empathically. Sometimes an objective party who serves as mediator can help.

Hint 6: Acquire Outside Experience

Acquiring outside experience is very important for potential heirs of a family business. It allows them not only to learn from a different vantage point, but it also provides a basis of comparison with the family business. It is possible to make an analogy between this and dating and marriage: How many times have you been told that it's better to date several people rather than just one before you marry? Similarly, if you have only worked in one business, how can you know how good you have it?

Hint 7: Show Maturity and Responsibility

Clearly, if you are interested in being a successor in the family business someday, you will probably have to prove that you are capable of such a position. Showing maturity and responsibility are therefore critical. Often, heirs of family businesses are considered immature and spoiled since they act as if they can "get away with things" because of their membership in the family. However, if you are truly interested in the business, this is a dangerous strategy that really isn't fair to anyone, including yourself.

Hint 8: Avoid Bringing Personal Problems to Work and Business Problems Home

Personal or family problems should be discussed outside the business. Business problems should be kept in the business. There is a distinction between family and business that needs to be maintained by the heirs as well as their parents and other relatives.

Hint 9: Work on Collaborating with Your Siblings (Relatives) in the Business

Since you might be working alongside your siblings and other relatives, it is important that you try to build a business relationship with them. This will make your life in the business both more rewarding and more enjoyable.

Hint 10: Evaluate Your Performance and Personal Objectives Against Your Goals on a Regular Basis

Since many family businesses do not have performance reviews, it is very important that potential heirs personally evaluate their performance in the business. They need to be honest with themselves by asking the following types of questions:

1. What are my strengths, and on what do I need to work?
2. What aspects of the business do I need to learn?
3. Do I have the qualities it takes to be a leader in the business?
4. Am I happy working in the business?
5. Is there anything else I need to be doing to meet my goals?

Questions for Personal Reflection and Planning

In deciding whether to go into or remain in the family business, ask yourself the following questions:

Questions Associated with Career Needs

1. In what ways does this position satisfy my career needs?
   a. How long have I been in this position?
   b. Does the work excite me? Challenge me? Is it rewarding?
   c. What is it about the work that I find suitable for me?
   d. What is it about the work that I would like to change?
   e. Are there other areas within this firm that interest me?
2. To what extent am I aware of my own career goals?
3. Is this the career path that I want to be pursuing?
   a. How does this career compare with earlier life thoughts about what I would be pursuing at this time?
   b. What other career paths have I thought of pursuing? How attractive and how realistic are they?

Questions Associated with Personal Identity Needs

1. To what extent can I be my own person, capable of my own accomplishments, and accountable to myself, while involved in the family firm?
   a. To what extent am I aware of my personal development goals?
   b. To what extent am I pursuing these goals in the family firm?
   c. How are my goals related to the business goals and the former-generation owner's goals?
   d. To what extent do I feel good about myself at work?
   e. In what areas do I feel less than good about myself at work? Why?
2. What is necessary for the ongoing development of my own sense of self?
   a. What do I need to do
      1. in terms of task learning?
      2. in terms of personal learning?
      3. in terms of timing?
      4. in terms of relationships?
   b. What do others need to do?

This exercise was written by Wendy C. Handler. Used by permission.

Questions Associated with Life-Stage Needs

1. In what ways are my needs changing over time, and how can they be satisfied through the family firm?
   a. How can I fulfill my desire to explore life and career options available while entering adulthood? (Have I worked outside the family firm, traveled, pursued additional education?)
   b. How can I fulfill my desire to advance in life and career while in early adulthood?
   c. How can I fulfill my desire for balance between career and other life activities while entering middle adulthood?

Circular Questions About the Family Business System

Be sure that your answers include brief explanations.

Name of Family Business_____

Founder's Relation to You_____

Present Leader_____

1. How would I describe my own role in the family?

   _____
   _____

   How would my mother describe it?

   _____
   _____

   How would my father describe it?

   _____
   _____

   How would other family members describe it?

   _____
   _____

2. How would I describe my own role in the family business?

   _____
   _____

   How would my mother describe it?

   _____
   _____

   How would my father describe it?

   _____
   _____

   How would other family members describe it?

   _____
   _____

This exercise was written by Wendy C. Handler. Used by permission.

3. If I asked for one sentence about the family business, my mother would say

_____

_____

My father would say

_____

_____

I would say

_____

_____

My brothers and sisters would say

_____

_____

4. Who would be most upset if I didn't go into the family business? Least upset?

_____

_____

5. To whom do I talk most about the family business? Least?

_____

_____

6. What would the people to whom I talk to most (both inside and outside the family business) say I need to watch out for in terms of the family business?

_____

_____

7. When and if I join the family business, who do I think I could count on to help me most? Least?

_____

_____

8. Who would have the most confidence in my ability to succeed? Doubts?

_____

_____

9. Who could teach me the most about the business?

_____

_____

10. What obstacles would I need to overcome in the family business? What internal (i.e., personal) and external (i.e., friends, information, consultants, etc.) strengths could I draw on?

_____

_____

11. Who in my family is most confident that women can be as effective leaders as men?

_____

_____

12. If I do join the family business, what would my mother say are some of the reasons?

_____

_____

What would my father say are some of the reasons?

_____

_____

What would other members of the family say?

_____

_____

13. If I didn't join the family business, what would my mother say are some of the reasons?

_____

_____

What would my father say are some of the reasons?

_____

_____

What would other members of the family say?

_____

_____

Succession in the Family Firm: Personal Assessment Questionnaire

What makes the family firm a unique institution in our society is the fact that its future is ultimately in the hands of the family in control. This means that members of the family must eventually face the decision to plan for succession. Recent research indicates that the opportunity to systematically reflect on one's style of coping with succession issues may have important implications for the future of the firm. This brief questionnaire, designed for your own use and not meant to be shared, is to assist in such reflection.

1. Briefly describe what you have been doing, if anything, to prepare for succession. What roles have other members of your family played?

    _____
    _____
    _____
    _____
    _____
    _____

2. How do you feel about the way succession is being planned for in your organization?

    _____
    _____
    _____
    _____
    _____
    _____

3. What hopes and concerns exist concerning succession? What answers would you like to have?

    _____
    _____
    _____
    _____
    _____
    _____

This exercise was written by Wendy C. Handler. Used by permission.

4. To what degree is succession discussed and decisions concerning succession shared in your family? In your organization? How do you feel about this?

_____
_____
_____
_____
_____
_____

5. What need to be the next steps in preparing for succession?

_____
_____
_____
_____
_____

6. What else is important to note?

_____
_____
_____
_____
_____
_____

Succession:
An Unfinished Piece of Business for John Smith

John Smith is proud of his accomplishments. He has a chain of retail stores in Boston that together brought in over $5 million in sales last year. Just recently, he purchased another store that he would like to open by the end of the year; he's not sure who he will find to manage it.

John Smith believes that his business success has been due to his own total involvement. His primary philosophy is "turn your back, and you never know what might happen." He is in good health at the age of sixty-five, and he still works a minimum of eighty hours a week overseeing the whole business.

John Smith's three sons and two daughters have all been involved with the business. His oldest son and daughter have left to pursue their own interests, one in medicine and the other in psychological counseling. That has left the two younger sons, James and David, and his younger daughter, Sandra. They are both still in college but work in the business over their summer vacations. Recently, James announced that he is considering taking the LSATs and applying to law school. David is still undecided about the career he will pursue; he is only a sophomore. Similarly, Sandra, a freshman, is also undecided.

John Smith has often thought about what is going to happen to the future of the business. He never talks about it to his children, although he does bring it up to his wife from time to time. John was concerned when he heard that James was thinking of law school. He had always thought that James would never leave the business. As he puts it, "I'm traditional; I believe that a son's place is by his father in business, and a woman's place is in the home." He is aware that his values are somewhat old-fashioned, but he says, "I can't help but feel this way; after all, what would happen to a business owned by a woman if she got pregnant?"

Questions for Discussion

1. What's going on here? Why aren't things turning out the way John Smith intended?
2. In what ways do you identify with John Smith, his wife, and his children?
3. Why does John Smith seem to be reluctant to bring up succession with his children?
4. If you were John Smith, what would you do now?
5. If you are part of a family that has a family business, how is your situation similar to or different from John Smith's?
6. What recommendations would you make to stimulate succession?
7. What lessons can be learned from John Smith?

This case was written by Wendy C. Handler. Used by permission.

Anthony Deluca

Anthony Deluca is founder and president of a successful real estate development firm in Los Angeles, California. He has designed and built over $50 million of residential and commercial real estate in some of the most desirable areas in and around Los Angeles. Deluca has seen his business grow and prosper since he started it thirty-five years ago, something he attributes to his active and constant involvement. He believes that "things run best when the owner is there," and he has even been known to visit a site at 4 A.M. just to make sure the security guard isn't sleeping. Deluca is also proud of the confidence and respect that he has engendered over the years in an industry where bullying and deception are commonplace. As he explained in a recent article in the Los Angeles *Times*, "I'm not going to be pushed around by anybody." This includes his family.

Now 63 years old, Anthony has been married for thirty-one years and has ten children, six boys and four girls, ranging in age from 19 to 30. The oldest and youngest are boys, while the middle children are equally divided between boys and girls. Six of the children have gone to USC, which is Anthony's alma mater and where he taught law for almost a quarter of a century. However, only two have graduated, despite the fact that Anthony is a big believer in education.

All ten of Anthony's children have worked in the family business, several having been sidetracked into it while still in college. For example, Cindy left USC after a year to work in the office of the family business, but after awhile, deciding that she was too sensitive to handle her father's temper, she left to become a secretary in the school of management of a leading university.

Timothy, the oldest son, only worked for the family business for a short time while getting his college degree. After graduating from Stanford, Timothy left the business saying he wanted more challenge and responsibility. He enrolled in a master's degree program in real estate development at MIT and is now working for a large development firm in Boston.

The other Deluca children are involved in occupations such as nursing and retail store management. The second-oldest boy, like his father, has decided to become an entrepreneur. He owns three bakeries and has recently recruited his youngest brother, who is interested in being a chef, to work for him.

Only three children are presently contemplating their futures in the business. Two are working there now: Jason, who is twenty-seven, has been working for his father since he was eleven. He is a maintenance man, and he has been called "the most intimidated and influenced by Dad" by people who know him. The other son, Jerry, worked many hours in the business while still in college. He is twenty-one, and he recently graduated from USC. His senior year was complicated by his working for the business and being required to carry a beeper around on his belt so that he could be contacted while at school. It was not unusual for him to get called out of class to answer a page and then have to report to work.

This case was written by Wendy C. Handler. The author would like to thank John P. DiGiovanni for his assistance in preparing this case. Used by permission.

Jerry admires his father, saying that he is great as an entrepreneur although not as good as an organizer and planner. He's glad to be helping his father out in the business because he feels he owes him something. "After all," says Jerry, "he raised and supported ten kids." He also notes that his Dad is "tougher on the family than with the business."

After spending a week with his oldest brother in Boston over spring break, Jerry says he understands why Timothy hasn't gone into the business and probably never will. Jerry also notes, "Personally, I never thought I would be one of the kids in line for the business, given that I am second youngest."

Although his title is Manager of Commercial Properties, Jerry explains, "I have a hard time trying to figure out what the hell I'm doing sometimes." He is excited, however, at his recent purchase of a boat, which will be his summer diversion.

Finally, there is Karen, who has just graduated from Duke Law School and has accepted a job with a local law firm. For her, it was a reluctant decision made with a good deal of guilt over her father's subtle hints that "the business could use a lawyer." On accepting the job, she explained, "I'll work for the law firm for a couple of years, and then I might go work for Dad."

Lately, Anthony Deluca has been increasingly complaining that he is growing tired. He talks about cutting back his sixty-five-plus hours per week in the business, but so far he hasn't. The long hours have been part of his schedule—what he has grown used to. In the interview with the LA *Times*, Deluca explained, "I even gave up teaching, which was my first love, for business." However, the business has also taken its toll on Deluca's health and his marriage. He and his wife have long ago grown apart: There is little sharing between them. Both are aware of this, but it has received little discussion. Silence is preferred over conflict in the Deluca family.

Questions for Discussion

1. What stands out for you about this family—its members, relationships, and so forth?
2. What are the implications for succession?
3. What needs to be done to enhance the chances for a smooth succession? (I.e., What would you do if you were Anthony Deluca?)

The Family Hotel

In this role play, you will be assigned one of three roles to play: Charlie Greene, the sixty-four-year-old founder of a hotel business; Pat Greene, Charlie's only child, age 24; or Veronica Greene, Charlie's 60-year-old wife. Some people may be asked to serve as observers.

Your family-run hotel has been in operation for ten years, and it has been doing well. Today, however, Pat has asked for some time with Charlie and Veronica to have a serious talk.

PROCEDURE

Step 1   (5–10 minutes)

Read your part carefully, making notes about those areas of concern that you would like to raise when you meet with the other members of your "family."

Step 2   (15–20 minutes)

Working in groups of three, with each person having a different role, present the problem as you see it through the role you have been given. Working together, develop a solution that is acceptable to all three family members.

Step 3   (10–15 minutes, depending on size of class)

Have a spokesperson from each group report on his or her "family's" solution. Solutions should be listed in a place visible to all.

Step 4   (open-ended)

Discuss the various solutions, considering the merits and drawbacks of each.

Step 5   (15–20 minutes)

Combine each group with one or two others and consider the following questions:

a.   What does it take to gain credibility in a family business?
b.   What are the factors and conditions needed for this to happen?

Working in these combined groups, develop a list of the factors associated with gaining credibility in a family business. Present these to the class.

Step 6   (open-ended)

Class discussion.

This exercise was written by Wendy C. Handler. Used by permission.

The Family Hotel
Observer Sheet

1. List the concerns and interests of each of the family members.

    Pat: _____

    _____

    _____

    Charlie: _____

    _____

    _____

    Veronica: _____

    _____

    _____

2. What resistances to the situation does each family member demonstrate in cooperating with each other?

    Pat: _____

    _____

    _____

    Charlie: _____

    _____

    _____

    Veronica: _____

    _____

    _____

3. What can each family member do to gain credibility with the others?

    Pat: _____

    _____

    _____

    Charlie: _____

    _____

    _____

    Veronica: _____

    _____

    _____

PART VII

INTERNATIONAL ASPECTS OF
ORGANIZATIONAL BEHAVIOR

OVERVIEW

In this section, we consider a relatively new phenomenon, the global marketplace. Although trade has been going on between the world's nations for a considerably long time, modern methods of communication and transportation have made such trade more efficient and more desirable.

In the United States, as in many countries, domestic markets alone can no longer provide adequate marketplaces. To the degree that companies must grow to prosper, growth beyond one's borders—international trade—is not only useful, it may also be necessary for survival.

International Gaffes

For more than a few companies, forays into the world marketplace have proven to be embarrassing. When Chevrolet boldly introduced their Nova model in Spain, for example, they overlooked an important fact: In Spanish, the phrase *"No va"* means "It doesn't go." This didn't exactly make Spaniards rush out to their local dealerships.

Coca-Cola has been one of the most active companies in the world market. As of 1990, Coke's American sales represented only 15 percent of their total sales volume. Though the international marketing of Coke was a success, the early days were marked by a few mishaps. Coke officials were startled to learn that the phrase "Coca-Cola," when translated into Chinese, means, "Bite the wax tadpole." Imagine turning on your TV and seeing Paula Abdul sing, "Just for the taste of it: Diet Bite the Wax Tadpole." Coke quickly decided to change their name into a Chinese phrase that means, "May your mouth rejoice."

Coke also stumbled when they first introduced their product to West Germany. When the "Coke Adds Life" slogan from a few years ago was translated into German, it was somehow transformed into a very different motto: "Coke brings your ancestors back from the grave." If it could live up to that claim, Coke would surely send all of its competitors to the grave.

As you might have concluded from these anecdotes, maneuvering in the international marketplace must be done cautiously. Language barriers and cultural differences between the United States and Japan, for example, can make business ventures extremely tricky, and negotiating can be difficult.

Not long ago, an American company formed a joint venture with a Japanese distributor. The basis for the partnership was solid: The U.S. firm had manufacturing and technological expertise; the Japanese firm had a grip on the intricate Japanese distribution network.

The American company had a hard time collaborating with its new partner because of vast differences in corporate culture. The American firm wanted its Japanese partner to appoint a young and aggressive marketing manager, Yoshi Mitsui, to the position of joint venture president. However, in Japan, promising managerial candidates are kept within the structure of the parent company, so the "promotion" probably would have hurt Mitsui's career. It would also have been inappropriate to appoint a young manager ahead of several candidates with more seniority.

Accordingly, the Japanese company appointed a veteran manager who was mild mannered and nearing retirement. He wasn't entrepreneurial and assertive. Much to the surprise of the American partners, however, the veteran manager's style proved to be appropriate because the function of the Japanese manager is to be a facilitator in a participative decision-making process.

After Operation Desert Storm, salespeople from around the world flooded into Kuwait City, but their lack of understanding of the culture often meant failure to sell their wares. A frequently reported story was of a cellular telephone salesman from the United States who explained the use of his phone system to his potential customer by noting, "You can speak into it in Arabic at this end, and it comes out in Arabic at the other end." An insulted Kuwaiti asked reporters, "Does his think we've been living in tents in the desert all these years? We've had more sophisticated equipment than he has before they even saw it in the U.S."

McDonald's, on the other hand, has seemed to balance their successful formula with a cautious willingness to embrace local norms. McDonald's opened in late 1990 in Moscow and has had lines extending down the street every day it has operated, even though its charges are high by Russian standards. In some McDonald's franchises in Europe, where attitudes towards alcohol sales and consumption are quite different from those in the U.S., beer is sold.

International Resources

Some companies have taken advantage of significantly cheaper labor costs by building plants in places like Korea and Mexico. As natural resources such as oil, coal, and various minerals are depleted in North America, many American companies have sought and found new sources in such places as Indonesia, Brunei, and Australia. If oil drilling is not allowed in the wildlife refuge in northern Alaska, the quest may well intensify elsewhere.

While many opportunities for worldwide expansion exist, the global marketplace is infinitely complex and unpredictable. The economic ramifications of a united Europe by the turn of the century, for example, are just beginning to be understood. Before an American company forms business partnerships with a firm in another country, its leaders will have to reconsider virtually every aspect of organizational behavior. Not just language, but differences in acceptable leadership styles, worker norms, decision-making styles, negotiating styles, "groupism" versus individualism, and so forth make the global marketplace not just more complex, but more interesting and challenging as well.

The Culture Quiz

Few, if any, traditions and values are universally held. Many business dealings have succeeded or failed because of a manager's awareness or lack of understanding of the traditions and values of his or her foreign counterparts, With the world business community so closely intertwined and interdependent, it is critical that managers today become increasingly aware of the differences that exist.

How culturally aware are you? Try the questions below.

1. In Japan, loudly slurping your soup is considered to be
    a. rude and obnoxious.
    b. a sign that you like the soup.
    c. okay at home but not in public.
    d. something only foreigners do.

2. In Korea, business leaders tend to
    a. encourage strong commitment to teamwork and cooperation.
    b. encourage competition among subordinates.
    c. discourage subordinates from reporting directly, preferring information to come through well-defined channels.
    d. encourage close relationships with their subordinates.

3. In Japan, virtually every kind of drink is sold in public vending machines except for
    a. beer.
    b. diet drinks with saccharin.
    c. already sweetened coffee.
    d. soft drinks from U.S. companies.

4. In Latin America, managers
    a. are most likely to hire members of their own families.
    b. consider hiring members of their own families to be inappropriate.
    c. stress the importance of hiring members of minority groups.
    d. usually hire more people than are actually needed to do a job.

5. In Ethiopia, when a woman opens the front door of her home, it means
    a. she is ready to receive guests for a meal.
    b. only family members may enter.
    c. religious spirits may move freely in and out of the home.
    d. she has agreed to have sex with any man who enters.

This exercise was written by Janet W. Wohlberg.

6. In Latin America, business people
   a. consider it impolite to make eye contact while talking to one another.
   b. always wait until the other person is finished speaking before starting to speak.
   c. touch each other more than North Americans do under similar circumstances.
   d. avoiding touching one another as it is considered an invasion of privacy.

7. The principal religion in Malaysia is
   a. Buddhism.
   b. Judaism.
   c. Christianity.
   d. Islam.

8. In Thailand
   a. it is common to see men walking along holding hands.
   b. it is common to see a man and a woman holding hands in public.
   c. it is rude for men and women to walk together.
   d. men and women traditionally kiss each other on meeting in the street.

9. Pointing your toes at someone in Thailand is
   a. a symbol of respect, much like the Japanese bow.
   b. considered rude even if it is done by accident.
   c. an invitation to dance.
   d. the standard public greeting.

10. American managers tend to base the performance appraisals of their subordinates on performance, whereas in Iran, managers are more likely to base their performance appraisals on
    a. religion.
    b. seniority.
    c. friendship.
    d. ability.

11. In China, the status of every business negotiation is
    a. reported daily in the press.
    b. private, and details are not discussed publicly.
    c. subjected to scrutiny by a public tribunal on a regular basis.
    d. directed by the elders of every commune.

12. When rewarding an Hispanic worker for a job well done, it is best not to
    a. praise him or her publicly.
    b. say "thank you."
    c. offer a raise.
    d. offer a promotion.

13. In some South American countries, it is considered normal and acceptable to show up for an appointment
     a.   ten to fifteen minutes early.
     b.   ten to fifteen minutes late.
     c.   fifteen minutes to an hour late.
     d.   one to two hours late.

14. In France, when friends talk to one another,
     a.   they generally stand about three feet apart.
     b.   it is typical to shout.
     c.   they stand closer to one another than Americans do.
     d.   it is always with a third party present.

15. When giving flowers as gifts in Western Europe, be careful not to give
     a.   tulips and jonquils.
     b.   daisies and lilacs.
     c.   chrysanthemums and calla lilies.
     d.   lilacs and apple blossoms.

16. The appropriate gift-giving protocol for a male executive doing business in Saudi Arabia is to
     a.   give a man a gift from you to his wife.
     b.   present gifts to the wife or wives in person.
     c.   give gifts only to the eldest wife.
     d.   not give a gift to the wife at all.

17. If you want to give a necktie or a scarf to a Latin American, it is best to avoid the color
     a.   red.
     b.   purple.
     c.   green.
     d.   black.

18. The doors in German offices and homes are generally kept
     a.   wide open to symbolize an acceptance and welcome of friends and strangers.
     b.   slightly ajar to suggest that people should knock before entering.
     c.   half-opened, suggesting that some people are welcome and others are not.
     d.   tightly shut to preserve privacy and personal space.

19. In West Germany, leaders who display charisma are
     a.   not among the most desired.
     b.   the ones most respected and sought after.
     c.   invited frequently to serve on boards of cultural organizations.
     d.   pushed to get involved in political activities.

20.   American managers running businesses in Mexico have found that by increasing the
      salaries of Mexican workers, they
      a.   increased the numbers of hours the workers were willing to work.
      b.   enticed more workers to work night shifts.
      c.   decreased the number of hours workers would agree to work.
      d.   decreased production rates.

The Culture Quiz
Answers

1. b. Slurping your soup or noodles in Japan is good manners in both public and private. It indicates enjoyment and appreciation of the quality. (Source: Eiji Kanno, Japan Solo, Nitchi Map-Publishing Co., Inc., Ltd., Tokyo, 1985.)

2. b. Korean managers use a "divide-and rule" method of leadership that encourages competition among subordinates. They do this to ensure that they can exercise maximum control. In addition, they stay informed by having individuals report directly to them. This way, they can know more than anyone else. (Source: Richard M. Castaldi and Tjipyanto Soerjanto, Contrasts in East Asian management practices, *Journal of Management in Practice* 2 [1], 1990, 25–27.)

3. b. Saccharin-sweetened drinks may not be sold in Japan by law. On the other hand, beer, a wide variety of Japanese and international soft drinks, and so forth, are widely available from vending machines along the streets and in buildings. You're supposed to be at least eighteen to buy the alcoholic ones, however. (Source: Eiji Kanno, Japan Solo, Nitchi Map-Publishing Co., Inc., Ltd., Tokyo, 1985.)

4. a. Family is considered to be very important in Latin America, so managers are likely to hire their relatives more quickly than hiring strangers. (Source: Nancy J. Adler, *International Dimensions of Organizational Behavior*, 2nd ed. [Boston: PWS-Kent, 1991].)

5. d. The act, by a woman, of opening the front door, signifies that she has agreed to have sex with any man who enters. (Source: Adam Pertman, "Wandering no more," *Boston Globe Magazine*, 30 June 1991, 10 ff.)

6. c. Touching one another during business negotiations is common practice. (Source: Nancy J. Adler, *International Dimensions of Organizational Behavior*, 2nd ed. [Boston: PWS-Kent, 1991].)

7. d. Approximately 45 percent of the people in Malaysia follow Islam, the country's "official" religion. (Source: Hans Johannes Hoefer, ed., *Malaysia* [Englewood Cliffs, N.J.: Prentice-Hall, 1984].)

8. a. Men holding hands is considered a sign of friendship. Public displays of affection between men and women, however, are unacceptable. (Source: William Warren, Star Black, and M. R. Priya Rangsit, eds., *Thailand* [Englewood Cliffs, N.J.: Prentice-Hall, 1985].)

9. b. This is especially an insult if it is done deliberately, since the feet are the lowest part of the body. (Source: William Warren, Star Black, and M. R. Priya Rangsit, eds., *Thailand* [Englewood Cliffs, N.J.: Prentice-Hall, 1985].)

10. c. Adler suggests that friendship is valued over task competence in Iran. (Source: Nancy J. Adler, *International Dimensions of Organizational Behavior,* 2nd ed. [Boston: PWS-Kent, 1991].)

11. b. Public discussion of business dealings is considered inappropriate. Kaplan et al. report that "the Chinese may even have used a premature announcement to extract better terms from executives" who were too embarrassed to admit that there was never really a contract. (Source: Frederic Kaplan, Julian Sobin, Arne de Keijzer, *The China Guidebook: 1987 Edition,* Houghton Mifflin, Boston, 1987.)

12. a. Public praise for Hispanics and Asians is generally embarrassing because modesty is an important cultural value. (Source: Jim Braham, "No, You Don't Manage Everyone the Same," *Industry Week*, 6 Feb. 1989). In Japan, being singled out for praise is also an embarrassment. A common saying in that country is, "The nail that sticks up gets hammered down."

13. d. Whereas in the United States, being late is frowned upon, being late is not only accepted but expected in some South American countries. (Source: Lloyd S. Baird, James E. Post, and John F. Mahon, *Management: Functions and Responsibilities* [New York: Harper & Row, 1990].)

14. c. Personal space in most European countries is much smaller than in the United States. Americans generally like at least two feet of space around themselves, while it is not unusual for Europeans to be virtually touching. (Source: Lloyd S. Baird, James E. Post, and John F. Mahon, *Management: Functions and responsibilities* [New York: Harper & Row, 1990].)

15. c. Chrysanthemums and calla lilies are both associated with funerals. (Source: Theodore Fischer, *Pinnacle: International Issue* [March–April 1991], 4.)

16. d. In Arab cultures, it is considered inappropriate for wives to accept gifts or even attention from other men. (Source: Theodore Fischer, *Pinnacle: International Issue* [March–April 1991], 4.)

17. b. In Argentina and other Latin American countries, purple is associated with the serious fasting period of Lent. (Source: Theodore Fischer, *Pinnacle: International Issue* [March–April 1991], 4.)

18. d. Private space is considered so important in Germany that partitions are erected to separate people from one another; privacy screens and walled gardens are the norm. (Source: Julius Fast, *Subtext: Making Body Language Work* [New York: Viking Penguin Books, 1991], 207.)

19. a. Whereas in the United States, political leaders especially are increasingly selected on their ability to inspire, according to international organizational behavior expert Nancy J. Adler, charisma is a suspect trait in West Germany, where Hitler's charisma is still associated with evil intent and harmful outcomes. (Source: Nancy J. Adler, *International Dimensions of Organizational Behavior*, 2nd ed. [Boston: PWS-Kent, 1991], 149.)

20. c. Paying Mexican workers more means, in the eyes of the workers, that they can make the same amount of money in fewer hours and thus have more time for enjoying life. (Source: Nancy J. Adler, *International Dimensions of Organizational Behavior,* 2nd ed. [Boston: PWS-Kent, 1991], 30, 159.)

Who to Hire?

PROCEDURE

Step 1 (10–15 minutes)

Read the background information and descriptions of each of the applicants. Consider the job and the cultures within which the individual to be hired will be operating. Rank the candidates from 1 to 5, with 1 being your first choice, and enter your rankings on the ranking sheet in the column marked "My Ranking." Briefly, list the reasons for each of your rankings.

Do not discuss your rankings with your classmates until told to do so.

Step 2 (30–40 minutes)

Working with four to six of your classmates, discuss the applicants, and rank them in the order of group preference. Do not vote.

Rank the candidates from 1 to 5, with 1 being the group's first choice, and enter your group rankings on the ranking sheet in the column marked "Group Ranking." Briefly list the reasons for each of the group's rankings.

If your group represents more than one culture, explore the ways in which each person's cultural background may have influenced his or her individual decisions.

Step 3 (open-ended)

Report your rankings to the class, and discuss the areas of difference that emerged within your group while you were trying to reach consensus. Consider the following questions:

a. Was your group able to explore openly any culturally based biases that came up—for example, feelings about homosexuality, religion, personality traits, politics?
b. Did you make any comments or observations that you feel would have been fully acceptable in your own culture but were not accepted by the group? Explain.
c. If the answer to (b) was yes, how did the reaction of the group make you feel about your membership in it? How did you handle the situation?
d. What implications do you believe these cultural differences would have in business dealings?

BACKGROUND

You are a member of the management committee of a multinational company that does business in twenty-three countries. While your company's headquarters are in Holland, your offices are scattered fairly evenly throughout the four hemispheres. Primary markets have been in Europe and North America; the strongest emerging market is the Pacific Rim. Company executives would like to develop what they see as a powerful potential

---

This exercise was written by Janet W. Wohlberg.

market in the Middle East. Sales in all areas except the Pacific Rim have shown slow growth over the past two years.

At present, your company is seeking to restructure and revitalize its worldwide marketing efforts. To accomplish this, you have determined that you need to hire a key marketing person to introduce fresh ideas and a new perspective. There is no one currently in your company who is qualified to do this, and so you have decided to look outside. The job title is "vice-president for international marketing"; it carries with it a salary well into six figures (US$), plus elaborate benefits, an unlimited expense account, a car, and the use of the corporate jet. The person you hire will be based at the company's headquarters and will travel frequently.

A lengthy search has turned up five people with good potential. It is now up to you to decide whom to hire. Although all of the applicants have expressed a sincere interest in the position, it is possible that they may change their minds once the job is offered. Therefore, you must rank them in order of preference so that if your first choice declines the position, you can go on to the second, and so on.

APPLICANTS

Park L., Age 41, Married with Three Children

Park L. is currently senior vice-president for marketing at a major Korean high technology firm. You have been told by the head of your Seoul office that his reputation as an expert in international marketing is outstanding. The market share of his company's products has consistently increased since he joined the company just over fifteen years ago. His company's market share is now well ahead of that of competing producers in the Pacific Rim.

Mr. Park started with his present company immediately after his graduation from the University of Seoul and has worked his way up through the ranks. He does not have a graduate degree. You sense that Mr. Park has a keen understanding of organizational politics and knows how to play them. He recognizes that because the company he works for now is family controlled, it is unlikely that he will ever move much higher than his present situation. Mr. Park has told you that he is interested in the growth potential offered at your company.

In addition to his native tongue, Mr. Park is able to carry on a reasonably fluent conversation in English and has a minimal working knowledge of German and French. His wife, who appears quiet and quite traditional, and his children speak only Korean.

Kiran K., Age 50, Widow with One Adult Child

Kiran K. is a Sikh woman living in Malaysia. She began her teaching career while finishing her D.B.A. (doctorate in business administration) at the Harvard Business School and published her first book on international marketing ten months after graduation. Her doctoral dissertation was based on the international marketing of pharmaceuticals, but she also has done research and published on other areas of international marketing.

Two months after the publication of her book, Kiran went to work in the international marketing department of a Fortune 500 company, where she stayed for the next ten years. She returned to teaching when Maura University offered her a full professorship with tenure, and she has been there since that time. Her academic position has allowed her to pursue a number of research interests and to write authoritative books and papers in her field. At present, she is well published and internationally recognized as an expert on international marketing. In addition, she has an active consulting practice throughout Southeast Asia.

You have learned through your office in Kuala Lumpur that Kiran's only child, a twenty-three-year-old son, is severely mentally and physically disabled. You sense that part of her interest in the job with your company is to have the income to guarantee his care should anything happen to her. Her son would go with her to Holland, should she be given the job, where he will need to be enrolled in special support programs.

In addition to fluency in Malay, English, and Hindi, Kiran speaks and writes German and Spanish and is able to converse in Japanese and Mandarin.

Peter V., Age 44, Single

Peter is a white South African. He had worked in a key position in the international marketing division of an American Fortune 100 company until the company pulled out of his country eight months ago. While the company wanted to keep him on, offering to move him from Johannesburg to its New York headquarters, Peter decided that it was time to look elsewhere. He had begun to feel somewhat dead ended in his position and apparently sees the position at your company as an opportunity to try out new territory. Like your other candidates for the position, Peter has a long list of accomplishments and is widely recognized as outstanding in his field. People in your company who have had contacts with him say that Peter is creative, hard working, and loyal. In addition, you have been told that Peter is a top-flight manager of people who is able to push his employees to the highest levels of performance. And, you are told, he is very organized.

Peter has a Ph.D. in computer science from a leading South African university and an M.B.A. from Boston University.

Peter had been a vehement opponent of apartheid and is still very much a social activist. His high political visibility within South Africa has made his life there difficult, and now he would like to get out. His constant male companion, P. K. Kaahn, would be coming with him to Holland, and Peter would like your personnel office to help P. K. find an appropriate position.

Peter speaks and reads English, Dutch, Afrikaans, and Swahili and can converse in German.

Tex P., Age 36, Divorced with One Child

Tex is currently job hunting. His former job as head of marketing for a single-product high-technology firm—highly specialized work stations for sophisticated artificial intelligence applications—ended when the company was bought out by Texas Instruments. Tex had been with his previous company virtually from the time the company was started six years earlier. Having to leave his job was an irony to Tex as it was largely due to the success of his efforts that the company was bought out. You sense that he is a little bitter, and he tells you that jobs offered to him by TI were beneath him and not worthy of consideration.

Tex has both his undergraduate and M.B.A. degrees from Stanford University. In addition, he was a Rhodes Scholar and won a Fulbright scholarship, which he used to support himself while he undertook a two-year research project on the marketing of high-technology equipment to Third World countries.

You have learned through your New York office that Tex has a reputation for being aggressive and hard driving. Apparently he is a workaholic who has been known to work eighteen to twenty hours a day, seven days a week. He seems to have little time for his personal life.

In addition to his native English, Tex has a minimal command of French—which he admits he hasn't used since his college days.

Zvi C., Age 40, Married with Five Children

Zvi began his career after receiving his M.B.A. from the Sloan School of Management at the Massachusetts Institute of Technology (MIT). His first job was as marketing manager for a German company doing business in Israel.

Zvi's phenomenal success with this company led to his being hired away by an international office equipment company in England. Again, he proved to be outstanding, boosting the company's market share beyond all expectations within two years. After five years, Zvi was offered a chance to go back to Israel, this time to oversee and coordinate all of the international marketing programs for an industrial park of fourteen companies run as an adjunct to Israel's leading scientific research institution. It has been his responsibility to interface the research component with product development and sales as well as to manage the vast marketing department. Again, he has shown himself to be a master.

You have learned through your Haifa office that Zvi is highly respected and has extensive contacts in the scientific and high-tech worlds. He is exceptionally creative in his approach to marketing, often trying bold strategies that most of his peers would dismiss as too risky. Zvi, however, has made them work and work well.

Zvi is a religious man who must leave work by noon on Friday. He will not work Saturdays nor any of his religion's major and minor holidays—about eighteen a year. He will, however, work on Sundays.

In addition to his native language, Dutch (Zvi and his family moved to Israel from Holland when Zvi was six), he speaks and writes fluent Hebrew, English, German, and Arabic.

Who to Hire?
Ranking Sheet

Applicant	My Ranking	Reasons	Group Ranking	Reasons
Park L.				
Kiran K.				
Peter V.				
Tex P.				
Zvi C.				

Rank the candidates from 1 to 5, with 1 being the first choice.

The International Cola Alliance

This exercise introduces some of the complexities involved in doing business across international borders. What happens when countries seeks to do business with one another without the benefit of a common language and customs? As we have seen, even with a common language, communication can break down, and interpretations of words and actions can confound understanding and incur often-negative attributions of purpose. Add to this the differences of personal needs that exist from individual to individual, as well as national and cultural needs that exist from country to country. These limitless variables make cooperation across borders even that much more complex.

OVERVIEW

You are a delegation from a country that would like to enter into a large cooperative effort with a number of other countries for the production and distribution of a popular soft drink produced by the American company International Cola. In the past, countries in your region of the world have been resistant to allowing foreign soft drinks into their markets, despite consumer demands. However, recent thinking is that the advantages of allowing this competition outweigh the disadvantages.

International Cola has expressed an interest in setting up a bottling plant, a regional corporate headquarters, and four distribution depots. Their goal, of course, is to do this in the most economically efficient way possible to maximize profits. However, because the executives at International Cola believe this area to be a rich new market with outstanding potential and are therefore anxious to get in, they have ceded to the demands of the various governments in the proposed alliance. These require International Cola to allow for local control of the facilities; to maintain only 49 percent interest in the facilities with local partners holding 51 percent ownership; and to allow the participating governments to work out among themselves the details of where the facilities will be located.

For the countries involved, having one or more of these facilities located within their borders will bring jobs, revenue, and a certain amount of prestige. (It is possible for a single country to have all six of the facilities: regional headquarters, bottling plant, distribution depots.)

Each of the countries involved shares at least two borders with the other countries. This has not always been the most peaceful area. Border skirmishes are frequent, most stemming from minor misunderstandings that became inflated by vast cultural and religious differences.

These distinct cultural differences between your country and your neighbors will likely become even more evident as you pursue the negotiation. It will be up to you to decide how to respond to them. While it is important for you to retain your own cultural integrity—for example, when you first meet a delegate from another country you will likely greet him or her in the cultural style of your country—you understand the importance of being sensitive to one another. If you understand, for example, that the

This exercise was written by Janet W. Wohlberg.

cultural style of another country is to bow on meeting, whereas you shake hands, you may wish to bow instead.

Since you are negotiating the venture across borders, and each country has a different primary language, you have agreed to negotiate in English, but none of you is entirely fluent. Therefore, a few phrases will creep in from your own languages.

Wear your country's flag in a visible place at all times.

PROCEDURE

Step 1   (30–40 minutes—may be done before class)

Working in small groups (5–7), develop a profile of your country and its people based on profile sheets 1 and 2.

You will also be given a third profile sheet that details cultural norms within your country. Information given will include the ways in which people in your country deal with areas such as time, personal physical space, gender, social mores, and oral communication.

After you have completed profile sheets 1 and 2 and everyone in your group has read profile sheet 3, briefly discuss them to be sure there is mutual understanding of what the group's behavior and negotiating stance are to be during the negotiation.

Step 2   (20 minutes—may be done before class)

Based on the profile sheets, decide which International Cola facilities you believe you should have in your country and why you believe they should be in your country rather than one of the others that will be represented. For example, if you have a highly educated population, you may argue that you should be the home of the regional corporate headquarters; be aware, however, that another country might argue that you should not have bottling and distribution facilities because these do not require a highly educated or skilled labor force.

On the negotiation sheet, make a list of the facilities you believe your country should have and some notes as to what your arguments will be for having them. Also make some notes on what you believe the other countries' counterarguments will be and how you expect to respond to them.

Step 3   (30–45 minutes—in class)

Everyone in your group should pin a copy of your country's flag and motto on himself or herself in a visible place. One to three representatives from your group (delegation) should negotiate the arrangements for International Cola's facilities with the representatives from the other delegations. Be sure to use the cultural norms of your country during the negotiation, but **do *not* tell** the others what your social norms are.

Representatives should introduce themselves to one another on an individual basis. After personal introductions, representatives should form a circle in the center of the room with their delegations behind them, briefly describe their countries, state their positions, and begin negotiations. During negotiations, representatives should make an effort to use their new language at least three times. They should not use English for any of the six phrases listed.

Delegation representatives and the other members of their groups may communicate with one another at any point during the course of the negotiation, but only in writing.

Group members may also communicate among themselves, but only in writing during the course of the negotiation.

Any group or representative may ask for a side meeting with one or more of the other groups during the negotiation. Side meetings may not last more than five minutes.

At any time in the negotiation, the delegation may change its representative. When such a change is made, the new representative and the other delegates must reintroduce themselves and greet one another.

Those members of each delegation who are not directly negotiating should be active observers. Use the observer sheet to record situations in which other groups insulted them, shamed them, or otherwise were offensive.

At the end of 45 minutes, the negotiation should be concluded whether or not an agreement has been reached.

Step 4 (open-ended)

Class discussion. Each group should begin by reading their profile sheet 3 aloud. A reporter should note some of the events in which members of other delegations caused them shame, embarrassment, and so forth. Open discussion of the meaning of what took place should follow.

Questions for Discussion

1. What role did cultural differences play in the various phases of the negotiation process? Be careful not to overlook the introductory phase. Was the negotiation frustrating? Satisfying? Other? Why?
2. At any time, did delegations recognize the cultural differences between themselves and the others? If so, was any attempt made to try to adapt to another country's norms? Why? Why not? Would there have been a benefit in doing so? Why?
3. What role did language differences play during the negotiation? What was the effect of lack of understanding or miscommunication on the process?
4. Did the delegations from various countries attempt to find mutual goals and interests despite their differences? In what ways were the best interests of the overall plan subjugated to the individual interests of each country? What rhetoric was used to justify the personal interests?
5. To what degree did groups construct their countries to best justify their position? In situations where this happened, did it work? Why? Why not?

The International Cola Alliance
Profile Sheet 1

1. Select a name for your country: _____
   Be sure that the name of your country appears on or around the flag (see below).

2. In the space below, design your country's flag or emblem. Make enough copies so that each member of your group has one to wear.

3. Write a slogan for your country that best embodies your country's ideals and goals. Include the slogan on or around the flag.

   _____
   _____

4. Make up a partial language with a vocabulary of up to twenty-five words into which you should translate the following phrases for use during negotiations:

Phrase	Translation
I agree.	_____
I disagree.	_____
This is unacceptable.	_____
I don't understand your point.	_____
You have insulted me.	_____
Please repeat that.	_____

5. Briefly describe how people in your country react when they have been insulted.

   _____
   _____

The International Cola Alliance
Profile Sheet 2

Describe your country by selecting one element from each of the following lists. After you have made your selections, list the elements that make up your country's description on a separate piece of paper and add any additional elements you wish.

POPULATION DENSITY

_____ high density with overpopulation a problem
_____ moderate density—high end
_____ moderate density—average
_____ moderate density—low end
_____ low density

AVERAGE EDUCATIONAL LEVEL

_____ less than 3 years—large percent totally illiterate
_____ 3–6 years—widespread functional illiteracy
_____ 6–9 years—functional illiteracy a problem in scattered areas
_____ 9–12 years—most read and write at functional levels
_____ 12+ years—a highly educated and functioning population

PER CAPITA INCOME

_____ under $1,000 per year
_____ $1,000–5,000 per year
_____ $5,000–10,000 per year
_____ $10,000–20,000 per year
_____ $20,000–30,000 per year
_____ $30,000–40,000 per year
_____ $40,000+ per year

CLIMATE

_____ tropical
_____ arctic
_____ mixed in different areas
_____ runs range from season to season

The International Cola Alliance
Profile Sheet 2 (cont'd)

FORM OF GOVERNMENT

_____ socialist
_____ democratic
_____ communist
_____ monarchy
_____ dictatorship
_____ other (specify)

DOMINANT RACIAL-ETHNIC GROUP

_____ Asian
_____ black
_____ white
_____ other (specify)

DOMINANT RELIGION

_____ animist
_____ atheist/agnostic
_____ Buddhist
_____ Catholic
_____ Hindu
_____ Jewish
_____ Mormon
_____ Protestant (specify)
_____ other (specify)

The International Cola Alliance
Negotiation Sheet

1. What facilities do you believe your country should have?

   _____

   _____

   _____

2. What facilities of those listed above are you willing to relinquish to reach agreement?

   _____

   _____

3. On what bases will you justify your need or desire for having the facilities you have listed?

   _____

   _____

   _____

   _____

   _____

   _____

   _____

   _____

   _____

   _____

   _____

   _____

   _____

   _____

   _____

   _____

The International Cola Alliance
Observer Sheet

1. List actions taken by members of other delegations that were insulting, created shame for you and your delegation, or were otherwise offensive based on your country's norms. Include notes on the context in which the actions were taken.

   _____
   _____
   _____
   _____
   _____
   _____
   _____
   _____
   _____
   _____
   _____
   _____
   _____
   _____
   _____
   _____
   _____

2. Based on the above list, what happened to your interest in forming an alliance and your belief that a mutual agreement could be reached?

   _____
   _____
   _____
   _____
   _____
   _____
   _____
   _____
   _____
   _____
   _____
   _____
   _____
   _____
   _____
   _____

Frederick International

In July of 1979, Gordon Frederick and Lewis Naehring, president and vice-president, respectively, of Frederick Engineering in Brookfield, Connecticut, decided to form a new division of their safety products company. The goal of the new division, Frederick International, would be to broaden the market for the company's main product, the Proxagard, a high-tech safety device, beyond the borders of the United States.

The Proxagard is used in such manufacturing equipment as punch presses. Punch presses are extremely dangerous. Around the world, many punch press operators have lost parts of fingers and hands when they have become careless and have allowed their hands to get in the path of the powerful machines. As a result, the punch press industry, and operators of hazardous equipment as well, were getting slapped with lawsuits when employees lost fingers or suffered other damage to their hands. In addition, OSHA, which regulates occupational safety and health in the United States, has the power to fine a company if an inspection or complaint reveals that the organization is jeopardizing the well-being of employees.

By electromagnetically sensing fingers when they come dangerously close to a press, the Proxagard provides customers with a fail-safe method of preventing injuries and does so at a competitive price. Another plus for the Proxagard is that help with installing and servicing this device is just a phone call away for customers in the United States. As companies have begun to see the rising costs of worker's compensation and costs associated with defending themselves against liability claims, they have started to weigh the bottom-line costs and benefits of safety equipment such as the Proxagard. In the United States, Frederick had been selling seven hundred to nine hundred of the machines per year.

Frederick's first sale to a foreign customer had been in September of 1976. Lapin Industrielle, a large company that specialized in importing American equipment, had seemed like a promising sales representative for the fledgling company. Frederick and Naehring were surprised and delighted when Lapin bought thirty Proxagards, which, at that time, cost about $450 each. All were installed in a company that used dozens of punch presses.

In addition to buying thirty Proxagards, Lapin Industrielle helped Frederick's cause by beginning the process of obtaining the necessary federal approval for the product in France. Without government approval, a product was supposedly not allowed to be sold in France. The early model of the Proxagard—the PG 101—that Lapin had purchased, had not received approval. Unlike OSHA in the United States, French federal inspectors have the authority to shut down a plant if equipment is considered unsafe. Lapin had installed the thirty Proxagards at the punch press company without telling anyone, so it was especially important that they keep up their efforts to gain federal approval. At this point, however, Lapin had lost interest in continuing to seek approval. As Frederick's engineers refined and improved a new PG 110 model of the Proxagard—which did eventually receive approval—Lapin did very little.

This case was written by Scott Weighart.

"We told Lapin that they had to get one salesman completely committed to the Proxagard," Frederick's sales people contended, "but they told us that they didn't have the resources to send one man out to sell and install the Proxagards to ensure they would pass inspection."

In early 1979, Rick Knackert, a navigator for Fresh Airlines and a personal friend of Frederick's, met salesman Pierre Vachon during a trip to Brussels. Upon hearing Knackert describe Frederick Engineering's Proxagard, Vachon was intrigued and extremely confident that he could sell a high volume of the machines.

Then came a curious turn of events: Vachon injured his back and was ordered to bed by his doctors for six weeks of rest. As Vachon was a workaholic, this was something he wouldn't take lying down—even if he was flat on his back. Vachon had his wife set up a Proxagard and its sensing antenna at the foot of his bed. For weeks, he experimented with the machine by wiggling his toes around to determine the size of the sensing field. He also read every piece of sales literature and other information that Frederick could provide for him.

After spending six weeks in bed with the product, Vachon had fallen in love. Back on his feet, he began new negotiations for getting the French government's approval, and he was successful. Then in 1985, Vachon met Jean-Claude Laperrière, who, on seeing the Proxagard in action, also became a devotee of the product. Laperrière was a tinkerer who loved to build gadgets and toy with new ideas. He had recently separated from his wife and was more than happy to go around the countryside installing Proxagards and building antennas that were perfectly tailored to each customer's needs.

Meanwhile, a French federal inspector discovered the thirty Proxagards that Lapin had quietly installed seven years earlier.

"What is this thing?" the inspector had demanded to know. "Who sells this?" After learning that the machines had been working for years without failures or accidents, he became fascinated by the device. He eventually traced the product to Frederick Engineering and to Laperrière and Vachon.

Suddenly all the pieces began to come together for Frederick International. When the French inspector found unsafe equipment, he would threaten to close down the plant and recommend a call to Pierre Vachon. By now, Frederick was charging $700 for the Proxagard, but Vachon and Laperrière could sell it for the equivalent of $2,500 to French companies, plus a charge for Laperrière's meticulous installations. This was steep compared with the American price, but consistent with prices charged by companies that made optical scanners or light curtains, which perform roughly the same function as the Proxagard but with different technology.

Laperrière installed between 125 and 150 Proxagards; he had made a great deal of money doing what he liked. Likewise, Vachon had earned substantial commissions, while Frederick had profited as well.

Since Frederick International's first venture was so successful, Lewis Naehring was very excited when the possibility for a similar arrangement in Japan arose. Mitsui Products, a maker of safety equipment in Japan, expressed serious interest in the Proxagard. Mitsui made palm buttons and light curtains for protecting punch presses: Palm buttons force the machine operator to keep both hands away from the path of the press; light curtains are similar to electric eyes. However, some of Mitsui's applications could only be carried out with something like the Proxagard.

Unlike Europe—where worker safety is a reasonable priority—some observers believe that Japanese claims of placing a high priority on safety are weakly supported by barely enforced standards. In comparison with the United States, Japan has far fewer lawyers per capita, and employee lawsuits are extremely rare.

"If an accident occurs, the individual is considered stupid for letting it happen," Naehring says. "Also, unions are not powerful because Japan is still basically a caste society and the socialized medical system covers any costs from injuries."

As was the case with France, government approval of the Proxagard had to be obtained, and while the approval processes were similar, it soon became clear that the Japanese government disapproved of imports unless it was proved that no comparable product could be built domestically.

When Naehring went to Japan's Department of Labor to secure approval, the official he spoke with got right to the point: "In selling your Proxagard in our country, are you attempting to replace light curtains?"

"No," Naehring replied. "This is for other applications."

"Good," the official replied. "Now the meeting can continue."

As he had once done with Lapin Industrielle, Naehring told Mitsui's executives that it would be crucial to find a person who could be an antenna design expert and who would make a full commitment to the project. The Mitsui president and engineers consistently said yes to whatever Naehring raised.

"Would you send your antenna expert to the U.S. for training?" Naehring asked. His question was met with vigorous nods of agreement. Naehring had been led to believe that twenty to twenty-five Proxagard orders per month would be possible.

A few months later, a Mitsui official came to Connecticut and expressed much enthusiasm for the project. That was in 1988. Since then, however, the Mitsui connection has resulted in very few orders for Proxagards, an average of fewer than fifty per year.

Through correspondence and occasional phone calls, Naehring tried to figure out what was going wrong.

"Are you really making an effort to sell these things?" he asked.

"Oh, yes," was the reply. "But we have not sold many yet, although we remain hopeful."

When he tried to determine if they had really followed through by assigning a person to travel the country, Naehring received a vague and roundabout letter in return, stating that Mitsui officials were taking appropriate action to ensure success in their mutual endeavors.

Today, Naehring remains unclear as to why the product is so successful in America and France but has failed to meet expectations in Japan. Was it really Mitsui's fault? Should Frederick sink some money into advertising in Japan? Would Frederick International be successful in Japan with a different partner? In the maze of government regulation, cultural differences, worker's compensation, and competition, Naehring couldn't be sure exactly where Frederick International had gone down the wrong path. He assumed that companies across the world would want to protect their workers from accidents with the best available technology, so it must be something else that went wrong.

Questions for Discussion

1. What has kept Frederick International from being as successful in Japan as it has been in the United States and France? Would finding a different Japanese representative be a good idea?

2. Do you believe it is possible to make Frederick International more successful and profitable in Japan? How?
3. What overall advice would you give Frederick and Naehring for making Frederick International more successful?

Force Field Analysis

Goal: Successful Sales of Proxagard in United States

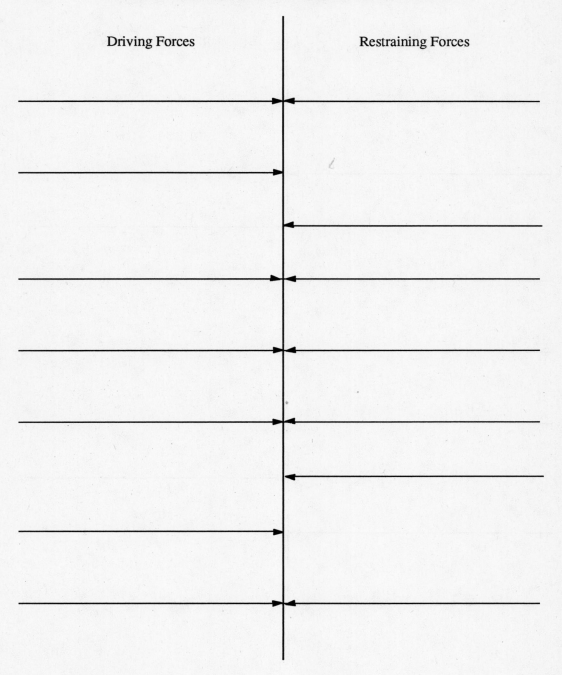

Driving Forces   Restraining Forces

Force Field Analysis

Goal: Successful Sales of Proxagard in Japan

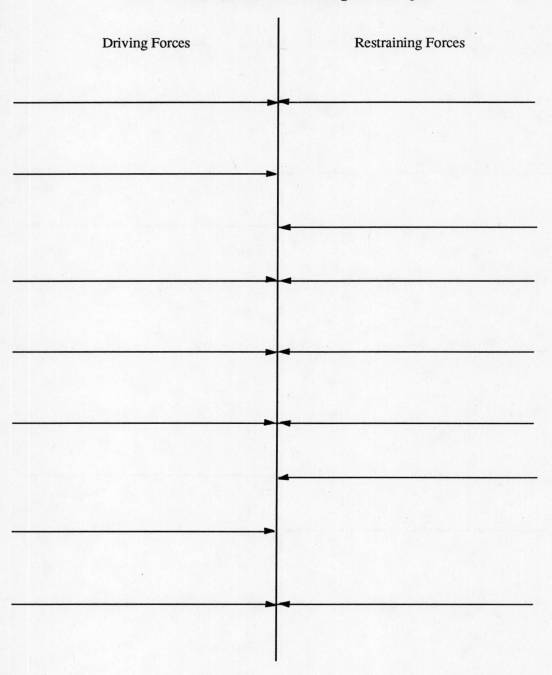

Driving Forces   Restraining Forces

Force Field Analysis

Goal: Successful Sales of Proxagard in France

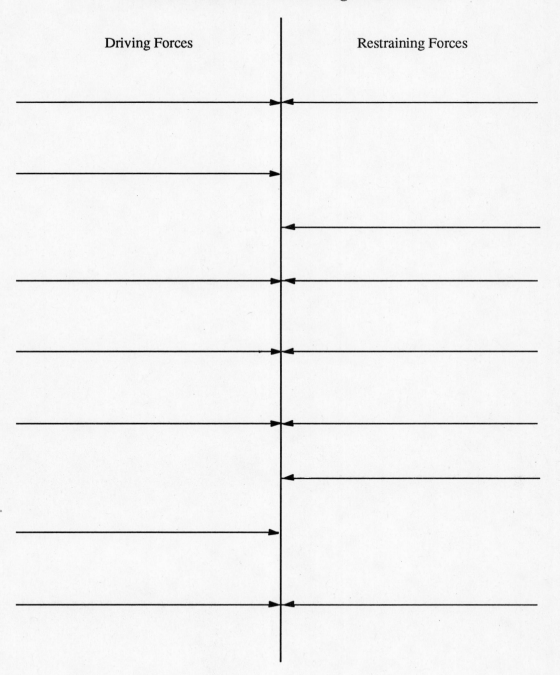

Driving Forces   Restraining Forces

PART VIII

CAREER MANAGEMENT

Bruce Leblang

OVERVIEW

Career planning can be discussed on an individual or group (organizational) level. This part focuses on the importance of good career planning for individuals preparing to enter the job market, as well as for organizations seeking to effectively manage their human resources.

This part begins by exploring the *dynamics*, or processes, of career planning and management. The 3-step process of the Career Planning Process is described, and the importance of good decision-making is discussed. The choices facing each person, i.e., choosing an occupation, an organization, and a particular type of work environment, also are examined.

The second section emphasizes people in organizations and the role of organizations in career management. Most employees go through a series of *Career Stages*, beginning with entry into and ending with withdrawal from the organization. Managing the career needs of workers plays a critical role in terms of meeting the future needs of an organization. All organizations—businesses, universities, non-profit agencies, government, etc.—must train and develop their increasingly diverse work forces to encourage teamwork and a sense of mission on behalf of the organization.

Finally, the results of good career planning as compared to ineffective career planning on both individual and organizational levels are explored.

Following the discussion is a series of short exercises and cases, as well as a list of books/articles, which will support and guide you as you begin your own career exploration.

Career Planning

As you are probably now thinking about your own future plans, you are probably beginning to realize that you must take primary responsibility for your own careers.

A career is a series of jobs, usually but not always paid, that allows individuals to express themselves, earn a living, and satisfy key values. While some people follow "traditional" career paths, starting from the bottom and aiming for the top of an organization, other alternatives are available.

There are a number of new realities in the workplace that must be recognized and for which individuals must plan:

- New workers entering the work force will, on average, change careers two to three times and change jobs about seven times.[1]
- In this era of down-sizing and foreign competition, job security is increasingly rare. Workers must be prepared to be flexible; change is unavoidable.
- Since the heyday of the 1980s, many people have searched for meaning in their work and in their personal lives. This has led to a great number of career transitions and an increased emphasis on how work and overall lifestyle mix. This new focus, which takes into account the whole individual, is known as life/work planning.

The above points emphasize the need for each person to practice effective career planning. Career planning involves three essential steps:

This overview was written by Bruce Leblang. Used by permission.

Bruce Leblang teaches courses in career management and organizational behavior at Boston University's School of Management, where he has also been a career counselor.

1. Richard Bolles, *What Color is Your Parachute?* (Berkeley: Ten Speed Press, 1991).

1. Self-assessment
2. Career exploration
3. Job search/placement

Personal career planning involves examining one's interests, skills, and values; looking at the types of work that match these characteristics; and finding, or creating, such a position. By completing this process, you will be more likely to find work that satisfies your unique goals and values. A key point to remember is that career planning should not end when you find a job; you will still need to guide your career within an organization. Career planning is an ongoing process that will prepare you for future decisions, either within your initial place of employment or in another company or agency.

From the point of view of a company or organization, there are many benefits to be derived from supporting the career-planning processes of employees. For example, workers are more likely to stay with an organization, have more positive attitudes, and be more productive if there is a good fit between the requirements of the job and the interests and skills of the workers.

While your future employer may provide assistance to you when making career decisions, you will be primarily responsible for each step of this process; therefore, it is useful to look at each stage in more detail.

Self-Assessment. Self-assessment is the most important stage of career planning,[2] yet students often try to shortcut, going straight to the job search and protesting that they "already know this stuff." Identifying your values (key beliefs of which you may not consciously be aware), interests, and skills (what you're good at) is necessary before you can move on to step 2, looking at any possible careers that might fit your self-assessment profile.

Part of self-assessment should involve life/work planning. You must consider how important you want your career to be in the overall scheme of your life. Chances are you have already engaged in some life/work planning. For example, you have had to make decisions about how to manage your time. You have also determined when to schedule—and attend—your classes and decided how much you wish to study. You also may have been involved in campus activities or obtained a part-time job to cover expenses. Integrating the various areas of your life—social, work, personal growth, and so forth—has given you a taste of the complex process of life/work planning.

Career Exploration. Career exploration can be completed in a number of ways and is an enjoyable process if you are interested in "what's out there" in the world of work. John Holland, a noted psychologist who has studied the concept of vocational choice—or how people choose their careers—has identified six basic personality types related to job preference. Holland found that people naturally look for work environments that fit their personalities and interests. People also enjoy working with others who have similar values and interests. This is called personality-job fit. By completing a vocational interest inventory, such as the Self-Directed Search, you can discover your personality type and identify additional career areas to explore. For more information on Holland's theory and the Self-Directed Search, see the resource list at the end of this chapter.

In addition, self-assessment exercises, such as compiling an autobiography that details key events in your life and completing the exercises in this chapter, will allow you to choose a number of fields to investigate. Then, by reading and through informational

---

2. Ibid.

interviewing—that is, meeting professionals to learn about their careers—gradually you will be able to focus in on one or two fields to explore in depth.

Informational interviews provide an excellent way to assess potential work environments and provide a chance to find out "what's really going on" in a particular company or job. Informational interviewing will allow you to meet the people involved in the kind of work you might find interesting. It will also give you the chance to examine the work environment and decide if it's really for you. Could you work in a cubicle for eight hours a day? Do you enjoy working in a hectic environment? Do you need other people around?

Informational interviewing should be the first phase of the networking process—that is, meeting people in your field of interest. The second phase of networking occurs when you are trying to meet people in a particular career—the one you have decided you most want to enter. During this stage, you will want to hear about job openings and meet individuals with the power to hire you. Since most college graduates do not find jobs through newspapers or on-campus recruiting programs, you will probably obtain your position through networking. Most jobs are never advertised, and many positions are created for specific job seekers who have impressed an employer. The process of networking and discovering the "hidden job market" provides about 75 percent of the professional jobs in the United States. As of this writing, most of these jobs are in small companies—that's where the growth is.

Placement. Placement (job search) involves your actual job hunt. Clearly you will be more likely to find satisfying work by locating a position that fulfills your self-assessment profile. After completing step 1 (self-assessment) and step 2 (career exploration), you should have a goal and a plan to reach that goal. Recruiters who hire college graduates usually prefer individuals who have a focus—that is, people who "know themselves" and have considered what they want. An important part of the placement process is the choice of work environment, something you explored in the self-assessment and career exploration steps when you looked at particular industries, companies, types of people, and so forth to consider where and with whom you would like to work.

The decision-making skills gained through completing the three essential steps of career planning will help you both immediately and in the future. As noted earlier, career changes and transitions within a particular career are becoming extremely common. Career planning is a cyclical process; chances are, you will need to reassess your career path sometime after graduation. In fact, many recent college graduates, based on their "real world" experiences and revised career goals, have changed their fields of work within two to three years after graduation. Failing to take seriously the importance of self-assessment and career exploration can significantly increase the likelihood of a poor initial job choice and hasten the need to change jobs or career paths.

Career Stages

Regardless of the type of career you choose, you will go through a number of stages within your field. As with the stages of career planning, you will probably enter more than one organization during your career, and you may change fields as well. The following discussion will focus on the needs and expectations in each career stage and the responsibility of organizations for meeting these needs.

The career stages most workers will go through are entry, socialization, advancement, maintenance, and withdrawal. Some employees become mentors; this is a separate stage.

Entry.   Your initial entry into a company represents a major transition into the world of work. New workers spend the entry phase getting to know the culture of the organization through discussions and research. College graduates often join companies with unrealistic expectations that may be aggravated by recruiters' sales techniques. Jeffrey Greenhaus, in his book *Career Management* has identified a number of key issues related to career entry:

- Your transition involves a major change from the "job" of being a student to becoming a company employee. For example, instead of having a professor who provides regular feedback, new workers may have managers who are too busy to discuss work or give much guidance.
- New employees often have inaccurate views of their initial positions in a company. It is up to the employee to find out as much as possible about the organization, to learn about the organization's culture, and to decide if a good fit exists between personal needs and the responsibilities and rewards the company provides to its employees.
- From a company perspective, recruiting people who are motivated, enthusiastic, and who fit in with the existing work force is crucial for success. Recruiters and line managers must provide prospective hires with accurate information about training programs and entry-level positions, and also give real information about the potential for growth and new responsibilities in the organization. Failure to do this will lead to unhappy recruits and high turnover costs for the organization.

Socialization and Advancement.   During socialization, new employees learn about the goals, values, and general operating style of an organization. In essence, you'll learn about the culture of a particular company or organization; you'll find out what's really going on, and you'll determine how to get things done within a particular environment. The main purpose of the socialization stage is to become a productive member of the organization, learn how things get accomplished, and work with others as a member of a team. Some accommodation has to be made between the wants/needs of the new employee and the needs of the organization. For example, a major retailer may want new trainees to immediately assist store managers, while the new employees need and expect a training program to outline their responsibilities and socialize them to the company.

As Greenhaus points out, both the employer and the employee have expectations of one another. Over time, you will test your employers and determine if they meet your needs, just as your employers will evaluate your performance. Both parties will look for a good match, or the employee may leave the organization. Clearly, organizations have a major incentive to socialize new workers in an effective manner.

While the socialization stage focus deals with fitting into the work environments, the advancement stage occurs when workers feel they are connected to an organization and can begin to focus on "moving up." Frequently, organizational entry and socialization take place when a worker is in his or her twenties. The achievement period generally occurs later, in the late twenties and thirties, as individuals commit themselves to particular careers and organizations. The impact of age and its importance in career decision making is presented most effectively in Daniel Levinson's *Seasons of a Man's Life.*

During the advancement period, employees become aware of what they want to accomplish and what type of contribution they want to make to the organization. The development of an area of expertise and an identification of important work values often occur during this time. Edgar Schein, a professor at MIT, has identified five "career anchors" that guide individual career decisions. Most employees have one or possibly two anchors that provide their motivation at work:

1. *Autonomy and independence.* People with this career anchor require a lot of freedom and avoid structured situations. They search for flexibility and freedom to do things their way.
2. *Security and stability.* People with this career anchor value a sense of safety and belonging to an organization. They like being closely tied to a particular company or geographic region.
3. *Creativity and entrepreneurship.* People with this career anchor want to create something of their own and "make it." This often involves introducing new products or services.
4. *Technical or functional.* People with this career anchor are driven to become experts in particular areas—for example, a function such as marketing or accounting—or to develop a skill area, such as an engineer who specializes in nuclear engineering for power plants. They are motivated by the work itself, not career management.
5. *Managerial.* People with this career anchor emphasize the development of management skills, wish to obtain key positions of power and influence, and focus on refining general skills such as communication and decision-making abilities.

Three additional anchors have been found: *service*, which involves focusing on a cause or ideal; *challenge*, which involves a search for competition; and *lifestyle*, which involves an attempt to have a balanced life with time for personal, social, and work life.

As you go through your career, it will be useful to identify your "career anchors" and to become aware of the career stages as you pass through them. For an organization, knowledge of employees' motivations and values will lead to more effective career planning. Organizations must identify possible career paths and provide opportunities for all workers, including those who are not focused on becoming presidents or CEOs.

Maintenance and Withdrawal. The next two career stages are often connected in terms of workers' experiences within an organization. The maintenance stage occurs when individuals are no longer rising in their companies; for many, this takes place during middle age, often during the forties and fifties. However, due to the down-sizing of many large companies and the elimination of many middle-management positions, you may reach a plateau or point of leveling off at a relatively young age. Maintenance involves accepting "where you are at" or creating a new dream or goal to pursue outside of your current organization. For companies that want to keep their plateaued workers, it is important to find ways to provide additional challenges or rewards. Failure of companies to address the needs and concerns of their workers will lead to withdrawal, either through firing, low productivity, or midlife career change, a common occurrence, according to Levinson.

If withdrawal does not take place during Levinson's midcareer stage, it will most likely occur during late career stage when workers are preparing for retirement and disengaging from the organization. The attitudes of employers toward late-career-stage workers often impacts the timing and the level of goodwill that workers feel when leaving an organization. Older workers can remain involved in their work and be useful assets to their companies by participating in special projects and by developing mentor relationships with younger workers.

During the maintenance stage and when workers are preparing for withdrawal, serving as a mentor to a younger worker can provide considerable satisfaction for the experienced individual. Employees in the entry and socialization periods often benefit from the wisdom and inside information possessed by the experienced worker who knows what's going on in the organization. This exchange of information and support of the younger individual can be useful in a newcomer's career, while reinforcing the commitment and interest of the mentor. Organizations may want to provide mentors for new employees as a means of socializing younger workers and keeping older employees involved.

Conclusion

This introduction has presented some of the concepts that form the basis of the career-planning process for individuals and organizations. The following points reinforce some of the main ideas presented:

1. Good career planning requires a commitment on the part of both you and your employer; however, you are still primarily responsible for managing your career.
2. Career planning is really a decision-making process; good decisions require a willingness to go through a process and examine various alternatives—in short, to accept uncertainty for a period of time.
3. Career planning is an ongoing cyclical process. Effective planning means assessing your needs every few years and developing an action plan and career goals based on your revised assessment and exploration.
4. While career planning is useful both for individuals and for organizations, it should not become a rigid lock-step process. Your career goals and strategies for obtaining these goals should be adjusted as you go through the various career stages from entry to withdrawal. In a similar manner, organizations must continually assess their needs and develop trained employees who possess the skills to keep the organization competitive. At the same time, managers must consider the career stages and anchors of their workers to maintain their interest and commitment.

Career planning is a decision-making process that will involve each of you in a challenging, sometimes frustrating, but ultimately rewarding experience. The following career exercises and cases will enable you to begin your own process of making decisions and to examine and evaluate the decisions of others. By discussing the upcoming cases and completing the exercises, you will be taking your first steps to getting prepared for life after graduation and for your future career.

RESOURCE LIST

Tests and Inventories:

Career Map Inventory, Novations, Inc., Provo, UT 84601.
Self-Directed Search, John Holland, Ph.D., PAR Inc., P.O. Box 998, Odessa, FL 33556.
Firo-B, Consulting Psychologists Press, 577 College Ave., Palo Alto, CA 94306.
Strong Interest Inventory, Consulting Psychologists Press, 577 College Ave., Palo Alto, CA 94306.

Books:

Bolles, R. *What Color is Your Parachute?* Berkeley: Ten Speed Press, 1991.

Greenhaus, J. *Career Management.* Chicago: Dryden Press, 1986.

Lathrop, R. *Who's Hiring Who?* Berkeley: Ten Speed Press, 1990.

Powell, C. R. *Career Planning Today: Hire Me.* 2nd ed. Dubuque, Iowa: Kendall Hunt, 1990.

Sinetar, M. *Do What You Love: The Money Will Follow.* New York: Paulist Press, 1987.

Stumpf, S. *Choosing a Career in Business.* New York: Simon & Schuster, 1984.

Self-Assessment Diagram

The Venn diagram below sums up the process of personal exploration. The interlocking format illustrates the overlapping nature of each of the four categories: values, interests, personality, and skills. Self-exploration should not ignore any of these components.

The exercises that are presented in the part tie in with this Venn diagram: As you complete the exercises, take the most important components from each and enter them on the diagram. The Work Values Planning Board will reveal your most significant values; Choosing Your Favorite Challenges and Problems will help you to isolate interests; and Peak Experiences will help you identify your key skills. One way to identify your personality traits is to talk with friends and family members, making a list of the adjectives they use to describe you. After obtaining a list of twenty-five or more adjectives, and adding some of your own, you can prioritize these personality traits in order of importance, placing the top four or five in the appropriate circle of the diagram.

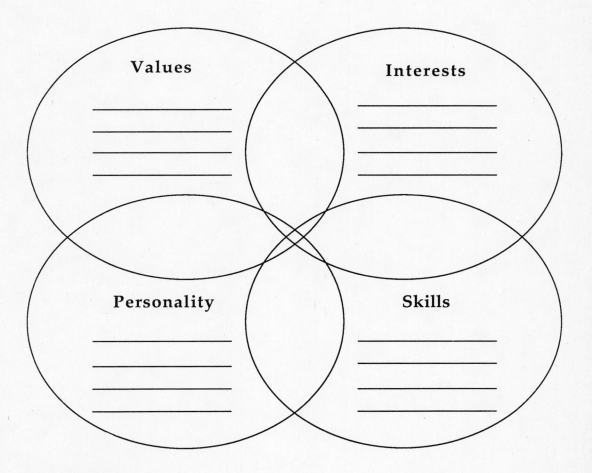

Prepared by Bruce Leblang. Used by permission.

Work Values Planning Board

Career seekers frequently underestimate the importance of considering their values when examining prospective careers. Values are the kinds of things we want from our work. Some are physical and/or tangible, some are social, some are psychological. Most of us want it all, but that is often difficult if not impossible to achieve. If you can't have it all, it is important to set priorities. The following activity was designed to help you decide which of your work-related values take precedence over others.

PROCEDURE

Step 1

The following page is divided into ten strips. One each of nine of the strips is listed a work-related value. On the tenth strip of paper, write a value of your own choice. Cut or tear the strips apart along the dotted lines.

Step 2

Rank-order the slips according to your personal priorities, from highest to lowest. In other words, if earning a high salary is the most important of the values listed, rank "Salary" number 1. Continue the ranking until you have positioned all ten values. Write the values on the planning board below in order of preference.

Planning Board

1. _____
2. _____
3. _____
4. _____
5. _____
6. _____
7. _____
8. _____
9. _____
10. _____

This exercise was adapted by Bruce Leblang from *Instructor's Manual* for *The Life Career Planning Program*, second edition, published by Northeastern University Custom Textbook Series, 1980. Reprinted by permission.

(Separate along dotted lines.)

Prestige

Salary

Relations with co-workers

Variety

Relations with supervisor

Advancement

Geographical location

Creativity

Challenge

_____
(value of your own choice)

The Career Fantasy

Imagine that you have just won a major contest, the right to spend an entire day with someone who has a job that you would love to do—your ideal job. You may spend your day with that person anywhere in the world.

During your day, you will be able to work with your "ideal person" at his or her job. Close your eyes for a minute, breathe deeply, and put yourself in this environment. As you breathe deeply, hold this image in your mind.

Spend about 10 minutes experiencing this vision, fantasizing about it, mentally living it. Then, answer the questions below. Do not talk to anyone until your instructor has told you to do so.

1. Whom would I most like to meet and why? What kind of job does he or she have?

2. What would I enjoy most about doing this type of work?

3. What is there about this type of work that I might not enjoy?

4. What special training would I need to do this job?

5. Could I really get a job like this? Why or why not?

When you have completed this part of the exercise, your instructor will give you further instructions.

This exercise was written by Bruce Leblang. Used by permission.

Choosing Your Favorite Challenges and Problems

Listed below are six types of problems or challenges. Facing these issues and dealing with them can be enjoyable, depending on the type of problem and your attitude toward the particular situation.

Imagine that you have a job that occupies 100 hours of your time. Look at the six types of problems below, and decide how you would like to divide your time. For the best results, do not divide your hours equally among categories, but rather weight them according to just how much time you would really want to spend on each area. In fact, you could choose to use all of your time solving one or two problems.

_____ Problems involving orderly use of data—including manipulation of numbers, words and forms of information—often in large organizations.

_____ Problems requiring persuasive ability and/or motivating others to reach organizational goals, often in business settings.

_____ Problems involving people—helping others with personal problems; leading others to inform or encourage; giving advice, support, and guidance.

_____ Problems involving creative ideas, new methods of getting something done, or creative problem solving using painting, drawing, art, music, or other artistic means as part of a solution.

_____ Problems requiring analytical ability, concentration, and combination of ideas to come up with a solution. These problems often involve mathematical and/or scientific skills and keen observation.

_____ Problems using your hands or other physical skills to fix or create something; to build a house, fix a tractor, work on a car. Usually involves "hands on" and/or outdoor work.

_____ Total Score (must equal 100)

This exercise was adapted by Bruce Leblang based on material from "Your Career: Choices, Chances and Changes," Bouchard, Kelly, and Weaver, 1984. Used by permission.

Peak Experiences

PROCEDURE

Step 1   (5–10 minutes)

Think back over the years of your life. Think about your "peak experiences,"[1] the times when you enjoyed a sense of accomplishment and felt happy and proud. Your accomplishment could be work related, connected with school, part of a hobby or sport, or anything in which you feel you played a meaningful role. Remember that your peak experiences are defined by you alone. The fact that another person may or may not consider your achievement as significant is not relevant.

Use one or two words to list five peak experiences:

1. _____
2. _____
3. _____
4. _____
5. _____

Step 2   (5 minutes)

Now, pick the two experiences from the above list that gave you the greatest sense of satisfaction, and list them below:

1. _____
2. _____

Step 3   (25–30 minutes)

Working with one other person, describe your first experience listed in step 2. Describe the events in detail. Explain how the event was planned, what you did, and describe the result. How did you feel? Relive the experience!

While you are the "storyteller," your partner, the "listener," should note the skills that you demonstrated in your experience, using the skills list below to locate the skills. When you are finished, have the listener share his or her findings with you.

After you have finished the discussion, switch roles. Repeat this cycle for your second experiences.

This exercise was written by Bruce Leblang. Used by permission.

1. See R. Bolles, *What Color is Your Parachute?* (Berkeley: Ten Speed Press, 1991).

Work Related Skills Checklist

1. Leadership

Plan for the future
Promote change
Assert yourself in groups
Initiate new activities
Present new ideas/proposals
Make decisions as necessary

Set goals
Persuade others
Bring people together
Motivate self/others
Analyze and solve problems
Serve as a role model

2. Management

Negotiate to reach consensus
Motivate others
Supervise others
Improvise/solve problems
Accept significant responsibilities
Make decisions within deadlines
Learn new skills as needed

Be self-disciplined
Encourage diverse people to work together
Review and evaluate information
Manage a number of different tasks at once

3. Administrative/Organizational

Manage time effectively
Follow through on plans
Put data in order
Develop systems

Classify, record, and file information
Create and administer work schedules
Coordinate detailed assignments
Prioritize work assignments

4. Quantitative

Manipulate numbers
Manage money
Keep records
Develop budgets

Estimate costs/plan for the future
Use financial planning techniques
Pay attention to details

5. Analytical

Understand how things work: people, machines, and systems
Research and gather information
Find causes of problems
Diagnose problems and identify solutions

Compare similarities and identify differences
Screen data
Prioritize information/evaluate courses of action

6. Counseling

Accept differing points of view
Interact with people in accepting ways
Advise and support others in decision making

Increase others' self-esteem
Demonstrate patience with people
Show empathy

7. Interpersonal

Develop positive relationships
Observe and evaluate peoples' needs
Be specific and clear when conveying
    information
Express self effectively in speech and
    writing

Use humor as appropriate
Accept differing points of view
Listen actively
Influence others through words and
    behaviors
Answer questions clearly

8. Training

Motivate others
Provide encouragement
Demonstrate curiosity and interest
Summarize information effectively
Communicate knowledge of different
    fields

Evaluate others' performance
Listen and speak to needs of others
Observe people, things, and surroundings
Help people learn; show enthusiasm

9. Creativity/Original Thinking

Express ideas and feelings openly
Create new procedures, products, and
    ideas
Use imagination
Create images using various media

Be flexible and adaptable
Prefer unstructured work environments
    and variety of tasks
Be non-conventional

Ted Johnson A & B

TED JOHNSON A

Ted Johnson is a twenty-year-old sophomore at Hurry State, a large university in the Northeast. Since he had to declare a major by the middle of his junior year, Ted decided to take a "Self-Assessment and Career Planning" course as an elective. Through the course, Ted hoped to get more focused beyond his general interest in business.

Since Ted was halfway to graduation—and the dreaded "real world"—he decided to examine the self-assessment exercises he had recently completed with the hope that he could locate some trends or themes. Ted chose his interests survey, skills exercises, and his autobiography as starting points.

Ted's "story" showed a love of the outdoors. Having grown up in western Nebraska, Ted was used to a horizon that stretched as far as the eye could see—a view best appreciated from atop a horse. On his family's thousand-acre cattle ranch and farm, Ted helped with odd jobs almost from the time he could walk. In addition to herding cattle, he loved to sit down with his father and go over the books. A farmer had to be an effective businessperson, and Ted seemed to have a natural talent for bookkeeping and finding "missing" entries. By age sixteen, Ted was handling the books and tracking the ranch's expenses. In high school, Ted excelled in his science and math courses, including biology, chemistry, and calculus. Although he had little time for extracurricular activities, Ted played on the soccer team and was the star of the chess club.

As Ted looked back on his life in Nebraska, which seemed awfully far away, his attention shifted to his interests survey. Many of Ted's experiences fell into the "realistic" area, but his highest scores were "investigative." His scores were supported by his behavior as a child; he was always asking "why?" Questions like why people ate cows when cows did not eat people always seemed to pop into his head. His problem-solving ability was very useful on the farm, but Ted wanted to experience life "back East" and get the broader perspective of a business education. On the interests survey, Ted scored 5s on solving math problems, predicting what people would buy, solving a mystery, and organizing information.

Ted's key skills from his exercises included tending animals; planning and organizing; observing; initiating and changing; making decisions; analyzing problems; and generating ideas. Ted felt this information was accurate; he saw himself as a bit of a loner who was not afraid to take risks, such as coming east to go to school. Ted's parents were already pushing for his return after graduation, if not to the ranch, at least to their part of Nebraska. Ted had decided, however, that while visits to the farm were fine, he needed to work in a faster-paced environment. His mother suggested an accounting position in Scottsbluff, a town of 20,000 people near the ranch. He thought he might consider Omaha, a city of 500,000 people, about four hundred miles from the ranch. An accounting position was not, however, attractive to Ted; he had no interest in sitting at a desk all day.

Now Ted was facing a number of major questions:

Both parts of this case were written by Bruce Leblang. Used by permission.

1. What subject areas within business might he study that would best fit his interests?

2. How could he find a summer job or internship that would use his problem-solving skills but not chain him to a desk?

3. What types of jobs would allow Ted to use the skills and interests he had identified?

4. What do Ted's parents want him to do after graduation? Do you think this will pose a problem for Ted? Why or why not?

TED JOHNSON B

Ted Johnson recently completed his junior year at Hurry State and now is enrolled as a first-semester senior. At this time, he is facing a number of major life decisions, including deciding on what type of work to go into, where to locate, and how to balance personal and family commitments.

At his parents' urging, Ted returned to the family ranch this past summer. Through friends of his parents, he was able to land a job as an assistant to Dave Jackson, an insurance claims adjuster whose territory includes most of western Nebraska. During the previous year, Ted had done a lot of thinking about different jobs he might want to try; he also had talked to numerous alumni through his school's alumni advising network. Now, through a stroke of luck, he'd found a possible answer to his career questions. Working with Dave, figuring out how accidents really happened, and learning a lot about human nature, Ted felt he had discovered a job that wouldn't "chain him to a desk." At the end of the summer, Ted received an informal job offer from Dave, as well as an excellent letter of reference.

Although Ted wasn't planning to go back to Nebraska, he was very interested in becoming a claims adjuster. But after getting back to Hurry State and talking to some friends, Ted began to question his plan. Denny, Ted's roommate and best friend, had a typical reaction. "Ted, insurance adjusters are the scum of the earth, and besides, you don't even need a degree to be one." Clearly, insurance adjusting was not a high-status profession, at least not among his friends back East. Ted felt that he could accept their comments as long as he was doing something he liked. Still, if Denny got a job with a company like P&G or in a major bank—well, he didn't really know how he'd react.

Ted was also dealing with the issue of where to live. After his "internship" with Dave Jackson, Ted felt he could learn how to be a claims adjuster and get a job in many areas of the country. Living on the ranch, or in the nearby town of Scottsbluff, seemed terribly boring after being in Boston, the home of Hurry State. After the summer, Ted realized he needed the excitement of living in a big city. Recently, he had visited friends in Chicago and had "fallen in love" with the city. Even though the city was huge, it still had a midwestern down-to-earth feeling that made Ted feel at home.

Soon after his visit, Ted described his visit to Chicago to his parents during their weekly phone call. As soon as Ted had finished breathlessly describing his trip—"it was awesome"—Ted's father expressed his disappointment.

"Gee, son," he said, "we only want what's best for you. You know, Chicago is kind of far. What about Lincoln or even Omaha?" Ted's mother followed with, "Ted, isn't Chicago a bit dangerous? What's wrong with Nebraska? Isn't Lincoln big enough for you?"

Now, with just a few months before graduation, Ted felt overwhelmed and confused. Didn't he owe something to his parents? As the only son, should he take over the ranch or at least live nearby? Finally, could he accept a job in a field with low status?

Ted wondered what his friends and family would say about his decisions and how much he might care about their reactions.

Questions for Discussion

1. What are the main decisions Ted is facing?

2. How would you resolve Ted's career dilemma?

3. How should Ted deal with his parents? What are his responsibilities toward them?

4. How should he decide where to live?

DJ Woods Writes His Resume

My name is David James Woods, but I've gone by "DJ" since I was a little kid. I grew up in Oceanside, New York, on Long Island, with two older brothers and my parents. Living near the shore, a lot of my time growing up was spent hanging out on the beach with my friends. When we weren't at the beach, you could usually find us in the schoolyard behind our house, playing basketball or softball.

Turning ten was a big deal for me because I got the chance to go away to overnight camp for six weeks. For the first few days I was homesick, until I realized that I could get away with staying up late and playing even more basketball than I did at home. I also started to make friends with some of the other kids in my tent. I went to camp each summer until I was sixteen, eventually becoming a counselor-in-training, which basically meant I was paid a little bit to have some fun. Anyways, at camp I earned the name DJ— a friend of mine said that I "made music" on the basketball court. At camp, I also learned to play tennis, and we had an archery range where I would sometimes go and practice for hours at a time.

I've always liked to move around and do a number of different things at once. In high school, my friends and I would get a group of people together and have parties. Sometimes, I'd just get out a stack of my older brothers' records from the sixties and seventies and get everybody dancing. To me, dancing is like playing basketball—it just feels right.

When I turned sixteen, I started working part-time. I've always liked fast cars, and with money saved from my job, I got my first car later that year—a 1968 red GTO convertible. When I wasn't working on my car, I did some studying, though I tried to avoid that as much as possible. I had to keep my grades up, though, so I could stay on the baseball and basketball teams. During my senior year, I was elected captain of the baseball team and was the starting third baseman. I was also a volunteer fireman in my town during my last two years of high school. I actually got to help put out a few fires. At times, it was a little scary, but I liked the excitement of being a firefighter, and I felt I was doing something useful.

My grades in high school weren't great, but I graduated with about a B average. I got mostly A's in my math and science courses. Language and writing have always been difficult for me. It's like I have the words in my mind but can't seem to get them out on paper. One of my high school English teachers suggested I take a creative writing class, which I did during freshman year. It helped a little—but not too much. Neither of my parents is into science. My Dad is a stockbroker in New York; I guess we're both addicted to excitement. I get my "hyper" side from him. My Mom is a calm person; she can spend hours sitting in one place and drawing/writing the greeting cards that she designs and sells. Sometimes I help her. I guess I get my patience from her.

I really kind of drifted into going to college. My folks had started saving when I was born, and most of my friends were going to school. I went with a few friends to look at Boston University and was really impressed by Boston—everybody seemed to be young, either a college student or an aspiring young professional. My SATs turned out better

---

This exercise was written by Bruce Leblang. Used by permission.

than I expected, especially in math, and I applied for admission to the School of Management since I figured management skills would be useful if I ever wanted to run my own business.

During my freshman year, I really got into Boston. I went to some clubs and listened to a lot of local bands. We had a lot of parties in my dorm. I made some friends through intramurals, and I played on our dorm basketball and baseball teams. Our baseball team only won three games, but we had a great time. Our basketball team did a little better, but I was no longer a big star. The following summer, I went back to Oceanside and worked in a friend's garage. I was almost like an apprentice mechanic, but I also got to see how the business was run. We did a lot of work on sports cars, and I thought about opening my own place after graduation.

In my sophomore year, I took the usual business classes, including Intro to Marketing, Finance and Operations, and Cost Accounting. I hated accounting, but at least I got through the classes more or less in one piece. I really enjoyed my operations class: One day a plant manager from General Motors came in to talk about careers in manufacturing operations. That really sounded like the right area for me—I'd actually be involved in a hands-on situation where I could get something done. The auto industry seemed especially interesting to me.

Eventually, I spoke with Bob Lane, the manager who had come to class, and I was able to set up an internship for the next summer at the GM plant in Framingham. Bob's responsibilities at the plant involved supervising all phases of manufacturing at the plant where GM's small cars are made. I spent most of my time working as his assistant—checking inventory lists, ordering materials, and doing some supervision of line workers when changes were being set up. Fortunately, Bob had a good relationship with most of the workers, and they accepted me pretty easily.

Junior year really flew by. I was still on two intramural teams, and I was taking higher-level courses. I also took a course in the organizational behavior department in which we had to do a career research project. My group interviewed people involved in operations careers in manufacturing, and I had the chance to learn more about possible career paths. It was especially useful to see the different manufacturing plants. Some were definitely not for me; others seemed great. During spring semester, I stopped into the career planning and placement office to talk with a counselor and check out their listing of summer jobs. I saw a listing for a production supervisor intern at Honeywell Bull, which was here in Boston. The computer industry was a long way from the automotive industry, but I thought it would be an interesting experience to try something different.

At Honeywell, I had the chance to be an assistant to the plant manager in charge of manufacturing. This was a great experience, because I got to do a little bit of everything—helping my boss set up his personal time schedule, revising our production quotas, checking inventory, and ordering materials as needed. I've gotten to the point where I believe I have some valuable experience that I can offer to an employer, but the idea of hunting for a job after graduation—yech!

During this semester (fall of my senior year), I have been thinking about life after graduation. Lately, I've been playing a lot of basketball, but also I've been talking with my folks, my operations professors, and a career counselor to get organized for the interviewing and job search stuff that is facing me. I don't want to be like some of my friends who seem to be waiting for an act of God or fate to deliver an answer about their life's work.

At this point, I'm looking for a job in manufacturing operations. I think that I would like to get into a training program that would allow me to learn a lot about the operations function. I'm especially interested in working for an auto manufacturer. I know that may mean moving to the Midwest or the Sunbelt, but I guess I'm ready for a change. Right now, I need to get a strong resume together to help me "get my foot in the door."

For the purposes of this exercise, you are DJ. Working with three or four other students, fill out the resume worksheet that appears with this exercise to help DJ get his interviews. He needs your help!

DJ Woods Writes His Resume

Local Address _____   Permanent Address _____

_____

_____

_____

Phone: (   ) _____   Phone: (   ) _____

Career Objective: _____

_____

_____

Education: Boston University School of Management, Boston, MA

Graduate Degree (if any): _____   Date: _____

Academic Data (Awards/Activities)

_____

_____

Undergraduate Degree _____   Date _____

Academic Data (Awards, Scholarships, Activities, Honors)

_____

_____

_____

_____

_____

This worksheet has been supplied courtesy of the Boston University School of Management Career Planning
Office and is used with permission.

Employment Experience:

Name of Organization   _____

Location of Organization   _____

Job Title _____

_____

Dates: From_____   To:_____

Duties and Responsibilities _____

_____

Name of Organization   _____

Location of Organization   _____

Job Title _____

_____

Dates: From_____   To:_____

Duties and Responsibilities _____

_____

Publications   _____

and/or   _____

Professional Memberships   _____

_____

Personal   _____
Interests   _____

_____

Comments and other related skills: _____

_____